Can the
Free Market
Pick Winners?

Can the Free Market Pick Winners?

What Determines Investment

Paul Davidson

Editor

Routledge
Taylor & Francis Group

LONDON AND NEW YORK

First published 1993 by M.E. Sharpe

Published 2015 by Routledge
2 Park Square, Milton Park, Abingdon, Oxon OX14 4RN
711 Third Avenue, New York, NY 10017, USA

Routledge is an imprint of the Taylor & Francis Group, an informa business

Library of Congress Cataloging-in-Publication Data

Can the free market pick winners?:
what determines investment/ edited by Paul Davidson.
p. cm.
Includes bibliographical references and index.
ISBN 1–56324–306–7. — ISBN 1–56324–307–5 (pbk.)
1. Investments. 2. Keynesian economics.
3. Keynes, John Maynard, 1883–1946.
General theory of employment, interest and money.
I. Davidson, Paul.
HG4515.C36 1993
332.6—dc20
93–35885
CIP

ISBN 13: 9781563243073 (pbk)
ISBN 13: 9781563243066 (hbk)

Contents

PAUL DAVIDSON

Introduction

In October 1990, the Nobel prize in economics was given for the first time to theorists working in the field of financial analysis and private investment theory for work done primarily in the previous two decades. Moreover, some of the theories had been widely acknowledged and endorsed by public policy makers and put into practice by capital market participants in Tokyo, Wall Street, and London. In other scientific fields where Nobel prize–winning work has been absorbed into real-world practice, the recipients in the area are able to demonstrate an accelerated progress toward improving the lot of mankind. Yet, compared with the quarter-century since the end of World War II, the era since the beginning of the 1970s has been marked by a declining rate of growth of labor and capital productivity, slower economic growth, and massive speculative investment bubbles (e.g., real estate bubbles in the United States, Japan, and London) that have handicapped modern economies with nonproductive excess capacity while public infrastructure in all modern cities collapses in front of our eyes. How is it possible that our advances in investment theory are so ingenious that they are worthy of Nobel prizes, while the institution of these theories into practice has generated such poor economic performance?

   In the election campaign of 1992, President Clinton emphasized the need for government to marshal substantial resources to expand investment in public infrastructure and provide an investment tax credit to induce additional private investment. He implicitly raised the issue of the failure of deregulated financial markets of the 1980s' to allocate capital in a manner that could have substantially improved the lot of the average family "working by the rules and paying their taxes."

   The science fiction literature of the 1940s and 1950s pictured a global economy in the twenty-first century where investment projects had become so productive that for the first time in the history of mankind, humans were free to pursue leisure. Work was done almost entirely by "robot" production processes. Even during the Great Depression, Keynes believed that if the economy could maintain a full-employment environment, capital accumulation would be sufficient (presuming population was kept under control) to eliminate entirely the scarcity of capital goods "within a single generation" (Keynes, 1936, p. 221) and to change people's preoccupation from the "economic problem" to the more civilized one of "how to occupy" leisure time through the appreciation of beauty, art, and culture (Keynes, 1972).

Today, as the second generation after Keynes approaches retirement years, the age of capital abundance seems almost as distant as it did in the 1920s. Even more threatening is the fact that if current investment and the resulting productivity trends continue, this generation of children may end up with a lower standard of living than their parents—an almost unheard of phenomenon since the Industrial Revolution and its reliance on capital accumulation for progress.

Capital accumulation and investments have not been able to provide the increasing fruits of progress for developed economies whose population growth appears to be substantially under control. Have the Nobel prize–winning developments in mainstream investment theory contributed to progress or merely re-created economics as "the dismal science"? Can human ingenuity provide a theory that will be a realistic foundation to create a twenty-first century in which humans no longer have to worry about the economic problem (as Keynes suggested over a half-century ago)?

Until we get our theory of investment and accumulation "right," we will be unable to promote public policy that has any potential to create a twenty-first-century economic garden of Eden. This book is dedicated to the task of analyzing the pros and cons of the current fashionable mainstream theory of finance and investment and comparing it with an alternative approach that has its roots in the scientific revolution of economics that Keynes attempted to engineer with his *General Theory of Employment, Interest, and Money.*

Economic proponents of various schools of thought (e.g., Monetarism, Keynesianism, Radical Political Economy, and Post Keynesianism) were invited to write an essay reflecting their views of mainstream versus alternative approaches to analyzing investment theory and the real world. The first article by M.J. Gordon on "The Neoclassical and a Post Keynesian Theory of Investment" provides a useful framework for organizing the articles. Professor Gordon lists five propositions that he argues are the essential elements in the foundations of the mainstream economic theory that won a Nobel prize. These propositions are:

(1) Real persons are portfolio investors who only hold financial assets, while corporate persons hold and invest in the real productive assets of the economy. (2) Each corporation serves its stockholders by making the maximization of its current market value the sole criterion in its investment and financing decisions. The value of a corporation is independent of its financing decisions, that is, (3) its capital structure, and (4) its dividend policy. The latter is the choice between retention of earnings and sales of shares in financing its investment. (5) Most important is the equal opportunity assumption, that the investment opportunities a corporation will have on any future date are independent of its prior investment and other decisions. These opportunities arise from random strokes of good fortune.

Professor Gordon discusses each of these propositions, explains why he believes them faulty, and suggests alternatives that are more in tune with the facts of experience.

The essays of Douglas Vickers, Joel Fried, and James R. Crotty, together with Gordon's, were originally published in the Summer 1992 issue of the *Journal of Post Keynesian Economics* as a minisymposium on investment theory. Vickers, who represents the approach of English economist G.L.S. Shackle, focusing on the uncertainty of the future, produces five propositions of his own that he believes are necessary "to establish a sound macrofoundation for microeconomic argument." Vickers compares his criticisms of mainstream theory with those of Gordon. Although Vickers believes Gordon has raised important analytical issues and is on sound ground in criticizing mainstream theory, Vickers explains why he believes Gordon has failed to provide an analysis of the fundamentals of real-world investment decisions. Vickers then provides economic tools which he claims are more in tune with real-world economic phenomena.

Joel Fried agrees that the neoclassical propositions enumerated by Gordon "are not met in capital markets of record." He argues that mainstream investment theory is not dependent on these five propositions for its applicability to the real world. Professor Fried provides a stirring defense for using and further developing mainstream theory for the important economic problems of the real world.

James R. Crotty examines Gordon's arguments and provides speculation about an "alternative Keynesian investment theory based on more realistic assumptions." Crotty believes that although his criticisms of mainstream theory are sympathetic to Gordon's, they are significantly different and his alternative provides a different approach for modeling the real world.

The response of readers to the original *Journal of Post Keynesian Economics* symposium was very enthusiastic. To encourage others to delve more deeply into this important area, we have opened the discussion up to others in order to provide a wider perspective in this volume.

Peter L. Bernstein is not only a trained economist but a well-regarded financial and economic analyst, who operates a very successful consulting firm in New York. Bernstein was recently the recipient of an award given by financial analysts for the best economic forecasts of the year. His article provides a practitioner's view of the conventional theory of investment.

Edward E. Williams has always had one foot in academia and the other in the real world of high finance and speculation. In addition to his position at Rice University, Williams has been on the board of various corporations that attempt to make profits from financial investment in securities and foreign exchange. Williams builds on the financial aspects of the essays of Gordon, Vickers, Fried, and Crotty to distinguish between corporate and entrepreneurial theories of investment. In the corporate sphere the separation of ownership and control raises questions regarding the role of agencies in financial markets. Williams develops an investment/financing model for large publicly held corporations operating in a world of Keynesian uncertainty. He also develops a second model—an entrepreneurial theory of the firm based on psychological as well as economic factors. A participant in small corporate investment firms, Williams brings a wealth of practical experience to his models.

Robert Chirinko, like Joel Fried, is more sympathetic to mainstream investment theory than the other contributors to this book. He is also well aware of the subtleties of the less well known Post Keynesian approaches to investment. He attempts to provide a synthesis between these two approaches.

Finally, Johan Deprez discusses the implication of expectations upon user costs and the supply and demand functions for capital goods in a Keynes—The General Theory—model. Deprez, an expert on the implications of the existence of fixed, long-lived capital plant and equipment in constraining entrepreneurial decisions, provides an innovative and intriguing analysis for resurrecting Keynes' user-cost concept into public policy discussions.

The purpose of this volume is to reopen the discussion of how to develop the economic theory of investment to better model the facts of experience and to provide policy makers with a better understanding of how capital markets work. In this final decade of the twentieth century, almost everyone agrees that human progress will be closely related to the decisions regarding the investments made to promote economic growth of output. Despite the Nobel prize work done in recent decades, economic performance in this area seems to have worsened. Clearly, a reopening of public discussion on what is required is necessary. Until we get our theory right, it is impossible to get our public policy right. This book does not promise to provide "the" correct theory. Instead, it hopes to stimulate the reader into an understanding of where we may have gone wrong, and how we might rectify our mistakes.

REFERENCES

Keynes, J.M. *The General Theory of Employment, Interest, and Money.* New York: Harcourt, 1936.

———. *Essays in Persuasion: The Collected Writings of John Maynard Keynes*, vol. 9, ed. D. Moggridge. London: Macmillan, 1972.

Can the
Free Market
Pick Winners?

1

The neoclassical and a Post Keynesian theory of investment

M.J. GORDON

Under the neoclassical theory of investment (NTI), the marginal rate of return on investment is equated with an interest rate. Prior to Keynes (1936), the NTI was based on the assumption that the future is certain, in which case that interest rate is the risk-free rate. Keynes was, of course, familiar with the NTI, but he argued at great length and very convincingly in Book IV that uncertainty and risk aversion severely limit the empirical relevance of the theory.[1] The neoclassical response involved the answers to two questions: (1) When do the ideal properties of the investment decision under certainty hold under uncertainty and risk aversion? (2) What "market imperfections" would cause the real world to depart from this ideal world? The answer to the first question was "perfectly competitive capital markets" (PCCM), where there are no taxes, no transaction costs, and equal information for all market participants. The only departure from the NTI was the addition of a risk premium to the risk-free rate. The answers to the second question that were found will be discussed shortly.

The NTI is a cornerstone of the micro foundation for neoclassical macroeconomics, particularly for its synthesis with Keynes' theory initiated by Hicks (1937). In neoclassical macroeconomics, output is a

The author is Professor of Finance at the University of Toronto. He has benefited from comments on earlier drafts of this paper by Trevor Chamberlain, Paul David-son, Lawrence Gould, Harry Markowitz, and Alan White. The ideas presented here are developed more thoroughly in Gordon (1994).

[1]Here uncertainty means that a future payment may have more than one value, and risk aversion means that the payment's present value varies with its mean and in-versely with its variance. There is ample evidence that shares and other assets are priced on the basis of estimates for means and variances of uncertain future payments or surrogates for these quantities. For alternative definitions of risk and uncertainty, see Shackle (1955) and Davidson (1991). They argue correctly that much of capital theory under uncertainty has no empirical relevance because it is based on probabil-ity distributions that cannot be estimated.

function of employment given the capital stock, and output growth is determined in the capital market by the interest rate that equates the demand for investment with the supply of savings. Keynes argued convincingly that changes in the wage rate have little influence on employment and changes in the interest rate have little influence on saving. His consumption function made the level of output as well as its growth determined in the capital market. His theory of national income determination was incomplete, however, because it had no theory of investment since investment expenditures depended on the animal spirits that determined future profit flow expectations.[2]

Under the Hicks synthesis, Keynes' theory on employment and saving was joined with the neoclassical theory on investment. "Market imperfections" may prevent the interest rate from moving rapidly enough to keep investment at the full employment level in the short run, but the NTI realizes that goal in the long run (see Mankiw, 1988; R.J. Gordon, 1990; and standard textbooks such as Dornbusch and Fischer, 1990). This synthesis was not burdened with Keynes' questions on investment. The neoclassical theory of finance "was attractive because it provided researchers with a rigorous justification for abstracting from the complications induced by financial considerations" (Gertler, 1988, p. 565). The classification of assets in macroeconomics remained money and all other assets, notwithstanding the fact that it should be the degree of risk.[3]

Unfortunately, the neoclassical theory of finance on which the NTI relies for its validity depends upon the truth of five propositions or theorems, all of which are false, some grievously so. These propositions are: (1) Real persons are portfolio investors who only hold financial assets, while corporate persons hold and invest in the real productive assets of the economy. (2) Each corporation serves its stockholders by making the maximization of its current market value the sole criterion in its investment and financing decisions. The value of a corporation is independent of its financing decisions, that is, (3) its capital structure, and (4) its dividend policy. The latter is the choice between retention of

---

[2]For some time thereafter and to this day the Post Keynesians treat investment as an exogenous variable. It cannot be predicted, and full employment requires the management of the economy by government. See Davidson (1978), Minsky (1975), and Eichner and Kregel (1975).

[3]E. Roy Weintraub could write: "From Hicks, through Lange and Klein, to Patinkin, we have seen a growing agreement about the particular microeconomic structure that is supposed to underlie all intelligent discourse about macroeconomic theory. This neo-Walrasian model is a certainty-based general equilibrium framework" (1979, pp. 67–68).

earnings and the sale of shares in financing its investment. (5) Most important is the equal opportunity assumption, that the investment opportunities a corporation will have on any future date are independent of its prior investment and other decisions. These opportunities arise from random strokes of good fortune.

Neoclassical financial economists have been concerned primarily with the two financing propositions (3) and (4). They have shown that these propositions are true under the PCCM assumptions. Their efforts have advanced in two directions. One is to present theory and evidence that a financing theorem remains true notwithstanding the presence of "market imperfections" that make it clear to all but the faithful that the proposition is false. The other is to explore the consequences of one or another market imperfection within a framework that accepts the truth of the other assumptions and the theory as a whole. The market imperfection is looked on as a failure not of the theory but of the real world, that will be cured in the long run, with the passage of time. The other three propositions, of which the second and the last are most critical, are simply assumed true without question.

This paper has two objectives. One is to show how the NTI requires the truth of all five propositions and to demonstrate that they are all more or less false, with two fatally false. The other purpose is to present an alternative superior theory of the investment and saving behavior of real and corporate persons. This alternative may be called Post Keynesian in that it gives voice in a meaningful way to Keynes' reservations about neoclassical investment theory. It is possible that Keynes would not be completely happy with this theory of investment, but it is quite likely that Keynesians such as Michal Kalecki, Joan Robinson, and Sidney Weintraub would be quite comfortable with it.

I. Portfolio investors and corporations

The first proposition of the NTI is that real persons hold only financial assets and corporate persons hold and invest in all real-risky assets. Consider an economy in which the future is certain and there are perfectly competitive capital markets (PCCM). Under these conditions there is no need for corporations. Regardless of how investment opportunities are distributed among the system's proprietors, each one is able to and does borrow or lend whatever amount equates the marginal rate of return on investment with the interest rate. That investment decision maximizes current wealth (net worth). Real persons maximize utility, not wealth, but, with the future certain, wealth and utility maximization result in the same decision, and we have the NTI under certainty.

Unfortunately, when uncertainty and risk aversion are recognized, utility and wealth maximization need not be equal. Utility maximization may persuade a risk-averse proprietor to borrow and invest less than the amount that maximizes net worth. There also are circumstances where a conservative policy guarantees bankruptcy, and it is rational for a proprietor to borrow and invest more than the amount that equates the marginal rate of return with the cost of capital (see Gordon and Kwan, 1979). Even when a proprietor's investment decision is optimal, it may not be possible to obtain the necessary credit when it requires a high debt-equity ratio.

Real people must be removed from the investment in real assets. With PCCM we have the world described in Markowitz (1959) and Sharpe (1964), where a proprietor becomes a portfolio investor who invests in a diversified portfolio of shares, lending or borrowing the difference between the amount invested and net worth.[4] In PCCM all shares are fairly priced, so that the portfolio investor's net worth is independent of the amount invested in risky shares. However, the expected return and risk on net worth both increase with the fraction invested, and the investment decision that maximizes utility will vary among investors with their risk aversion. Utility maximization is a very personal decision in neoclassical economics, and we, therefore, cannot say what any individual or people in aggregate will do without discovering what most people including neoclassical economists are unable to articulate—their utility functions. This is no problem because people's decisions only influence the risk premium in the cost of capital. What is important is what the corporations do, because they invest in real assets.

II. The value maximization theorem

The second proposition necessary for the truth of the NTI is that the objective of the corporation in its investment and financing decisions is the maximization of its current market value. That is what portfolio stockholders want the corporations to do. An investment or financing decision that raises the price of its shares may change the risk and return on a shareholder's portfolio, but that is of absolutely no concern to the

---

[4]Markowitz demonstrated that aversion to risk is general if not universal. Indifference would result in all wealth in the most profitable asset regardless of risk, while aversion could be expected to result in diversification. He also established the mathematics for optimal diversification policy. Sharpe showed that in PCCM, a portfolio investor invests in the market portfolio.

shareholder, who enjoys the increase in net worth that results from the price increase, and a few minutes on the telephone to a broker creates a portfolio that restores the previous or achieves any other risk-return position on her or his net worth.

Corporate managements have the legal obligation to serve stockholders, but as long ago as Berle and Means (1932) it was recognized that the separation of ownership and control creates a principal agent problem. That is, a corporation's management has considerable freedom of action to subordinate stockholder interests to its own interest. A corporation's management does not hold a well-diversified portfolio of jobs, so that bankruptcy is very costly to management. It will be seen shortly that raising share price today is accomplished by very high debt ratios and dividend payout rates that raise the probability of bankruptcy tomorrow. Hence, self-interest persuades corporate managements to follow conservative leverage and dividend policies. As Crotty (1990, p. 533) observes:

> The primary objective of top management is the *long-term reproduction, growth, and safety of the firm itself*, and, through these, its own status and security. Stockholder interests are not an objective pursued by management but rather a constraint upon it.

Long-run survival also requires the avoidance of a hostile takeover in the short run. The developments in the "market for corporate control" over the past few decades have increased the profitability and reduced the barriers to corporate raiding. A rise in leverage and dividend rates along with the adoption of "poison pill" arrangements have taken place to deal with the short-run threat to corporate managements.

Prior to a paper by Jensen and Meckling (1976), the principal agent problem was ignored by most neoclassical financial economists. It was simply assumed that managements maximize the *current* market value of their corporations' shares. Since 1976, Jensen and Meckling has become the standard treatment of the principal agent problem, but they trivialized it. They treated the problem as a conflict between inside and outside stockholders. The former have control and they use their power to take income from the corporation in the form of salary or payments in kind instead of dividends. The invidious term for payment in kind is perquisites. If the inside ownership is 100 percent, the allocation between dividends and other forms of payment is irrelevant apart from tax consequences. However, as outsiders are brought in, insiders gain at the expense of the outsiders by increasing the income taken in the form of perquisites or excessive salaries, which are treated as expenses in calculating profit.

For a number of reasons, this is a trivilization of the principal agent problem. The corporation could not survive as an institution unless perquisites beyond those that can be explained by tax considerations are trivial in amount or exceptional. More important, Jensen and Meckling assumed that the insiders maximize the market value of their net worth in their decisions, but, as shown in Chamberlain and Gordon (1991), insider assets are not diversified and, like proprietors, they maximize utility, not net worth. Insiders behave like proprietors.

Jensen and Meckling acknowledged that they had nothing to say on the central problem of the separation of ownership and control, that is, the investment and financing of a corporation with a management that has little or no ownership interest.

> One of the most serious limitation [*sic*] of the analysis is that as it stands we have not worked out in this paper its application to the very large modern corporation whose managers own little or no equity. We believe our approach can be applied to this case but space limitations preclude discussion of these issues here. They remain to be worked out in detail and will be included in a future paper. [Jensen and Meckling, 1976, p. 356]

That future paper has still not appeared. It is therefore most surprising that this paper has become generally accepted in the literature of financial economics as the definitive treatment of the principal agent problem, and not merely as an elaboration of the special issues involved in the corporation, usually small, where the principal owners are also the management.

III. The capital structure theorem

The Modigliani–Miller (1958) capital structure or leverage theorem is that the value of a corporation is independent of its capital structure in PCCM. This theorem is necessary for the validity of the NTI, for without it the investment decision that maximizes value would be compromised by leverage policy to realize the objective. The intuition behind the theorem is that an investor can create the risk and return that shares in a levered corporation provide through personal leverage on shares in an unlevered corporation. The theorem is true in PCCM, because the assumptions of PCCM make personal leverage a *perfect substitute* for corporate leverage. The relevant empirical question, therefore, is the nature and significance of the limitations on the use of personal leverage as a substitute for corporate leverage.

In a correction to their 1958 paper, Modigliani and Miller (1963) found that the value of a share increases continuously with leverage, when interest is treated as an expense under the corporate income tax, and when the personal tax rate on bond and share income is lower than the corporate tax rate. In addition, Brigham and Gordon (1968) found that the increase in value with leverage exceeds the amount that could be attributed to the tax system. The explanation in Gordon and Kwan (1979) is that the institutional arrangements that govern the terms under which individuals and corporations borrow make personal leverage a very poor substitute for corporate leverage. These terms persuade investors to value corporate leverage very highly. Value maximization at an infinite leverage rate is quite ridiculous, and it stimulated interest in market imperfections that make leverage costly, and a finite capital structure optimal. The imperfections found were in the expected costs of bankruptcy, monitoring, and the moral hazard of violating me-first rules, all of which increase with leverage (see Stiglitz, 1969; Gordon and Kwan, 1979; and Bradley, Jarrell, and Kim, 1984). However, these considerations still leave as optimal policy leverage rates that are exceedingly high relative to the range of rates ordinarily employed by corporations.

Nonetheless, a number of papers by financial economists have "demonstrated" capital structure irrelevance, notwithstanding the market imperfections that produce the contrary result. Miller (1977) is the most striking and influential of such papers. He found that with a corporate income tax and a progressive personal income tax, there is a finite optimal amount of leverage for the economy as a whole, but once this equilibrium is reached, the value of each corporation is independent of its capital structure as in PCCM. Gordon (1982b) examined the exact same tax regime described by Miller and found that the value of a corporation increases with its leverage rate as before. The only basis for Miller's conclusion is the assumption that investors are indifferent to risk. But how can one dare claim empirical relevance for results obtained under that assumption?[5] It is either a tribute to Miller's authority or an index of the confusion on the subject that Miller's 1977 paper has been

---

[5]That is, investors are satisfied with the same expected return on a share as on a risk-free bond. Miller (1977, p. 267) stated: "If, therefore, the personal tax on income from common stocks is less than that on income from bonds, then the *before tax* return on taxable bonds has to be high enough, other things equal, to offset this tax handicap." Ross (1985) introduced a paper with the title "Debt and Taxes and Uncertainty" with the statement: "The purpose of this article is to extend Miller's argument by recognizing the differences between debt and equity when the environment is not certain."

extensively referenced over the years as an important contribution to the theory of capital structure.[6]

Finally, a brief comment on the flood of papers that examine the influence of asymmetric information and signaling on the relation between leverage and value. It is argued that when the market places a lower value on a corporation than the value its management "knows" is correct, debt financing may be used to communicate management's superior knowledge or capture a benefit for the existing shareholders (see Harris and Raviv, 1990). What can be done empirically with this theory is open to question. Nonetheless, it would seem to be of no relevance for the relation between leverage and value in *equilibrium*. At any point in time the equilibrium relation should prevail for most corporations, and to ascertain it we have to look elsewhere.

In sum, the present state of knowledge on capital structure is as follows. The Modigliani–Miller theorem is true in PCCM. The tax system and the institutional arrangements that make investors prefer corporate to personal leverage make the value of a corporation increase with leverage initially. The expected value of bankruptcy, agency, and moral hazard costs make the value turn down at very high leverage rates. The great majority of corporations under ordinary conditions have leverage rates that are more or less below the rates that maximize the value of their shares. Why that is so we saw in section II.

IV. The dividend policy theorem

The Miller–Modigliani (1961) dividend policy theorem is that in PCCM the value of a corporation is independent of its choice between retained earnings and the sale of additional shares to finance a given investment plan, with all other attributes of the corporation such as its capital structure held constant. A corollary is that the value of a corporation is also independent of its choice between dividends and the repurchase of shares in making distributions to shareholders. The theorem and its corollary are true under the stated assumptions. The simple intuitive proof is that in PCCM the dividend that a stockholder receives under one method of financing or payment is exactly matched by a capital gain under the other method, and a dollar is a dollar.

This conclusion is upset by the presence of taxes, transaction costs,

---

[6]The only subsequent reference to Gordon (1982b) has been a comment by Jaffee and Westerfield (1984) that did not find fault with the basic argument in Gordon. See also Gordon (1984).

and unequal information. Capital gains that are unrealized through the sale of shares are tax-free, and over long periods of time realized capital gains to most investors have been taxed at substantially lower rates than dividends. The transaction costs involved in a new share issue are substantially higher than the costs involved in retaining earnings. Both of these market imperfections therefore make retained earnings a substantially less expensive cost of equity capital than the issue of shares. Unequal information also contributes to the advantage of retention over the sale of shares.

The inescapable conclusion is that market imperfections make the value of a corporation depend upon its dividend policy. Maximization of value should lead corporations to pay no dividends. They should rely on share repurchases insofar as they wish to make distributions of earnings. However, we have a "dividend puzzle" recognized by Black (1976) and others. We not only have dividend relevance, but the relevance is exactly opposite to that predicted by the market imperfections that have been recognized. Corporations pay dividends and raise funds by issuing more shares. They rarely rely on share repurchases to make distributions. The simple and obvious explanation is that dividends have a favorable instead of an unfavorable influence on share price.

There are, however, financial economists who have managed to find that market imperfections do not violate the irrelevance of dividend policy or its corollaries. One is that the dividend and investment decisions of a firm are independent of each other. Fama (1974) claimed that he found the empirical evidence consistent with this corollary. Another corollary is that the expected return or yield at which a share is selling and its dividend yield should be independent of each other.[7] With capital gains taxed at a lower rate than dividends, yield and dividend yield would be *positively* correlated. Black and Scholes (1974) found no correlation between yield and dividend yield, while Litzenberger and Ramaswamy (1979) found the two were positively correlated. A debate followed on which of the two conclusions is correct. In Gordon (1989) I have argued that both papers, and Fama (1974) as well, are wrong or irrelevant. Here I will only note that these studies support the conclusion that a rise in the dividend payout rate has either no influence on price or

---

[7]Let the expected return or yield on a share be $k = d + g$, with g = expected growth rate in price, $d = D/P$ = dividend yield, D = dividend, and P = price. Also, $D = pY$ with Y = permanent earnings per share and p = payout rate, so that p is dividend policy. With $k = pY/P + g$, dividend policy irrelevance implies that P is independent of p. It also means that k is independent of p, since a change in g exactly offsets any change in pY/P, thereby making k and pY/P independent.

that it actually depresses the price! Does anyone in the real world believe that either of these propositions is true?

Miller and Modigliani are not among the believers. They accepted that the opposite is true. They then invoked the asymmetric information hypothesis to argue that the covariation between dividend and price "would not be incompatible with irrelevance to the extent that it was merely a reflection of what might be called the 'informational content' of dividends" with respect to future earnings (Miller and Modigliani, 1961, p. 429). Notwithstanding the questionable significance of this distinction between the dividend per se and the information it conveys, this argument has generated empirical research on the covariation in dividends, earnings, and price. If they all move together, the earnings change is responsible for the price change. If price and dividend change with no concurrent earnings change, the covariation is explained by the information in the dividend about earnings. Under what conditions is the proposition false?[8] (Note also that the relevant dividend policy variable is not the dividend but the fraction of earnings paid in dividends.)

For those who cannot accept what is evident to the naked eye, there is, of course, no lack of convincing econometric evidence, that price and payout rate are positively correlated so that yield and dividend yield are negatively correlated. Almost twenty-five years ago, Brigham and Gordon (1968) demonstrated the latter proposition. Malkiel and Cragg (1970) provided a direct proof that price and payout are correlated, using the regression:

(1) $$P/Y = a(o) + a(1)p + a(2)g + a(3)\beta,$$

where P/Y = price–earnings ratio; p = payout rate; g = expected rate of growth in earnings; and β = share risk measured by beta. This is a simple direct test on the existence and direction of the influence of dividend policy on price: the influence depends upon the coefficient of the payout rate, $a(1)$. Malkiel and Cragg found $a(1)$ to be positive in each of five years, and statistically significant in three of the years, which contradicts the findings of both Black and Scholes (1974) and Litzenberger and Ramaswamy (1979).[9]

[8]See Ross and Westerfield (1988, pp. 416–417) for references to this literature and an effort to rationalize a distinction between the dividend and the information it conveys.

[9]Lynch Jones and Ryan (1989) developed monthly estimates of the coefficients of equation 1, and they found $a(1)$ positive with exceptionally high t statistics in every month from November 1987 through August 1989. Clearly, raising the dividend payout rate raises price over the relevant range of variation in payout.

V. The equal opportunity proposition

The last of the five propositions necessary for the truth of the neoclassical theory of investment is the equal opportunity proposition. It is the most questionable and the most critical among the five, but it remains unrecognized by neoclassical financial economists. This proposition is the direct basis for the valuation model that is used to establish the NTI where the marginal rate of return is equated with the cost of capital.[10] That valuation model was first presented in Miller and Modigliani (1961, p. 416).[11] It is:

(2)
$$V(0) = \frac{X(0)}{\rho} + \sum_{t=0}^{\infty} I(t) \frac{[\rho*(t) - \rho]}{\rho} (1 + \rho)^{-(t+1)}.$$

In this expression, $V(0)$ = current value of the common equity; $X(0)$ = current earnings on the common equity; ρ = yield (discount rate) at which the shares are selling; $I(t)$ = investment in period t, and $\rho^*(t)$ = the annualized rate of return in perpetuity that $I(t)$ is expected to earn. The first term, $X(0)/\rho$, is the present value of the expected earnings in perpetuity on the existing net worth. The remainder of the expression is the present value of the return in excess of ρ that the corporation is expected to earn on investment in the current and all future periods. With the return on investment, $\rho^*(t)$, a decreasing function of $I(t)$, the investment in period t that maximizes the value of the equity is obtained by taking the derivative of $V(0)$ with respect to $I(t)$. For the current period:

(3)
$$\frac{\delta V(0)}{\delta I(0)} = \frac{m(0) - \rho}{\rho} (1 + \rho)^{-(t+1)}$$

where $m(0)$ is the marginal rate of return on investment. It is clear that $V(0)$ is maximized at the $I(0)$ that makes $m(0) = \rho$. That is the neoclassical theory of investment, where the cost of capital, ρ, is equal to the interest rate plus a risk premium.

Implicit in the above is the assumption that ρ is independent of $I(t)$,

[10]Notice that this theorem may be false without calling into question that the firm *ranks* investment opportunities according to their profitability in selecting among them.

[11] The value of a share of stock is the present value of its expected future dividends. Starting with this expression, the paper arrives at the above "investment opportunities" model under the PCCM assumptions. Other models consistent with this one are also presented but they cannot be used to arrive at the cost of capital and the value-maximizing investment decision. The assumption in this expression is that equity is the only source of funds to finance the firm. There is no essential change in the conclusions reached when the model is extended to include debt financing.

notwithstanding the evidence found by Fewings (1979) and others that ρ varies with growth. The other more important assumption, implicit in the summation sign in equation 2, is that the function that $\rho^*(t)$ is of $I(t)$ is independent of the investment in every other period. This means that the investment opportunities available to a corporation are independent of its history. Neoclassical economists do not explore very deeply the sources of investment opportunities with abnormal returns, but fundamental to this model is the assumption that the opportunities are simply given, due perhaps to good fortune in the past.[12] The assumption was characterized as follows:

> On the other hand, the position that the investment opportunities available to IBM, General Motors or any other firm are independent of their prior investment decisions means that IBM and General Motors would have the same investment opportunities today if they had undertaken no investment over the prior fifty years. What could be less true? [Gordon and Gould, 1978, p. 855]

Gordon and Gould established the investment that maximizes the market value of a corporation when corporate investment and other policies generate investment opportunities. The cost of capital as well as the return on investment prove to be functions of investment policy.

Does the empirical evidence support the neoclassical theory of investment notwithstanding the failure of all five finance propositions that are necessary for its theoretical validity? There is considerable evidence that profitability and investment are positively correlated, but every theory of investment is consistent with such correlation. Jorgenson has been a leading figure in the empirical representation of the NTI, and Jorgenson and Seibert (1968) tested his representation of the theory against a number of alternatives. They found that the neoclassical theory performed best, and a liquidity or long-run survival theory performed worst. However, all of the subsequent efforts at replicating their results were unsuccessful (see Eisner and Nadiri, 1970; and Chamberlain and Gordon, 1989). In addition, the latter found that investment models based on profitability variables, among them Tobin's q, performed far better than the neoclassical model. Chamberlain and Gordon also found that

---

[12] When real as well as financial capital markets are perfectly competitive, the value of a corporation is independent of its investment decision, just as the net worth of a portfolio investor is independent of her or his investment decision. The corporation may have profitable investment opportunities, but they are separable as well as independent. Hence, selling a valuable investment opportunity is a perfect substitute for undertaking it. Ordinarily, the perfect market assumptions are not carried that far.

the Jorgenson and Seibert model for liquidity theory misrepresented the liquidity variable, and the explanation of investment was improved when a model based on profitability variables was enlarged correctly to include liquidity properly measured.

VI. The Keynesian theory of investment

As a starting point for a theory of investment that can serve as a micro foundation for a complete Keynesian theory of national income determination, we will consider only a proprietor.[13] The proprietor is a member of a species—a socioeconomic species, not one in nature. Two conditions must be satisfied for the long-run survival of a species. One is a benign environment so that changes in the number and character of the species over time are very modest under feasible behavior by its members. The other condition is that the members follow the behavior necessary for long-run survival. A proprietor does this by maximizing the probability of long-run survival (PLRS) subject to reasonable constraints. This assumption is less general than utility maximization, but it certainly does not lack intuitive merit. The consequences for the savings and investment behavior of a proprietor are outlined below, and the bases for the conclusions reached are developed in greater detail elsewhere (Gordon, 1980, 1987).

Let the proprietor have a net worth of $W(t)$ and a capital of $K(t)$ at the start of t. The difference $K(t) - W(t)$ is financed by borrowing or lending at the interest rate $i(t)$. For simplicity, we let $i(t) = i$ for all t. The proprietor's debt-equity ratio is $w(t) = [K(t) - W(t)]/W(t)$. The return on capital in t is the random variable $x(t)$. For simplicity, $1 + x(t)$ is log normal and independently and identically distributed over time with mean $\bar{x}$ and variance v. The return on net worth in t is:

(4) $$r(t) = i + [x(t) - i][K(t)/W(t)].$$

The expected value of $r(t)$ is $\bar{r}(t)$, and it results from substituting $\bar{x}$ for $x(t)$ in $r(t)$. With risk aversion making $\bar{x} > i$, the mean and variance of $r(t)$ both rise with $K(t)/W(t)$.

The proprietor's consumption $C(t)$ is the fraction $c(t)$ of $W(t)$, so that:

[13] There are problems in extending the results obtained to a corporation and a portfolio investor with or without human capital. These problems should prove to be more interesting than difficult, in that their solutions are likely to enrich the theory's ability to explain the dynamic behavior of capitalist systems.

(5) $$I(t) = W(t)[r(t) - c(t) + d(t)];$$

(6) $$W(t + 1) = W(t)[1 + r(t) - c(t)];$$

(7) $$K(t + 1) = K(t) + I(t).$$

In addition, note the following properties of the environment. First, for a proprietor who has no monopoly power, the variance of $x(t)$ is very large in relation to its mean. Second, to ensure that debt is completely or substantially free of default risk, an upper limit is placed on the debt ratio $w(t)$. Finally, a proprietor's desire for consumption does not allow a value for $K(t)$ that is negligible in relation to $W(t)$.[14]

It is not possible for a proprietor to remain in a stationary state. Such a state requires that $c(t) = r(t)$ and $W(t + 1) = W(t)$ over time. With $x(t)$ and $r(t)$ random variables that can take on negative values, and with $r(t)$ unknown at the start of t, it is not physically possible to set $c(t) = r(t)$. What a proprietor can do is set $c(t) = \bar{r}(t)$, the expected value of $r(t)$, subject to $C(t) = c(t)W(t)$ being larger than $C(min)$, the minimum value for $C(t)$ necessary for survival during t.[15] However, a proprietor who follows this policy is practically certain to go bankrupt in the long run. Over a relevant finite horizon, say five to twenty-five years, the probability of bankruptcy increases with the probability of a negative growth in $W(t)$. The latter is in excess of one-half, and it rises with time, with $C(min)/W(0)$, with the ratio of the variance to the mean of $x(t)$, and with the leverage rate.[16]

It is clear that the probability of long-run survival increases with the

---

[14] Any proprietor may be a rentier who puts all net worth in risk-free loans. However, the only source of the output required to pay the interest is the capital of the borrower. Hence, proprietors who have $K(t)/W(t)$ at or close to zero are special cases that need not concern us.

[15] The minimum at the very least is the amount needed for survival. A proprietor can be expected to set a higher value on $C(min)$, if going on the dole or taking employment follow bankruptcy.

[16] If $c(t)W(t)$ is not constrained by $C(min)$, the arithmetic and geometric mean growth rates in $W(t)$ are zero and negative respectively. Then, as $t \rightarrow \infty$, it becomes almost certain that the actual growth rate will be negative, in which case $W(\infty)$ will be infinitely small. Also, over any finite time period the probability of negative growth in $W(t)$ will be in excess of one-half, that probability increasing with $\sqrt{x}$ and $K(t)/W(t)$. However, at $t = \infty$, there is an infinitely small probability that $W(\infty)$ will be infinitely large, so that the expected value of $W(\infty) = W(0)$ and the variance of $W(\infty)$ is infinite. Infinity is an elusive concept. With the $C(min)$ constraint, over any finite number of time periods, the probability of bankruptcy is less than the probability of negative growth, but the former approaches the latter with time, $C(min)/W(0)$, $\sqrt{x}$, and $K(t)/W(t)$.

probability of long-run growth in $W(t)$, and that probability increases with the fraction of expected income that is saved, that is, with the ratio $[\bar{r}(t) - c(t)]/\bar{r}(t)$. A policy that balances the desire for current consumption against the desire for long-run survival is to make $c(t)$ fall as $W(t)$ rises. With $c(t) = 1$ when $W(t) \leq C(min)$, $c(t)$ might reasonably fall asymptotically toward zero or the interest rate as $W(t) \to \infty$. We have thus a theoretical basis for the Keynesian consumption function with income $\bar{r}(t)W(t)$ the permanent income that determines the level of savings.

Monopoly power increases the mean and reduces the variance of $x(t)$. Hence, we might reasonably expect a proprietor to pursue monopoly power. A proprietor with no monopoly power has a return on capital with such a large variance in relation to its mean that survival beyond a few years has a very small probability. Kalecki (1971) argued that without monopoly power, the prices of a manufacturing firm's products fall to their marginal cost and fail to cover overhead costs, thereby resulting in bankruptcy. In the large modern corporation we find the pursuit of monopoly power institutionalized. Such corporations engage in production and a wide range of nonproduction activities that are intended to make the production profitable. These activities can be beneficial, benign, or malignant (see Gordon, 1982a, 1985).

The third and last variable that a proprietor can use to manage the PLRS is capital structure, $K(t)/W(t)$. It will be argued here that the PLRS is maximized by making $K(t)/W(t)$ vary inversely with $W(t)$. In other words, a proprietor becomes more conservative, moving from a debtor to a creditor position as wealth increases. The argument begins by recalling that when $c(t)$ is independent of $W(t)$, the actual growth rate converges on its geometric mean as $t \to \infty$. A policy of maximizing the geometric mean growth rate has, therefore, come to be called a growth optimal policy. Over a finite horizon, say twenty years, the geometric mean is the median growth rate, with the actual values dispersed around it to a degree that depends upon its variance. Growth optimal policy, therefore, also maximizes the probability of a positive growth rate, since that probability rises above one-half as the median rises above zero. Young and Trent (1969) have shown that a good approximation of the geometric mean growth rate is:

(8) $$g = \{(1 + \bar{r} - c)^2 - v(K/W)^2\}^{1/2} - 1,$$

which is maximized when:

(9)
$$K/W = \frac{[1+i-c]\,[\bar{x}-i]}{v-[\bar{x}-i]^2}.$$

As long as c is in the neighborhood of i, the growth optimal capital structure depends primarily on the relation between v and $\bar{x}-i$. Under a reasonable range of values for v and $\bar{x}-i$, we could have K/W as large as 2 and as small as 0.5.

What happens when we take account of our consumption function, which has $c(t) = C(t)/W(t)$ approach 1 as $W(t)$ falls to $C(min)$ and has $c(t)$ fall below $\bar{r}(t)$ to the interest rate or lower as $W(t)$ becomes large? A growth optimal policy when $W(t)$ is small would result in a negative growth rate and make bankruptcy practically certain. With consumption little if at all above the minimum, it makes sense to adopt a go-for-broke policy. Borrowing and investing to the limit or more (the moral hazard problem) increases the probability of bankruptcy in the immediate future, but the PLRS is also increased. A stroke of good fortune is possible and capitalizing on it raises $W(t)$ materially. A high PLRS is then made possible by moving to a conservative capital structure. As net worth rises, the capital structure that maximizes the PLRS falls to and then below perhaps the growth optimal value. Markowitz (1976) has argued that an investor may prefer a more conservative policy than the growth optimal policy, without making clear why that could be rational. Perhaps uncertainty about the parameters of the return on investment and the consumption constraint are at work here.

VII. Conclusion

A cornerstone in establishment macroeconomics is the neoclassical theory of investment, which equates the marginal rate of return with a risk-adjusted interest rate. That theory in turn depends on five propositions, all of which are more or less false, with some critically false. The failure of the two finance propositions, the irrelevance of leverage and dividend policies, was demonstrated, and the limitations of the theory and evidence created to support NTI exposed. Value maximization and equal opportunity were shown to be most critical, blatantly false, and nonetheless accepted without question by neoclassical financial economists.

An alternative and superior explanation of saving and investment behavior follows from the reasonable assumption that people are motivated by concern for long-run survival as well as current consumption. Proprietors who behave accordingly make the fraction of income saved rise and the fraction invested fall as net worth rises. Portfolio investors and corporations are likely to behave in a similar fashion. Exploration of the macro consequences of such behavior in Gordon (1994) illuminate the short-run fluctuations and the long-run development of capitalist systems.

REFERENCES

Berle, A.A., and Means, G.C. *The Modern Corporation and Private Property*, New York: Macmillan, 1932.

Black, F. "The Dividend Puzzle." *Journal of Portfolio Management*, Winter 1976, *2*, 5–8.

Black, F., and Scholes, M.S. "The Effects of Dividend Yield and Dividend Policy on Common Stock Prices and Returns." *Journal of Financial Economics*, May 1974, *1*, 1–22.

Bradley, M.; Jarrell, G.A.; and Kim, E.H. "On the Existence of An Optimal Capital Structure: Theory and Evidence." *Journal of Finance*, July 1984, *39*, 857–878.

Brigham, E.F., and Gordon, M.J. "Leverage, Dividend Policy, and the Cost of Capital." *Journal of Finance*, March 1968, *33*, 85–103.

Chamberlain, T., and Gordon, M.J. "Liquidity, Profitability and Long-Run Survival: Theory and Evidence on Business Investment." *Journal of Post Keynesian Economics*, Summer 1989, *11*, 589–610.

———. "The Investment Financing and Control of the Firm: A Long Run Survival View." *Cambridge Journal of Economics*, 1991, *15*, 393–403.

Crotty, J. "Owner-Manager Conflict and Financial Theories of Investment Instability: A Critical Assessment of Keynes, Tobin, and Minsky." *Journal of Post Keynesian Economics*, Summer 1990, *12*, 519–542.

Davidson, P. *Money and the Real World*. London: Macmillan, 1978.

———. "Is Probability Theory Relevant for Uncertainty? A Post Keynesian Perspective." *Journal of Economic Perspectives*, Winter 1991, *5*, 129–143.

Dornbusch, R., and Fischer, S. *Macroeconomics*. New York: McGraw-Hill, 1990.

Eichner, A.S., and Kregel, J.A. "An Essay on Post-Keynesian Theory: A New Paradigm in Economics." *Journal of Economic Literature*, December 1975, *13*, 1293–1314.

Eisner, R., and Nadiri, M.I. "Neoclassical Theory of Investment Behaviour: A Comment." *Review of Economics and Statistics*, May 1970, *52*, 216–222.

Fama, E.F. "Empirical Relationships between the Dividend and Investment Decision of Firms." *American Economic Review*, June 1974, *64*, 304–318.

Fewings, D.R. *Corporate Growth and Common Stock Risk*. Greenwich, CT: JAI Press, 1979.

Gertler, M. "Financial Structure and Aggregate Economic Activity: An Overview." *Journal of Money Credit and Banking*, August 1988 (part 2), *20*, 559–587.

Gordon, M.J. "Growth and Survival in a Capitalist System." *Journal of Post Keynesian Economics*, Summer 1980, *2*, 443–458.

———. "Corporate Bureaucracy, Productivity Gain and the Distribution of Revenue in U.S. Manufacturing, 1947–1977." *Journal of Post Keynesian Economics*, Summer 1982a, *4*, 483–496.

———. "Leverage and the Value of a Firm under a Progressive Income Tax." *Journal of Banking and Finance*, 1982b, *6*, 433–443.

———. "Leverage and the Value of a Firm under a Progressive Income Tax: Reply." *Journal of Banking and Finance*, July 1984, *8*, 495–497.

———. "Postwar Growth in Monopoly Power." *Journal of Post Keynesian Economics*, Fall 1985, *7*, 3–13.

———. "Insecurity, Growth and the Rise of Capitalism." *Journal of Post Keynesian Economics*, Summer 1987, *9*, 529–551.

———. "Corporate Finance under the MM Theorems." *Financial Management*, Summer 1989, *18*, 19–28.

———. *Finance Investment and Macroeconomics: The Neoclassical and a Post Keynesian Solution.* Cheltenham, UK: Edward Elgar, 1994.

Gordon, M.J., and Gould, L.I. "The Cost of Equity Capital: A Reconsideration." *Journal of Finance*, June 1978, *33*, 849–861.

Gordon, M.J., and Kwan, C.C.Y. "Debt Maturity, Default Risk and Capital Structure." *Journal of Banking and Finance*, 1979, *6*, 483–493.

Gordon, R.J. "What Is New-Keynesian Economics?" *Journal of Economic Literature*, September 1990, *28*, 1115–1171.

Harris, M., and Raviv, A. "Capital Structure and the Information Role of Debt." *Journal of Finance*, June 1990, *45*, 321–350.

Hicks, J.R. "Mr. Keynes and the Classics: A Suggested Interpretation." *Econometrica*, 1937, 147–159.

Jaffe, J.F., and Westerfield, R.W. "Leverage and the Value of a Firm under a Progressive Income Tax: A Correction and Extension." *Journal of Banking and Finance*, November 1984, *8*, 491–494.

Jensen, M.C., and Meckling, W.H. "Theory of the Firm: Managerial Behavior, Agency Costs, and Ownership Structure." *Journal of Financial Economics*, October 1976, *3*, 305–360.

Jorgenson D.W., and Seibert, C.D. "A Comparison of Alternative Theories of Corporate Investment Behavior." *American Economic Review*, September 1968, *58*, 681–712.

Kalecki, M. *Selected Essays on the Dynamics of the Capitalist Economy, 1933–1970.* Cambridge: Cambridge University Press, 1971.

Keynes, J.M. *The General Theory of Employment Interest and Money.* New York: Harcourt Brace, 1936.

Litzenberger, R.H., and Ramaswamy, K. "The Effects of Personal Taxes and Dividends on Capital Asset Prices: Theory and Empirical Evidence." *Journal of Financial Economics*, 1979, *7*, 163–195.

Lynch Jones and Ryan. "I/B/E/S, P/E Growth Model." *I/B/E/S Monthly Comments*, August 31, 1989, p. 29.

Malkiel, B., and Cragg, J.G. "Expectations and the Structure of Share Prices." *American Economic Review*, September 1970, *60*, 601–617.

Mankiw, N.G. "Recent Developments in Macroeconomics: A Quick Refresher Course." *Journal of Money Credit and Banking*, August 1988 (part 2), *20*, 436–449.

Markowitz, H. *Portfolio Selection: Efficiency Diversification of Investment*. New Haven, CT: Yale University Press, 1959.

————. "Investment for the Long Run: New Evidence for an Old Rule." *Journal of Finance*, December 1976, *31*, 1273–1286.

Miller, M.H. "Debt and Taxes." *Journal of Finance*, May 1977, *32*, 261–275.

Miller, M.H., and Modigliani, F. "Dividend Policy, Growth, and the Valuation of Shares." *Journal of Business*, October 1961, *34*, 411–433.

Minsky, H. *John Maynard Keynes*. New York: Columbia University Press, 1975.

Modigliani, F. and Miller, M.H. "The Cost of Capital, Corporation Finance, and the Theory of Investment." *American Economic Review*, June 1958, *48*, 261–297.

————. "Corporate Income Taxes and the Cost of Capital: A Correction." *American Economic Review*, June 1963, *53*, 433–443.

Ross, S.A. "Debt and Taxes and Uncertainty." *Journal of Finance*, July 1985, *40*, 637–657.

Ross, S.A., and Westerfield, R.W. *Corporate Finance*. St. Louis: Times Mirror/Mosby, 1988.

Shackle, G.L.S. *Uncertainty in Economics and Other Reflections*. Cambridge: Cambridge University Press, 1955.

Sharpe, W.F. "Capital Asset Prices: A Theory of Market Equilibrium under Conditions of Risk." *Journal of Finance*, September 1964, *19*, 425–442.

Stiglitz, J.E. "A Re-Examination of the Modigliani–Miller Theorem." *American Economic Review*, December 1969, *59*, 784–793.

Weintraub, E.R. *Microfoundations: The Compatibility of Microeconomics and Macroeconomics*. Cambridge: Cambridge University Press, 1979.

Young, W.E., and Trent, R.H. "Geometric Mean Approximation of Individual Security and Portfolio Performance." *Journal of Finance and Quantitative Analysis*, 1969, *4*, 179–200.

2

The investment function: five propositions in response to Professor Gordon

DOUGLAS VICKERS

I

The literature of dissent from the neoclassical traditions in our subject has reached significant proportions. Coming from the varied pens of Nobel laureates and the rank and file, not all of the dissent can be dismissed as what Hutchison has called "rather opaque verbiage" (1978, p. 212). Some of it no doubt is. Moreover, the neoclassical theory itself is seen as something other than monolithic. It means different things to different critics, as differing aspects of it attract analytical opprobrium. A calm reflection on the debate raises several perspectives from which the analytical significance and the empirical relevance of the earlier economic theory can be assessed. Among them is the question of which variables or identifiable forces can profitably be understood for analytical purposes as endogenous, and which may be regarded as exogenous. That exogeneity–endogeneity debate is directly relevant to the question of investment activity and its significance for the functioning of the economic system.

The issue is in no sense a new one. Certain styles of economic theorizing argue, for example, that progress is to be made most effectively by regarding the money wage as exogenous rather than holding to its neoclassical endogeneity. Similarly, the money supply, and particularly changes in the money supply, are best understood, it is claimed, to be endogenous rather than exogenous. The rate of interest, given the Central Bank's policy influence, is thought to be exogenous rather than

The author is Professor of Economics at the University of Massachusetts, Amherst. His thanks, without attribution of responsibility, are due to Professor Donald W. Katzner for his critical comments on an earlier draft of this paper.

endogenous. In each case, in relation to the money wage rate, the money supply, and the rate of interest, advances in theorizing have turned the neoclassical system on its head. Professor Gordon's highly insightful paper provokes a similar question (Gordon, 1992). Is it best, for purposes of analytical progress, to understand investment behavior as endogenously determined, or, to the contrary, to have regard to what might be thought to be, from other analytical perspectives, the high degree of exogenous determination of the worthwhileness of investment expenditures and capital formation, or the influence upon it of exogenous economic forces?

In order to address a number of questions related to the analytical issues raised by Professor Gordon, I shall submit five propositions which, in themselves, will bring into focus a small part of the relevant theoretical terrain. Three caveats are in order. First, my five propositions are not addressed directly to the five points of criticism of the neoclassical apparatus articulated by Professor Gordon. Their bearing is in some cases quite indirect. Second, my list of propositions is quite incomplete, both as to the issues that might be raised in this connection, and as to the extent to which the analytical significance of the propositions themselves is expressed. Third, the word "function" in the title of this paper is deliberately intended to be ambiguous. I have in mind not only the mathematical relation that is frequently envisaged under that heading—a relation whose existence, in a moment, I shall call in question—but also the part played by investment activity in the general economic scheme of things.

Casting a valuable light on the relevance of the endogeneity–exogeneity question, and bringing to focus the perception of Keynes as to the inherent instabilities of the system and the resultant volatility of investment expenditures, Shackle has observed, with relation to investment that he saw as "the key to all" (1974, p. 81), that:

> The message spelled out by all this creaking semiphore [the *General Theory*] is that intended (designed, ex ante) investment is a law to itself, dependent (if at all) on too elusive and involved a skein of subtle influences, too eagerly clutching at the straws of suggestion whirled along by "the news," to be ever captured in any intelligible, let alone determinable equation. It is not really the shapes of the curves, but their broad bodily shifts and deformations, that contain the meaning of the argument. [Shackle, 1972, p. 218. See also Vickers, 1979–80]

My five propositions follow:

1. It is necessary, reversing the frequent analytical plea, to establish a sound macroeconomic foundation for microeconomic argument.

2. The inherent instability of the system impinges in a uniquely significant way on the present question of investment behavior.

3. The foregoing propositions imply, along with the considerations of uncertainty and ignorance in real historical time, that the methodology of short-run, as distinct from long-run, analysis assumes signal importance.

4. The concept of the marginal efficiency of investment is a significant, meaningful, and usable concept in investment analysis and decision making.

5. Investment expenditures are subject not to a savings constraint but to a financing constraint.

II

The need to establish an adequate macroeconomic foundation for microeconomic analysis, and to call in question thereby the assumptions of methodological individualism on which neoclassical microeconomic theory rests, is illustrated by the fact that the microeconomics of a fully employed economy is quite different from that of an economy exhibiting degrees of unemployment. A macroeconomics that incorporates the assumptions of Say's Law, or any of the derivative implications of it, will throw open the possibility of microeconomic argument quite different from what is permissible or relevant where that classical assumption is not invoked. Consider two issues from among a number that might be adduced. First, and confining our argument for the moment to a strict neoclassical conception, the traditional demand curve for labor, with its dependence on the conceived relevance of marginal productivity and revenue magnitudes, assumes that firms can sell all they choose to produce in a fully employed economy. The firm is conceived to specify the marginal product of labor as applied to a fully employed capital base. Those analytically vital assumptions, however, might not in fact be viable, to the disruption of the supposed results of the demand for labor argument. The precedence of the macroeconomic analysis is clarified when it is recognized that the demand for labor cannot be specified until the aggregate demand for goods and services, or the aggregate level of effective demand, has been determined (see Davidson, 1983, on the proposition that "the marginal product curve is not the demand curve for labor").

Second, a corresponding proposition is relevant to the investment expenditure relation. In severely summarized terms, the argument can be put as follows. It has to do with what I referred to previously as the possibility of coherence in the aggregative system (Vickers, 1985). By "coherence" is meant the equilibration of all mutually determined markets at acceptably high and stable levels of employment and economic welfare. But saving, and the moderation of expenditure flows that accompanies saving, may very well imply a lack of coherence in the aggregate economy. The saving may, of course, flow into investment expenditures. Indeed, the assumption that there existed an automatic mechanism and, by implication, an efficiently functioning financial intermediary system, to transform saving into investment was an essential part of the implications of the Say's Law assumption. But when saving is made, no signal at all exists at that point in time to indicate what consumption goods might, at a later time, be demanded by those who are saving out of presently dated income. If, then, no signal exists for transmission to the consumption goods trades, no signal exists for onward transmission to the capital goods trades, and there is no way, prima facie, to know what capital goods investment should take place. It is precisely this that raises the relevance of economic ignorance in real time and the place of guesses, conjectures, and imagination in economic decision and behavior.

My first proposition is relevant to our present question of investment in two further respects. First, in contemplating investment expenditures, the question arises, "Where does the money come from?" Or where, in short, does the investing firm obtain the money capital it needs to finance its investment in real capital and other associated assets? Second, at what cost and on what terms is the firm able to obtain the money capital? The first point raises the highly significant fact that, unlike the traditional neoclassical textbook assumption, the firm does not enjoy the luxury of making its investment and operating decisions against what has been called "money capital saturation" (see the insightful paper of Lange, 1936, and the discussion of the argument that is here in view in Vickers, 1968). In the general case, the firm optimizes against the pressure of a "money capital availability constraint," and the effective cost of money capital is the "full marginal cost of relaxing the money capital availability constraint" (Vickers, 1968, 1970, 1987). For our present purposes, this requires a recognition of the relevance and importance of the structure of financial intermediary institutions through which the flow of money capital funds finds its way into the hands of prospective investing firms. An adequate macroeconomic foundation, therefore, is necessarily informed by a clear recognition of the institutional structure that actually exists.

On the second matter of the cost of money capital, the statement that has just been made clarifies the point adequately for present purposes, and I shall comment on it further in my final section on the financing constraint. But it is necessary to acknowledge that the effective cost of money capital is influenced by all the conditions that exist on the supply side of the money capital market. That may be considered in relation to either or both the debt capital sector and the equity capital sector of the money capital market. Relevant also, however, is the fact that the rate of interest, which Keynes referred to as a "highly conventional variable" (1936, p. 203) and Shackle spoke of as an "inherently restless variable" (1972, p. 199), is, by virtue of the Central Bank's policy influence, essentially an exogenous variable. Macroeconomic structures and policy possibilities again enter the picture in determining the framework of the decisions that are contemplatable and made by individuals and firms. Professor Gordon's paper does not address these important issues. He argues at the heart of his paper that, all else being given, an individual's investment activity should be conducted in such a way as to aim at "maximizing the probability of long-run survival (PLRS)." The argument is agile, provocative, and imaginative, and it provides valuable insight on the question it addresses. But in the light of our observations to this point, it might be seen, notwithstanding Professor Gordon's disclaimer, as a variation on the neoclassical theme. Perhaps the most important feature of the entire neoclassical edifice is its assumption of omniscience. The perfect knowledge postulate characterized economic argument from Ricardo onwards, and it was clearly implicit in Ricardo's argument about investment opportunities, the point we now have under consideration. Capital would migrate, Ricardo argued, from lines of employment offering lower to those offering higher rates of return. That movement would occur with a fluidity that took no account of either the uncertainties involved or the possible absence of relevant knowledge (see Hutchison, 1978, p. 48).

In similar vein, Professor Gordon's argument regarding the probability of long-run survival can be seen as a variant of the perfect knowledge assumption. Of course, it differs from the earlier neoclassical apparatus in that it purports to take explicit account of the risks that are inherent in investment decisions and outlays. But it clearly invokes the latter-day analog of the neoclassical perfect knowledge assumption in that it supposes that the probability calculus can be effectively employed to abolish the uncertainties that do in fact exist. The assumption of the form of a probability distribution, in the present case relating to the periodic return from investment, is itself an assumption of knowledge. But knowledge is the antithesis of the ignorance that characterizes the decision maker's stance in real time as the economic opportunities confronting him are imagined and contemplated. In the present case, the assumption of a random variable return that is "log normal and independently and identically distributed over time" with specified mean and variance, is an explicit employment of the probability calculus to abolish uncertainty and to escape into the domain of probabilistically reducible risk. That procedure is the traditional neoclassical method of purportedly extracting knowledge from ignorance. I shall return to further aspects of its significance.

Of course, Professor Gordon's procedure may be understood to be used for illustrative purposes only, and it does, in fact, make an important point. But the question protrudes as to whether, in actual economic environments and decision making, the frame of reference for investment decisions can bear any resemblance at all to the procedures that the PLRS model has envisaged. The question remains whether such a procedure is genuinely in the spirit of Keynes, as Professor Gordon states, rather than the neoclassicists. Keynes was, as his post–*General Theory* work insisted, primarily interested in the real uncertainties and the instabilities that abound. He was, as is now well known and widely recognized, disinclined to assume that those uncertainties could be corralled effectively by the probability apparatus.

These arguments point to the difficulty of maintaining analytically the assumptions and implications of methodological individualism, as that has generally informed the neoclassical analysis. It is beyond our present scope and objectives to enter the relevant methodological debate at length. But the priority of the macroeconomic foundations for which I am arguing implies a dissent from the postulates of methodological individualism, as that comes to expression, for example, in what has been referred to as psychologistic individualism. That system of thought insists that in the formulation of explanatory economic models or analysis, "psychological states are the only exogenous variables permitted beyond natural givens (e.g. weather, contents of the universe, etc.)" (Boland, 1982, p. 30), and that only individuals are reckoned to be decision makers in economic and social affairs. In fact, the "givenness" of economic states, forces, institutions, and what it is that determines the psychic and epistemic status of decision-making individuals varies, and it provides a changing, kaleidic environment that constrains the worthwhileness of contemplated actions. Joan Robinson has argued forcefully in this connection that the results of past decisions, and of past mistakes that cannot be undone, are exogenous for current decisions and actions (Robinson, 1974; see also Boland, 1982, p. 93). Not only do institutional structures exist and constrain individual decisions, but institutional actions, including policy actions, monetary and fiscal, impinge on economic affairs. The fallacy of composition, moreover, entraps economic argument. Macroeconomic depressions occur. The classical theorem of the impossibility of general overproduction does not, in the light of the facts, warrant rehabilitation.

III

My second proposition, relating to the inherent instability of the economy and its relevance for investment theory, opens the door to what has become a favorite hunting ground in Post Keynesian work. Our minimal comment at this point has to do with the fact that all of the decisions and economic actions that determine outcomes must necessarily accommodate the impacts of uncertainty and ignorance in their real-time context. As to the impacts of those phenomena on investment decisions, a most telling argument is contained in Loasby's work on *Choice, Complexity and Ignorance* (1976, chs. 9, 11, 12). Loasby takes up the Shacklean notion contained in our quotation at the beginning of this paper, and he reaches the conclusion that, in view of what Shackle has referred to as the "bodily shifts and deformations" of the investment demand curve, it is difficult to say that any such curve exists, in the sense in which the neoclassical apparatus has envisaged it.

This realization forces the conclusion that the probabilistic analog of the neoclassical scheme that Professor Gordon has worked with in his paper hardly gets at the real determination or causation of investment expenditures. The uncertainties that exist in a real-time economy, quite apart from inducing a profound analytical respect for historic time itself, induce also a recognition of the ignorance in which the human condition and accordingly economic decision making are bound. Marshall, in his respect for real economic time, has cautioned that "we cannot foresee the future perfectly. The unexpected may happen" (1920, p. 347), and Keynes observed, regarding many aspects of the future, that "we simply do not know" (1937a, p. 214). In making our judgments as to economic action, frequently based as they are on conventional valuations, Keynes continued, "we assume that the present is a . . . serviceable guide to the future . . . so that we can accept it as such until something new and relevant comes into the picture" (1937a, p. 214). Of course, he recognizes, that may be a "flimsy foundation," and it may be "subject to sudden and violent changes. The practice of calmness and immobility, of certainty and security, suddenly breaks down. New fears and hopes will, without warning, take charge of human conduct" (Keynes, 1937a, p. 214). It is that kind of argument that caused Shackle to speak felicitously of what he called "Keynesian Kaleidics" (1974).

The reasons why this line of argument calls in question the appropriateness of the probability calculus as applicable to investment decision making has been extensively explored (see Davidson, 1978, 1991; Vickers, 1987; Shackle, 1969). The most persuasive contribution on the point from the Nobel laureates is that contained in Sir John Hicks's recent and important *Causality in Economics* (1979). Hicks has argued not only that real time needs to be brought back into economic analysis, but also that the widespread employment of the probability calculus is misdirected and irrelevant to the questions and decision situations with which economics is concerned. Keynes was very much concerned with the inherent instabilities that made economic analysis the difficult, and the frequently tortured, undertaking that it is. He argued in connection with the liquidity preference function, for example, that "If . . . our knowledge of the future was calculable and not subject to sudden changes, it might be justified to assume that the liquidity preference curve was . . . stable" (Keynes, 1937a, p. 219). But in the conditions of the world he was at pains to examine, that was not the case.

The relevance of the point, however, is that if, for all of the reasons we have adumbrated, there is an analytical necessity to call in question the existence, or at least the manipulable stability, of the aggregate investment function, those same considerations call in question the assumption of stability, or of readily specifiable determinants, at the level of the decision-making firm. Professor Gordon is beyond doubt on very sound ground in insisting that the firm's investment decisions are not independent of its own history and, in particular, of its own capital investment history. But to argue from that point that a smooth and well-designed decision apparatus of the PLRS kind actually exists might well be a non sequitur. For at any point in the unfolding of the unidirectional time in which we are bound, not only is the future unknown and unknowable, but who is to say what new and hitherto unknown or inconceivable investment opportunities may arise? Firms change. They grow and mature and sometimes die. They change their product mix as they pursue their profit opportunities in kaleidic market environments, and they change their production technologies, market penetration, financing structures, and management philosophies. The extent to which bygones can always be treated as bygones in the matter of capital employment depends, of course, on questions of specificity of use of capital equipment and other issues that influence real capital and realizable money capital mobility, as well as on product market developments and trends. While, therefore, the current investment program of IBM or General Motors is not uninfluenced by its own corporate history, it is nevertheless true that investment decisions, and no doubt the medium-term or longer-term projection of them, are subject to pressures of immediate profitability that may imply a more or less radical variation from previously adopted patterns.

IV

The suggestions contained in my third proposition regarding the significance of short-run, as opposed to long-run, economic analysis have recently been discussed at length elsewhere (Vickers, 1991), where the relevant methodological and intellectual historical issues are explored. Three brief points of some significance may be noted. First, the preceding argument regarding the relevance to economic affairs, and therefore to an adequately structured economic analysis, of uncertainty, ignorance, historical time, and nonequilibrium or the possible absence of coherence in the aggregative system, points in the direction of a short-run economic analysis. This is because it is in the ever-present moment that stands, as has been said, between a "dead yesterday" and an "unborn tomorrow" (Shackle, 1969, p. 14ff), that decisions are taken. The present changes. Knowledge changes. The epistemic status of the decision maker changes with it, as do the scope for action and the imagination of what, in the times ahead, may result from actions that are taken in the present. An analytical focus on what are, or what it is imagined might be, the determinants of long-run economic outcomes, to the neglect of the ever-changing pressures, the kaleidic forces, that bear upon those outcomes and the plans that are made or are in course of unfolding in the short run, is in danger of neglecting the real causation of economic values and desirable courses of action. Dangers exist in locking into assumedly stable long-run forces and determinants that, it has been argued already, are in fact subject to kaleidic variation. The probability of long-run survival is conceivably itself subject to unexpected and unexpectable variation.

Second, the short run matters, and matters crucially in economic analysis, because our actions in the short run *create history*. History is not something out there waiting to be discovered. We are not determinists in that sense. It is the *creation of history* by the ever-unfolding conjuncture of short-run forces and the decisions precipitated in the context of them that needs to focus analytical attention. What emerges in the longer-run scheme of things is what it is because of the actions we take and the opportunities we cognize in the economic present that, in genuine time, continually passes before us.

Third, the analytical significance of the short run in the sense in which we have just connoted it can be set against the argument of the neo-Ricardians for what they have insisted upon as a so-called "traditional long-period method" of economic analysis (Milgate, 1982, p. 23; see also Vickers, 1991). That neo-Ricardian argument insists on identifying what it calls the long run "center of gravitation" of the system. For our present purposes, it can be observed that "uncertainty" has been substantially dismissed by the neo-Ricardians and the practitioners of the long-period method of analysis as "just one of those multitude of influences which cause the day-to-day circumstances of the economy to deviate from the long-run normal position. Uncertainty and expectations may thus be confined to the category of 'temporary' or non-systematic effects, as distinct from the persistent and systematic forces which act to determine the long-run position" (Eatwell and Milgate, 1983, p. 12). Uncertainty may be dismissed, from this point of view, as simply one of the "frictions" or "imperfections," the appeal to which, or the focus on which, "serves to deprive economic analysis of all definite content, thus reducing the discussion of economic policy to the status of guesswork" (p. 279).

The divergence of the neo-Ricardian analysis from what we have already advanced as relevant to the investment and capital formation decision will be clear. In a recent evaluation of the neo-Ricardian understanding of the marginal efficiency of investment, to which I shall refer in the next section, Brothwell has judiciously observed that "the neo-Ricardian notion of a long-period equilibrium, towards which the system gravitates . . . may have some relevance to a stationary economy or an economy which is subject to a slow rate of technical change . . . but it has little operational significance for the turbulent, rapidly changing, advanced economies of today" (1987, p. 501). Carvalho (1984–85) has provided a fruitful analysis of the senses in which the long run/short run dichotomy may be connoted, addressing the Garegnani–Eatwell, the Kaldor–Pasinetti, the Kalecki, the Davidson–Kregel–Minsky, and the Shackle alternatives.

V

The marginal efficiency of investment, my fourth proposition suggests, is a legitimate and usable concept that should enjoy a meaningful place in a Post Keynesian analytical scheme. Keynes' formulation of the related concept of the marginal efficiency of capital is well known. The concept in which we are now interested is a short-run concept, in the sense that it has to do with the rate of return which, at a given time and in the presence of the immediate forces of evaluation that bear upon it, can be expected to be obtained, with greater or lesser degrees of confidence and assurance, from immediate capital investment. In the computation of that possible rate of return, a good deal of imaginative anticipation of possible future events is involved. We have argued in the preceding sections that we cannot tie those future events down to a probabilistically defined time shape. In the presence of real time and genuine, residual uncertainties, decision criteria quite different from those that the neoclassical probability calculus has formulated are required. We can dissent from the claim of Hirshleifer and Riley (1979), for example, that the "economics of uncertainty" is concerned with "decisions made under fixed probability beliefs." Alternative decision criteria, such as Shackle's potential surprise apparatus, have already given rise to a large and expanding literature (Shackle, 1969, 1979; Ford, 1983; Vickers, 1987; Katzner, 1986, 1989–90).

Our concern at present is to rehabilitate the marginal efficiency of investment as a meaningful analytical notion in the light of the arguments against its usefulness that have been presented by, for example, the neo-Ricardian long-period method of analysis. In the course of presenting what he regards as an irreparably damaging critique, Garegnani addresses what he sees as the "deficiencies regarding the . . . marginal efficiency of investment" in Keynes' analysis. He sees the concept of the marginal efficiency of capital as "the Achilles' heel" of Keynes' critique of the neoclassical theory (Garegnani, 1983, pp. 59–60). Eatwell (1983, pp. 119, 121) joins in the critique.

The neo-Ricardian criticism is related to the widespread misconception that in a model in the spirit of Keynes the demand for investment necessarily reflects the neoclassical investment demand function. Eatwell claims, for example, that "the lack of any logical foundation for the construction of an elastic demand schedule for investment as a function of the rate of interest is simultaneously a critique of the neoclassical theory of output and of Keynes' concept of the marginal efficiency of capital—which was itself derived from the neoclassical schedule" (1983, p. 121). Keynes, it has been widely claimed, simply took over the neoclassical investment demand function. But quite apart from the consideration of uncertainty that has led us to believe that what Keynes was vitally concerned about was not so much the precise form of any such relation as the instability of it, there is no necessity at all to conclude that the macromodel or Keynes' construction of it necessarily embeds such a neoclassical function. The claim that it did so, and that it inherited damaging analytical deficiencies as a result, has followed from the Cambridge capital theoretic critique. It is this body of argument, with its conclusion, stemming initially from debates regarding the measurability of the capital factor of production, that capital reversal and reswitching may occur, that forces the conclusion that it is not possible to define an investment demand function, or a demand for investable funds, that is uniformly negatively elastic with respect to the rate of interest. An early summing up of the capital theoretic debate is available in Harcourt (1972, 1976) and Blaug (1975). A highly valuable recent interpretation of the significance of many of the relevant issues has been presented by Rogers (1989).

Rogers, in his illuminating and important *Money, Interest and Capital*, has seen the relevant point clearly. Without any surrender to the Cambridge critique at this point, the marginal efficiency of investment can be incorporated into the short-run macroanalysis simply as the discount factor that equates the demand price of a capital good with its supply price. Alternatively, it can be said that the present discounted value of the capital good's prospective income stream, when that income stream is discounted at a discount factor equal to the entrepreneur's required rate of return, or, in other words, his effective cost of money capital, establishes a demand price for the capital good. Investment can advisedly proceed when that demand price is no less than the supply price of the capital good as established, for example, as the Marshallian supply price in the capital goods market (see Davidson, 1978, ch. 4). In either formulation there is no reason to imagine that any logical neoclassical problem is involved. As Pasinetti has observed in relation to the Cambridge critique of the capital intensity issue,

> there is absolutely no need to consider Keynes' marginal efficiency of capital schedule as an expression of the [neoclassical] marginal productivity of capital. The theory necessarily entails an inverse monotonic relation between *capital intensity* and the rate of interest. But this is not

the case with Keynes' ranking of investment projects. In a slump situation the last project to be implemented might well be the least capital intensive of all, and therefore entail a decrease (not an increase) in the average amount of capital per employed labour. [Pasinetti, 1974, p. 43, quoted in Rogers, 1989, p. 170, emphasis added; see also Schumpeter, 1954, p. 1119n].

The Cambridge critique and Keynes' marginal efficiency of capital have quite different frames of reference and move on quite different levels of discourse.

What is necessary also, however, in order to make the marginal efficiency of investment usable as a meaningful investment decision criterion, is an understanding of the firm's cost of money capital. We have already referred to earlier work that established the relevant cost of money capital as the "full marginal cost of relaxing the firm's money capital availability constraint." This calls for an understanding of the manner in which the firm's decision to relax its money capital availability constraint by introducing additional equity capital or debt capital to the firm will change the risk profile of the firm and thereby react back on the costs of debt and equity capital. These, in turn, are reflected in the rates of return required by the suppliers of money capital. At the decision margin, therefore, room exists for a good deal of imaginative assessment by the firm of both the possible income stream that marginal investment outlays may generate and the impacts of such prospects, as seen by the supply side of the money capital market, on the financial market's required rates of return on the firm's capital securities. I shall make a further comment on that highly important set of relationships in the next section when addressing the fact that investment is in general constrained, not by saving, but by the availability of finance.

But in conjunction with the marginal efficiency of investment concept and its relation to money capital market conditions, it is apposite to recall our remark that the cost of corporate capital is not unrelated to the going rate of interest on riskless securities—say, government securities—in the financial asset market. That latter rate is influenced by Central Bank participation in the market and by the market conditions that result. It can be said, therefore, that the nominal rate of interest is, by virtue of the Central Bank's activities in the market, a policy-determined exogenous variable. In other terms, analytical attention can focus on the exogenous, or policy-determined, rate of interest at which the Central Bank is willing to provide reserves, or base money, to the monetary institutions, thereby determining the rate of interest at which those institutions will, in turn, make funds available to potential borrowers. The money supply thus created by the monetary institutions can be regarded as endogenously supplied at a rate of interest that is a markup from the monetary institutions' cost of funds, as that has just been seen to be determined by the Central Bank's policy decision.

VI

My fifth proposition states that investment expenditures are subject not to a savings constraint but to a financing constraint. This issue did not come within the scope of the argument that Professor Gordon presented. But it lies at the heart of the investment decision, the feasibility of expanded capital formation, and the processes by which investment activity impacts on the economic system. In an earlier section the question was raised, "Where does the money come from?" when new capital formation is contemplated. At this point two comments can be made.

First, at the aggregate level it is analytically inappropriate to state that newly contemplated investment expenditures, such as would raise the level of investment above that previously maintained, are constrained by the availability, or lack of availability, of saving. It is not necessary at this time of day to explain again that Keynes turned the classical system on its head and argued effectively that investment preceded saving, both in causation and time. The Ricardian system understood the saving out of capitalist incomes to be the source and the engine of economic growth. Say's Law was very much a part of the classical logic at that point. Saving flowed into investment, and depending on the rate at which profits fell, as occasioned by the diminishing marginal productivity in the wage goods industries, notably agriculture, and the attendant increase in the effective wage rate, the economic growth rate would taper off as the stationary state approached. But Keynes changed all that. The reality was that investment generated incomes and incomes generated saving. The saving that might be thought to finance investment did not appear until a later stage in the process. As Keynes observed,

> if there is no change in the liquidity position [following a decision to increase investment expenditure] the public can save ex-ante and ex-post and ex-anything else until they are blue in the face, without alleviating the problem in the least ... the banks hold the key position in the transition from a lower to a higher scale of activity ... The investment

market can become congested through shortage of cash. It can never become congested through shortage of saving. This is the most fundamental of my conclusions within this field. [Keynes, 1937b, pp. 668–669]

In another context, Keynes observed that "Credit expansion provides not an alternative to increased saving, but a necessary preparation for it. It is the parent, not the twin, of increased saving" (1939, p. 572, quoted in Kregel, 1984–85, p. 151).

At the level of the individual firm, it might be imagined that the financing constraint may be eased by employing retained earnings as a source of finance. But while, as is well known, retained earnings do in fact provide a large part of the money capital equivalent of investment expenditures, the statement that this eases the immediate financing problem can be quite misleading. For it has to be asked at the same time what might have happened to the cash flow counterpart of the firm's retained earnings that have been accumulated from profits during previous trading periods. That cash flow counterpart may have been used to build up liquid balances in the firm, to repay previously contracted short-term debt, or to acquire other assets. When, then, additional investment is contemplated, the question still arises, "Where does the money come from?" If, of course, the firm is able to liquidate marketable security holdings in order to acquire cash to finance investment expenditures, that will mean that no increase in the money supply has thereby occurred. But the fact that funds have been pried loose from previous asset balances implies that the velocity of circulation of money has increased. At the same time there will have been some pressure on asset market prices, with attendant upward pressures on market yields, interest rates, and the cost of corporate capital. This may have a feedback effect on the level of investment expenditures, depending, of course, on the impacts of proposed expenditures on the risk profile of investing firms and the attendant effects on their cost of money capital.

When it is said, therefore, as we have put it so far, that in the presence of investment opportunities, the firm will relax its money capital availability constraint by introducing additional debt or equity capital, that leaves unexamined the detailed *modus operandi*, or the interrelations that come into play between the real and the financial sectors that facilitate the anticipated investment expansion. That *modus operandi* does itself raise a number of issues demanding close analytical attention. Basil Moore has recently provided an extensive and insightful analysis of the relevant processes (Moore, 1988; see also Davidson, 1978, 1986).

My final point therefore relates to the procedures by which contemplated investment is in general facilitated. To a large extent, industrial firms will have available to them lines of credit or other arrangements with bankers that permit them to obtain short-term bank loans when investment outlays are planned. Those firms comprise part of what Hicks has referred to as the "overdraft sector" (1974, p. 51). The fact that banks in this way increase their loans against industrial lines of credit means that the money supply has thereby endogenously increased. The firm at that time will have made its plans in anticipation of the fact that at a later time, after additional incomes have been generated, it will go to the long-term money capital market and float either a new debt or a new equity issue. With the proceeds of the sale of such an issue, it will repay the short-term loans it has accumulated during the investment expansion process.

Two points, therefore, immediately become relevant. First, the firm will have formed, at the time of the investment expansion, an anticipation of the prices and terms on which it will be able, at the later time, to obtain the long-term money capital it has in view. Conditions in the money capital market when the time for the long-term flotation arrives may or may not be what were initially anticipated. The firm's estimate of its effective cost of permanent money capital funds may therefore be either confirmed or disappointed. Second, much will depend, for the emergence of money capital market conditions, on what Davidson has judiciously referred to as the marginal propensity of income earners to purchase long-term securities out of saving. In other words, we are necessarily very much concerned at that point with the structure, and with possible changes in the structure, of the financial intermediation process by which the entire investment and saving mechanism is, as we have just conceived of it, conducted (see Davidson, 1986).

If, of course, firms repay short-term bank loans, that will in itself reduce demand deposits and the money supply. Or it may be said that the banks thereby experience an increase in excess reserves that enables them to relend. A revolving fund of finance is thereby established. But if the investment expansion process in the economy as a whole is to continue, or if, that is, the economy's investment expenditures are to be raised to a permanently higher level, then it can be shown analytically that the money supply will have to increase in order to sustain the projected higher levels of overall activity. Admittedly, that necessary increase in the money supply may be moderated by a possible increase in the velocity of circulation of money attendant, perhaps, on innovations in the financial sector. But as the money supply increases, in the sense in which our earlier quotations from Keynes have envisaged, the additional money supply will accrue as savings in the hands of income earners. As Dennis Robertson put it half a century ago, "All the money that is anywhere must be somewhere" (Robertson, 1959, p. 125, quoted in Kregel, 1986, p. 95).

As the real multiplier works its way through the system, the level of voluntary saving will rise, and the need for additional money supplies diminishes proportionally. In the meantime, the newly created money gives rise to what Moore has labeled "convenience lending" or what I have referred to as "convenience saving" (Vickers, forthcoming). That convenience saving, representing the additional incomes generated by the new money flows, will, when added to the voluntary saving made out of the public's previously anticipated income, amount to the actual level of investment expenditure. Another way of describing the development of the expansion process is to say that as investment is raised to a permanently higher level, that investment expenditure will be financed to a progressively larger extent by traditionally conceived voluntary saving, and to a progressively smaller extent by convenience saving or new money creation. That was in fact the precise vision held by Robertson in his early essay on "Effective Demand and the Multiplier" (Robertson, 1940).

VII

Professor Gordon's paper and his tilting with the neoclassicists thus raise a large number of highly important analytical issues. He is profoundly correct in raising the importance of uncertainty, risk perception, and risk aversion. And he is on thoroughly sound ground in dissenting from many of the methodological strictures and irrelevancies of the neoclassical apparatus. His central proposition regarding the probability of long-run survival is meaningful and useful. My suggestion that, in its embrace of the probability calculus in what is, in many respects, a neoclassical formulation, and my suggestions as to a number of issues relevant to investment and the investment process that are provoked by his paper, should not be allowed to diminish the very welcome contribution his central thought has made.

Decisions as to economic action are made by individuals in an ever-changing, kaleidic milieu on which unforeseeable exogenous forces impinge with determinative effects. Decisions in real time and in the context of its attendant uncertainties are made, in an important sense, in conditions of ignorance. At decision points, the future cannot be known. Future knowledge cannot be known before its time (Lachmann, 1959). The aggregate scheme of things bears, with insistent pressure and frequently in mockery of our best imaginations, on the scope for economic action. The neoclassical omniscient economic man, an autonomous creature who is untouched epistemically by the forces that swirl around him and provide him with the brute facts that determine his ranges of choice, is unrecognizable in the world of real economic performance. The analytical strictures in the neoclassical apparatus that Professor Gordon has perceived confirm, in conjunction with the range of issues we have examined, that a markedly different conception of economic analysis is called for if it is to attain meaningful empirical relevance.

REFERENCES

Blaug, M. *The Cambridge Revolution: Success or Failure?* London: Institute of Economic Affairs, 1975.

Boland, L.A. *The Foundations of Economic Method.* London: Allen and Unwin, 1982.

Brothwell, J.F. "On the Nature and Use of the Concept of the Marginal Physical Product in Post Keynesian Economics." *Journal of Post Keynesian Economics,* 1987, *9* (4), 496–501.

Carvalho, F. "Alternative Analyses of Short and Long Run in Post Keynesian Economics." *Journal of Post Keynesian Economics,* 1984–85, *7* (2), 214–234.

Davidson, P. *Money and the Real World,* 2d ed. New York: Wiley, 1978.

———. "The Marginal Product Curve Is Not the Demand Curve for Labor and Lucas's Labor Supply Function Is Not the Supply Curve for Labor in the Real World." *Journal of Post Keynesian Economics,* 1983, *6* (1), 105–117.

———. "Finance, Funding, Saving, and Investment." *Journal of Post Keynesian Economics,* 1986, *9* (1), 101–110.

———. "Is Probability Theory Relevant for Uncertainty? A Post Keynesian Perspective." *Journal of Economic Perspectives,* 1991, *5* (1), 129–143.

Eatwell, J. "Theories of Value, Output and Employment." In J. Eatwell and M. Milgate, *Keynes's Economics and the Theory of Value and Distribution.* New York: Oxford University Press, 1983.

Eatwell, J. and Milgate, M. *Keynes's Economics and the Theory of Value and Distribution.* New York: Oxford University Press, 1983.

Ford, J.L. *Choice, Expectation and Uncertainty: An Appraisal of G.L.S. Shackle's Theory.* Totowa, NJ: Barnes and Noble, 1983.

Garegnani, P. "Notes on Consumption, Investment and Effective Demand." In J.

Eatwell and M. Milgate, *Keynes's Economics and the Theory of Value and Distribution.* New York: Oxford University Press, 1983.

Gordon, M.J. "The Neoclassical and a Post Keynesian Theory of Investment." *Journal of Post Keynesian Economics*, Summer 1992, *14* (4):425–443. Chapter 1 of this volume.

Harcourt, G.C. *Some Cambridge Controversies in the Theory of Capital.* Cambridge: Cambridge University Press, 1972.

———. "The Cambridge Controversies: Old Ways and New Horizons or Dead End?" *Oxford Economic Papers*, 1976, *28* (1), 25–65.

Hicks, J. *The Crisis in Keynesian Economics.* Oxford: Blackwell, 1974.

———. *Causality in Economics.* New York: Basic Books, 1979.

Hirshleifer, J., and Riley, J.G. "The Analytics of Uncertainty and Information: An Expository Survey." *Journal of Economic Literature*, 1979, *17* (4), 1375–1421.

Hutchison, T.W. *On Revolutions and Progress in Economic Knowledge.* Cambridge: Cambridge University Press, 1978.

Katzner, D. "Potential Surprise, Potential Confirmation, and Probability." *Journal of Post Keynesian Economics*, 1986, *9* (1), 58–78.

———. "The Shackle–Vickers Approach to Decision-Making in Ignorance." *Journal of Post Keynesian Economics*, 1989–90, *12* (2), 237–259.

Keynes, J.M. *The General Theory of Employment, Interest, and Money.* London: Macmillan, 1936.

———. "The General Theory of Employment." *Quarterly Journal of Economics*, 1937a, *51*, 209–223.

———. "The Ex-ante Theory of the Rate of Interest." *Economic Journal*, 1937b, *47*, 663–669.

———. "The Process of Capital Formation." *Economic Journal*, 1939, *49*, 569–574.

Kregel, J. "Constraints on the Expansion of Output and Employment: Real or Monetary?" *Journal of Post Keynesian Economics*, 1984–85, 7 (2), 139–152.

———. "A Note on Finance, Liquidity, Saving and Investment." *Journal of Post Keynesian Economics*, 1986, *9* (1), 91–110.

Lachmann, L.M. "Professor Shackle on the Economic Significance of Time." *Metroeconomica*, 1959, *11*, 64–73.

Lange, O. "The Place of Interest in the Theory of Production." *Review of Economic Studies*, 1936, *3*, 159–192.

Loasby, B. *Choice, Complexity and Ignorance.* Cambridge: Cambridge University Press, 1976.

Marshall, A. *Principles of Economics.* London: Macmillan, 1920.

Milgate, M. *Capital and Employment.* London: Academic Press, 1982.

Moore, B. *Horizontalists and Verticalists: The Macroeconomics of Credit Money.* Cambridge: Cambridge University Press, 1988.

Pasinetti, L. *Growth and Income Distribution: Essays in Economic Theory.* Cambridge: Cambridge University Press, 1974.

Robertson, D. "Effective Demand and the Multiplier." In *Essays in Monetary Theory.* London: P.S. King, 1940.

————. *Money*. Cambridge: Cambridge University Press, 1959.

Robinson, J. *History versus Equilibrium*. London: Thames Polytechnic, 1974.

Rogers, C. *Money, Interest and Capital*. Cambridge: Cambridge University Press, 1989.

Schumpeter, J.A. *History of Economic Analysis*. New York: Oxford University Press, 1954.

Shackle, G.L.S. *Decision, Order, and Time in Human Affairs*. Cambridge: Cambridge University Press, 1969.

————. *Epistemics & Economics, A Critique of Economic Doctrines*. Cambridge: Cambridge University Press, 1972.

————. *Keynesian Kaleidics*. Edinburgh: Edinburgh University Press, 1974.

————. *Imagination and the Nature of Choice*. Edinburgh: Edinburgh University Press, 1979.

Vickers, D. *The Theory of the Firm: Production, Capital, and Finance*. New York: McGraw-Hill, 1968.

————. "The Cost of Capital and the Structure of the Firm." *Journal of Finance*, 1970, *25*, 35–46.

————. "Uncertainty, Choice, and the Marginal Efficiencies." *Journal of Post Keynesian Economics*, 1979–80, *2* (2), 240–254.

————. "On Relational Structures and Non-equilibrium in Economic Theory." *Eastern Economic Journal*, 1985, *11* (4), 384–403.

————. *Money Capital in the Theory of the Firm*. Cambridge: Cambridge University Press, 1987.

————. *The Long Run and the Short*. Department of Economics, University of Western Australia, 1991.

————. "The Monetary and the Real." In Paul Wells (ed.), *Essays in Post Keynesian Economics*. Amsterdam: Kluwer, forthcoming.

3

Financial theory and the theory of investment

JOEL FRIED

Myron Gordon has provided readers five propositions that he believes are essential for the theory of finance. Having argued that there is reasonable doubt as to the empirical validity of each, he then goes on to provide an outline of a theory of investment that differs from that of neoclassical theory. While I may agree that the propositions necessary for the now traditional theory of finance are not met in capital markets of record, I do not believe the neoclassical theory of investment is dependent on the truth or falsity of financial theory as described by Gordon (1992). The neoclassical theory of investment takes from financial theory one element, namely the cost of capital, or, alternatively, the demand price of capital. The theory of finance itself simply provides one set of assumptions that can provide a measure of that cost. If the assumptions do not hold true, then an alternative measure can be derived if, for a theory of investment, an explicit formulation of the actual cost of capital is needed. I believe that the agenda in the finance literature has been to explore alternative formulations rather than to defend the assumptions stated by Gordon as an adequate description of reality.[1]

In what follows I want to concentrate on Gordon's distinction between proprietors and corporations and to link that to what I regard as the fundamental assumption of financial theory, that capital markets are free of transactions costs and are perfectly competitive. To do so I shall lay out the decision problem for an agent that operates in environments where some secondary asset markets are nonoperative (i.e., are characterized by arbitrarily large transactions costs) and compare (implicit)

The author is Associate Professor at the University of Western Ontario. He would like to thank, without implicating, Peter Howitt for helpful comments on an earlier draft of this paper.

[1] See, for example, Miller et al. (1988) and the subsequent discussion of his paper.

prices there to those generated in a system where markets are complete, the latter corresponding to the case of corporate ownership of all real assets. The case of incomplete markets corresponds to what can be viewed as a system of proprietorships.

The points I wish to make are that under both ownership systems, financial theory provides an interpretation of asset prices where the demand price of capital is well defined for the real investment decision, that there are economic incentives to proprietors to be able to broaden the markets for titles to their real assets, and that these gains come not only from the ability to reduce risk by diversification but also to avoid the costs of borrowing constraints. Finally, I would like to suggest that currently existing financial markets for corporate debt and equity are not yet in conformity with the neoclassical assumption of the perfectly competitive capital markets (PCCM) required for the empirical validation of received financial theory. Research in understanding the value of the firm and of investment should therefore look to theories of information and of market structure as methods of reconciling financial theory with financial markets of record. In doing so, I would conjecture that the resulting implications will give the neoclassical theory of investment a decidedly Keynesian twist.

The economic environment

Suppose an overlapping generations (OG) framework where agents live three periods. Let the size of each generation equal N. An agent is identified by the date of her or his birth and, for notational convenience, normalize $N = 1$. Agent t receives an initial known endowment of the amount $W_t = W$ which can be consumed, sold for financial assets to be detailed below, and/or invested in a real indivisible asset of the amount $K < W$ that will provide uncertain income over the next two periods of her life. If the agent chooses to invest she will have $\omega = W - K > 0$ available from her initial endowment plus V_t, the (implicit) market value of the investment, for consumption and/or asset purchases. If she chooses to invest in K, the firm will produce a stochastic income stream of $(\theta_{t+1}, \phi_{t+2})$ in the subsequent two periods of capital's economic life where θ and ϕ are distributed with the joint density $f(\theta, \phi)$ whose support is $\theta^*, \phi^* > 0$. At the end of $t+2$, the scrap value of K is nil.

To determine if it is desirable to invest, agent t compares the cost, K, of doing so to the demand price of the firm at date t.[2] This demand price,

---

[2]For the remainder of this paper I shall assume that V_t is always greater than K. To do otherwise would mean no firms.

V_t, is given by:

(1) $$V_t = P_{st} S_t + P_{dt} D_t + P_{bt} B_t + P_{lt} L_t + P_{qt} Q_t$$

where S_t and D_t are, respectively, riskless and residual claims on θ_{t+1}, Q_t is the residual, "equity," claim on ϕ_{t+2}, and B_t and L_t are bills maturing at $t+2$ that promise to pay the first $B+L$ of income from ϕ_{t+2}. L_t is subordinated debt, with owners of L_t paid only after B_t claims have been met. It is assumed that $S_t < \theta^*$ and $B_t < \phi^*$. P_{it} denotes the price in terms of consumption goods of asset i at date t. Agent t can hold any title to income from her own firm and, if markets for them exist, titles to income from firms managed by other generations. In the OG structure used here, the only other generation operating firms with future titles to sell are the middle-aged of generation $t-1$ who can sell some of their B_{t-1}, L_{t-1}, or Q_{t-1} if secondary markets for them exist. These will sell at secondary market prices of P_{st}, P^*_{lt}, and P^*_{qt}, respectively.

At the time of her birth, agent t has preferences characterized by:

(2) $$\Omega_t = U(C^1_t, C^2_{t+1}, C^3_{t+2}),$$

where C^i_j is consumption at date j by an age i agent and $i = 1, 2, 3$ refer to young, middle, and old age, respectively. She wishes to maximize the expected value of (2) subject to the budget constraints faced in one of the two following regimes:

Regime **P** is an economic environment where the costs of transacting in secondary markets are sufficiently large that agents are precluded from such transactions. In the context of this overlapping generations framework, this means that the demands for two-period assets by the middle-aged are zero.[3] I shall, however, assume that B_t titles can be "sold" in either the agent's youth or middle age, but because there is no secondary market, this means that B_t are effectively one-period securities that can be sold only in the seller's middle age. Despite this, in the agent's youth, B_t will be priced *as if* it was marketable in a PCCM because it can be sold at no cost at any future date where new information is available.[4] Finally, it is assumed that the market for D_t is closed. These assumptions mean that equilibrium in asset markets requires that:

---

[3] With no bequest motive, the middle-aged receive no utility from assets whose pay-out can only occur after their death.

[4] Alternatively, B_t can be viewed as a costless line of credit using ϕ_{t+2} as collateral and, as will be assumed, ω is sufficiently large that the agent has no desire to use B_t to borrow for first-period consumption.

(3p)
$$X^1_t = X_t, \quad X = B, D, L, Q,$$
$$S^1_t + S^2_t = S_t + B_{t-1},$$

where Z^i_t describes the demand for Z by age group i at date t. Although there are no formal markets for any asset other than S_t, (3p) implies an implicit price at which the agent is just willing to hold the existing stock of the nontraded security.

Regime **C** is an economy with perfectly competitive capital markets corresponding to the neoclassical "corporate" world. All agents are allowed to trade any title to future income. In this case, equilibrium requires:

(3c)
$$X^1_t + X^2_t = X_t, X = D, B, L, \text{ and } Q$$
$$Z^1_t + Z^2_t = Z_{t-1}, Z = L, Q, \text{ and}$$
$$S^1_t + S^2_t = S_t + B_{t-1}.$$

The proprietorship regime

Consider the **P** regime first. Here the young agent t wishes to maximize

(4p)
$$\omega + V^p_t - P_{dt}D^1_t - P_{st}S^1_t - P_{bt}B^1_t - P_{\ell t}L^1_t - P_{qt}Q^1_t - C^1_t = 0,$$
$$S^1_t + R_{dt+1}D^1_t - P_{st+1}(S^2_{t+1} - B^1_t) - C^2_{t+1} = 0,$$
$$S^2_{t+1} + \psi_{t+2}L^1_t + R_{qt+2}Q^1_t - C^3_{t+2} = 0, \text{ and}$$
$$S^2_{t+1} + B_t \geq 0.$$

the expected value of (2) subject to the constraints:

where:

$y_{t+2} = min(1, (\phi_{t+2} - B_t)/L_t),$
$R_{dt} = (\theta_t - S_{t-1})/D_{t-1},$
$R_{qt} = (\phi_t - B_{t-2} - \psi_t L_{t-2})/Q_{t-2},$ and
V^p_t is the date t value of the firm in the **P** regime.

From the first-order conditions of this problem and (3p), and noting that $E(xy) = cov(xy) + E(x)E(y)$, where $E(.)$ is the expectations operator conditional on all available information and $cov(x,y)$ denotes the covariance of x and y, the implicit prices of the various assets are:

(5 p) $\quad P_{st} = E(M_{21})$,

$$P_{dt} = P_{st}E(R_{dt+1}) + \text{cov}(M_{21}, R_{dt+1})$$

$$P_{bt} = E(M_{31} + \mu) = P_{st}E(P_{st+1}) + \text{cov}(M_{21}, P_{st+1}),$$

where $M_{ij} = U_i/U_j$, $i,j = 1,2,3$; $U_i = \partial W/\partial C^i$; and μ is the Lagrangian attached to the borrowing constraint, $S^2_{t+1} + B_t \geq 0$, divided by U_1. Using the above pricing relationships, the value of the firm can be evaluated as:

(6p)

$$V^p_t = P_{st}E(\theta_{t+1}) + \text{cov}(M_{21}, \theta_{t+1}) + P_{bt}E(\phi_{t+2}) + \text{cov}(M_{31}, \phi_{t+2})$$

$$- E(\mu)E(\phi_{t+2} - B_t).$$

With the exception of the last term in (6p), the value of a proprietorship reflects only tastes (the M_{ij}) and technology (the θ and ϕ)and does not contain any purely financial variables. Thus, for instance, we could carry out the conceptual experiment of the proprietor changing the "dividend" policy of the firm by issuing less S, and declaring that the firm will pay more dividends, and she would be unaffected in any material way.[5] Given an initial equilibrium, then, she would have neither a greater nor a lesser incentive to invest. Furthermore, if the firm changed the debt/equity ratio by altering L_t and Q_t, there would be no change in the value of the firm, even if the possibility of bankruptcy (i.e., the probability that $\phi_{t+2} - L_t - B_t < 0$) were increased. This is because the cost of bankruptcy is nil when the entrepreneur is the only agent who is affected by the "bankruptcy." Indeed, the "Robinson Crusoe" nature of the proprietorship suggests that the valuation of the firm does not require the necessity of me-first contracts or the absence of bankruptcy to obtain the irrelevance of the financing decision.

However, if there is any change in *marketable* risk-free debt for *either* risky *or riskless nonmarketable* claims on the firm, then financial policy does appear to matter. Why is this? It is not because L-type debt is subordinate to B-type claims on the firm: Even if, in equilibrium, the existing L_t is in the same risk class as outstanding B_t, a change in L_t/B_t will still change the valuation of the firm and thus the marginal investment decisions of the proprietor. Rather, it reflects the fact that I have

---

[5]One can think of the entrepreneur as having two sets of books, one for her firm and one for her household. The change in the firm's balance sheet will be reflected in the household accounts, but will not affect the choice set of the agent.

identified the B-type claims as marketable and, as such, they relieve the borrowing constraint that the firm, *and therefore the entrepreneur*, would face in "bad" states in period $t+1$. If L-type debt, riskless or not, were marketable, then changes in the mix of B_t and L_t would also be immaterial to the investment decision. Alternatively, if the likelihood of the firm being rationed is nil, then μ is zero and financial policy is entirely irrelevant to the valuation of the firm and the real investment decisions of its management/owners.

As it stands, however, the greater the likelihood that the borrowing constraint is binding, the greater will be the value of $E(\mu)$, and the lower the value of the firm. In the limit, the increased value of μ will lead to a decision not to invest. By not purchasing K, the agent would use those resources to purchase one-period securities to obtain the flexibility of consumption in period $t+1$ that is denied her with the purchase of "illiquid" capital. It is also worth observing that the borrowing constraint does not impact on V^P_t for compensated changes in nonmarketable D_t and marketable S_t. This is because, in this model, with ω sufficiently large, "dividends" are available to the agent at the next trading opportunity (middle age) and therefore have the same liquidity attributes as S_t. The constraint that they cannot be sold in period t means only that the risk associated with θ_{t+1} cannot be diversified away in the **P** regime.

One might ask why there should be any borrowing constraint on the firm. Possible reasons might include agency costs and the cost of monitoring the management of the firm.[6] These are precisely the same set of problems that arise in the finance literature relating to incentive mechanisms to direct the actions of corporate managers. For the proprietorship the principal is generally a financial intermediary but it, just like the equity and debt owners of the corporation, requires some method to ensure that management operates with its interests in mind.

An alternative interpretation is that the borrowing constraint serves as a measure of the cost of transacting in capital markets. What it does is insert a wedge between the valuation of a financial claim that is illiquid, such as Q_t or L_t, and a liquid claim such as B_t. The existence of transactions costs plays a similar role. To see this, suppose L_t assets can be sold at a proportional transactions cost of γ_t at $t+1$, and add $(P^*_{lt+1} - \eta\gamma_t)$ $(L_t - L^2_{t+1})$ to the middle-aged budget constraint, where $\eta = 1$ if $L^2_{t+1} < L_t$ and 0 otherwise. Suppose, for expositional purposes, that $\psi_{t+2} \equiv 1$ so that, for "seasoned" L, $E(P^*_{lt+1}) = E(P_{st+1})$. Then:

[6] See, for example, Fried and Howitt (1980) or Stiglitz and Weiss (1981).

(4b)

$$P_{\ell t} = E(P^*_{\ell t+1} - \eta\gamma_\ell)M_{21}$$

$$= P_{bt} - P_{st}E(\eta\gamma_\ell) + [\text{cov}(M_{21}, P_{st+1} - \eta\gamma_\ell) - \text{cov}(M_{21}, P_{st+1})].$$

Under the plausible assumption that low-income states for the middle-aged are positively correlated with low-income states in the aggregate economy, the term in brackets should be negative since transactions costs increase the variance of the effective sales price of L. This is because asset sales occur when P_{st+1} is low, and the transactions costs incurred in those states further depress the effective price received by the seller. For a small proprietorship, the cost of making a market in their debt instruments can be costly indeed, not only because of search costs in finding willing buyers and/or sellers, but also for the buyer in assessing the risks that might be incurred if the instruments were indeed purchased. These costs must ultimately be born by the issuer if expected effective yields of a similar risk class are to be equalized.

The corporate regime

Next consider the **C**, or "corporate," regime where perfectly competitive capital markets exist for all income streams. The representative generation t agent faces the decision problem of maximizing the expected value of (2) subject to the constraints:

(4c)

$$\omega + V^c_t - P_{st}S^1_t - P_{dt}D^1_t - P_{bt}B^1_t - P_{\ell t}L^1_t - P_{qt}Q^1_t - P^*_{\ell t}L^{*1}_t - P^*_{qt}Q^{*1}_t - C^1_t = 0,$$

$$S^1_t + R_{dt+1}D^1_t - P_{st+1}(S^2_{t+1} - B^1_t) - P^*_{\ell t+1}(L^{*2}_{t+1} - L^1_t) - P^*_{qt}(Q^{*2}_{t+1} - Q^1_t) + \psi_{t+1}L^{*1}_t +$$

$$R_{qt+1}Q^{*1}_t - P_{dt+1}D^2_{t+1} - P_{bt+1}B^2_{t+1} - P_{\ell t+1}L^2_{t+1} - P_{qt+1}Q^2_{t+1} - C^2_{t+1} = 0,$$

$$S^2_{t+1} + \psi_{t+2}L^{*2}_{t+1} + R_{qt+2}Q^{*2}_{t+1} + R_{dt+2}D^2_{t+1} + P_{st+2}B^2_{t+1} + P^*_{\ell t+2}L^2_{t+1} +$$

$$P^*_{qt+1}Q^2_{t+1} - C^3_{t+2} = 0,$$

where V^c_t is the date t value of the firm in the **C** regime. The first-order conditions combined with the equilibrium conditions (3c) generate the following equilibrium asset prices as seen by the young agent t:
(5c)

$$P_{st} = E(M_{21})$$

$$P_{dt} = P_{st}[E(R_{dt+1})] + \text{cov}(M_{21}, R_{dt+1})$$

$$P^*_{qt} = P_{st}[R_{qt+1}] + \text{cov}(M_{21}, R_{qt+1})$$

$$P^*_{lt} = P_{st}E(\psi_{t+1}) + \text{cov}(M_{21}, \psi_{t+1})$$

$$P_{bt} = E(M_{31})$$

$$P_{lt} = P_{bt}E(\psi_{t+2}) + \text{cov}(M_{31}, \psi_{t+2})$$

$$P_{qt} = P_{bt}E(R_{qt+2}) + \text{cov}(M_{31}, R_{qt+2}).$$

Substituting in the prices from (5c) into (1), the value of the firm becomes:
(6c)

$$V^c_t = P_{st}E(\theta_{t+1}) + \text{cov}(M_{21}, \theta_{t+1}) + P_{bt}E(\phi_{t+2}) + \text{cov}(M_{31}, \phi_{t+2}).$$

As this is the traditional neoclassical financial construct, it follows that financial policy is irrelevant in valuing the firm and the investment decision.[7]

Pricing differences in the P and C regimes

Of more interest is the question of the differences in pricing in the **P** and **C** environments. There are two differences on which I would like to comment. The first point to note is well known: if θ_t and ϕ_t are not perfectly correlated, then, because agents can diversify in the **C** regime, the variances of M_{21} and M_{31} are lower in that regime so that, *ceteris paribus*, the covariation of these with the real economic shocks to the firm that is managed will be reduced. This represents a welfare gain to the individual agent and, in equilibrium, a decrease in the risk premiums

[7]This statement carries the usual caveats of me-first contracts or no bankruptcy, etc. See Fama (1978).

on uncertain income streams.[8] The welfare gain represents an incentive for the individual proprietor to "go corporate," that is, attempt to make use of asset markets. To the extent that agents do not make use of the diversification possibilities, then it argues either that markets are costly to enter or that something other than wealth, *or* welfare, maximization is affecting the proprietor's choice.

The second point I wish to stress is that, if there are PCCM, the borrowing constraint facing the firm no longer operates to constrain the individual owners of the firm, and it is this constraint that places limits on the extent to which the value of the firm is independent of financial policy. This is not to say that corporations are not, in some cases, rationed as to the types of borrowing they can undertake in the real world, but rather that, with the assumption of PCCM, such constraints cannot bind individuals because all income streams of the firm are, by definition, marketable. It will, however, still be true that the agency problems that led outside agents to ration credit to the firm (and therefore to the individual proprietor) remain after incorporation. If such is the case, then the value of the corporation must, in some manner, reflect these agency costs. The work by Ross (1977) and others are attempts to indicate some mechanisms that can reduce these costs, and the link to financial policy itself represents a major insight. However, one could as easily think of a fee paid by the corporation to some monitoring agency that provided the same services but did not involve the financial structure of the firm, in which case financial policy would again become "irrelevant." Nonetheless, if signaling through financial policy is the least cost method of addressing the agency problem, then financial policy will appear to "matter."[9]

To see that it is indeed the absence of costless capital markets that causes the financing decision to be important, and not risk *per se*, it is useful to provide a modification to the **P** regime to allow for diversification opportunities. To do so, suppose the existence of futures markets for all income streams that were not previously tradeable, and assume that costs of operating in these markets is nil but that each proprietor

---

[8]The decrease in the risk premium may or may not increase the value of firms in the aggregate economy. As Barsky (1989) has shown, this is because the decrease involves an increase in the risk-free rate of interest and may or may not increase the price of risky assets. It nonetheless continues to be the case that, for the individual proprietor, the value of her firm will be greater if titles to the output are marketable than if they are not.

[9]An alternative interpretation is that agency costs represent a violation of the PCCM assumption because information on the firm's prospects is not costless to obtain.

must continue to own and operate her individual firm.[10] The budget restrictions that now face agent t in this "**F**" regime are:

(4f)

$$\omega + V_t^f - P_{st}S_t^1 - P_{dt}D_t^1 - P_{bt}B_t^1 - P_{lt}L_t^1 - P_{qt}Q_t^1 - C_t^1 = 0,$$

$$S_t^1 + R_{dt+1}D_t^1 - P_{st+1}(S_{t+1}^2 - B_t^1) + (R_{dt+1} - F_{dt})G_{dt}^1 + (R_{qt+1} - F_{qt}^*)G_{qt}^{*1}$$
$$+ (P_{st+1} - F_{bt})G_{bt}^1 + (F_{lt+1}^* - F_{lt})G_{lt}^1 + (F_{qt+1}^* - F_{qt})G_{qt}^1 + (\psi_{t+1} - F_{lt}^*)G_{lt}^{*1}$$
$$- C_{t+1}^2 = 0,$$

$$S_t^2 + \psi_{t+2}L_t^1 + R_{qt+2}Q_t^1 + (R_{dt+2} - F_{dt+1})G_{dt+1}^2 + (\psi_{t+2} - F_{lt}^*)G_{lt+1}^{*2} + (R_{qt+2} -$$
$$F_{qt+1}^*)G_{qt+1}^{*2} + (P_{st+2} - F_{bt+1})G_{bt+1}^2 + (F_{lt+2}^* - F_{lt+1})G_{lt+1}^2 + (F_{qt+2}^* -$$
$$F_{qt+2})G_{qt+1}^2 - C_{t+1}^3 = 0,$$

$$S_{t+1}^2 + B_t \geq 0,$$

where the F_{ij} is the price of the future contract for asset type i entered into in period j, and the G_{ij}^k is the quantity contracted for by age group k.[11] The first-order conditions from the decision problem of maximizing the expected value of (2) plus the equilibrium conditions, (3p) and $G_{it}^1 + G_{it}^2 = 0$ for all i, imply the following pricing relationships at date t:

(5f)

$$P_{st} = E(M_{21})$$

$$P_{dt} = P_{st}E(R_{dt+1}) + \text{cov}(M_{21}, R_{dt+1})$$

$$P_{bt} = E(M_{31}) + E(\mu)$$

$$P_{lt} = (P_{bt} - E(\mu)) E(\psi_{t+2}) + \text{cov}(M_{31}, \psi_{t+2})$$

---

[10] To maintain consistency with the **P** regime, it is assumed that actual delivery on futures contracts is not permitted. Rather, these contracts can best be seen as bets on the level of future prices with the difference between the contracted futures price and the actual price representing the payout on these bets. It should be noted that, on organized futures markets, few contracts are held to the point where delivery of the underlying good is actually made.

[11] Note that the x_{ij} in the terms $(x_{ij} - F_{ij-1})G_{ij-1}^k$, $x = R, P, \psi$ denotes the "delivery" price on contract G_{ij-1} so that $x_{ij} - F_{ij-1}$ denotes the payoff at j on each unit of futures contract G_{ij-1}.

$$P_{qt} = \{(P_{bt} - E(\mu)) \, E(R_{qt+2}) + cov(M_{31}, R_{qt+2})$$

$$F_{dt} = E(R_{dt+1}) + cov(M_{21}, R_{dt+1})/P_{st} = P_{dt}/P_{st}$$

$$F^*_{lt} = E(\psi_{t+1}) + cov(M_{21}, \psi_{t+1})/P_{st}$$

$$F^*_{qt} = E(R_{qt+1}) + cov(M_{21}, R_{qt+1})/P_{st}$$

$$F_{bt} = (M_{31} + E(\mu))/P_{st} = P_{bt}/P_{st}$$

$$F_{lt}^* = E(F^*_{lt+1}) + cov(M_{21}, F^*_{lt+1})/P_{st}$$
$$= \{P_{lt} + cov(M_{21}, F^*_{lt+1})E(P_{st+1}) - cov(M_{31}, F^*_{lt+1}) \}/(P_{bt} - E(\mu))$$

$$F_{qt}^* = E(F^*_{qt+1}) + cov(M_{21}, F^*_{qt+1})/P_{st}$$
$$= \{P_{qt} + cov(M_{21}, F^*_{qt+1})E(P_{st+1}) - cov(M_{31}, F^*_{qt+1}) \}/(P_{bt} - E(\mu)).$$

These futures contracts provide the individual agent with the same risk diversification opportunities as under the **C** regime, and, it can be shown, if the possibility of rationing or transactions costs are nil, prices in the **C** regime will be identical to the **F** regime futures prices multiplied by the cost of carry, P_{st}. However, if the borrowing constraint is binding in some states, prices in the C and F regimes will differ.

The way to understand why the two regimes differ is to consider the experiment of a young agent t contemplating a "bad," or low-income, state in middle age. Despite using the futures market to diversify risk, her net income from her firm plus net profits on her portfolio are such that she cannot optimally smooth her consumption in $t+1$ and $t+2$ without borrowing more than B_t. In a world with PCCM she could sell assets in order to achieve her optimal consumption path. Without a market for titles, or the ability to use her firm's $t+2$ income as collateral, she cannot. It then follows that prices in the two regimes will differ as the young agent chooses her portfolio to handle this contingency. It also follows that, if there is a shift from L_t to B_t in the firm's capital structure that alters the borrowing constraint, the consumption decisions of the young will be affected and, as a logical consequence, the value of the firm will change with changes in financial structure.

Evidence on perfectly competitive capital markets

The question to ask next is whether or not the perfectly competitive capital markets assumption is reasonably consistent with behavior in actual capital markets. To make this assessment, compare some of the implications of the PCCM assumption with actual asset pricing. The most apparent implication if PCCM does not hold is that the "risk-free" discount factor for "illiquid" assets, $P_b - E(\mu)$, is less than that for liquid securities. Further, if there is an inability to diversify fully, the perceived risk to the individual agent is greater than that for the economy as a whole, and will manifest itself, simultaneously, in too low a riskless rate and too large a risk premium relative to the predictions of a PCCM model. Both of these implications suggest that the place to look for evidence on the appropriateness of the PCCM assumption is in the yield spread between assets that are perceived to be liquid and those that are illiquid and/or risky.

The class of interest-bearing securities that most economists would agree are liquid and (reasonably) riskless are U.S. Treasury bills of short maturity. Thus, if these have yields that are substantially below what would be predicted by some general equilibrium model that made use of the PCCM assumption and of finance theory, one could argue that the PCCM assumption was violated.

The finance literature is replete with models that have consistently concluded that the U.S. Treasury bill rate is "too low." An early example is Fama and Macbeth (1973) who tested the capital asset pricing model (CAPM) using the one-month T-bill rate as the risk-free rate. They concluded that, while the CAPM was generally not inconsistent with their data, the risk-free rate predicted by equity prices was statistically significantly greater than the T-bill rate by almost 0.5 percent per month. More dramatic evidence is available in the seminal paper by Mehra and Prescott (1985) on the equity risk premium. Their model, based on the consumption CAPM, implied a maximum equity risk premium of under 1 percent for "reasonable" values of the coefficient of relative risk aversion. For the period 1889–1978, the actual equity risk premium calculated from the Standard and Poor 500 index and the three-month T-bill rate was over 6 percent.[12] Even had they correctly applied the Modigliani–Miller (1958) theorem to account for leverage in their model, it still would have left the implicit equity risk premium at less than 2 percent.[13] Subsequent to Mehra and Prescott, a variety of modifications to the consumption CAPM that maintained the PCCM assumption have fared somewhat better at mimicking the actual equity premium.

---

[12] To obtain the risk-free rate for the period prior to 1931, Mehra and Prescott used Treasury certificates or 60 to 90 day prime commercial paper instead of T-bills.

[13] See Benninga and Protopapadakis (1990).

Nonetheless, Weil's (1989) remark that the premium puzzle is likewise a puzzle of too low a risk-free rate suggests that some market incompleteness or transactions costs are an essential element in the explanation of relative asset pricing.

There is a third piece of information from the futures markets that suggests that the PCCM assumption is inconsistent with asset prices because actual rates violate the law of one price. If one compares the price of a thirteen-week Treasury bill futures contract for delivery t weeks in the future with the forward price, constructed from a t week and a $t+13$ week T-bill, for the same deliverable thirteen-week bill, one finds that the price of the futures contract is significantly greater than that of the forward contract.[14] For T-bill futures contracts deliverable 14 to 39 weeks in the future, this price premium translates into an average 37 basis point difference over the period August 1976 through August 1987. Over the period of the monetarist experiment, October 1979 to August 1982, when monetary tightness led to a general lack of "liquidity," it averaged over 75 basis points. Because risk premiums are present in both the spot and futures prices, this systematic difference cannot be accounted for by risk factors. Incomplete, or costly, markets for T-bills of maturities over six months would, however, be consistent with the empirical results. This is to say that, insofar as the individual investor is concerned, longer-term Treasury bills have the price characteristics of an illiquid, risk-free type-L asset instead of the liquid type-B asset in the P regime.[15] If this is the case for T-bills, where buy–sell spreads are normally under 5 basis points and brokerage costs are minimal, it seems logical to suppose that other financial assets also are characterized by total transactions costs substantially greater than the small explicit costs attached to their purchase and sale.

If it is costly for individual agents to operate in markets for some financial assets, financial policy will matter for the cost of capital, and firms will devote resources to choosing a financial structure. As innovations occur in the cost of using one form of financing or another, and/or as the tax structure changes, the new opportunities will be exploited to increase the value of the firm, or alternatively, to finance new investment in the least cost way.

Financial economists have directed some attention to analyzing inno-

[14] See Fried (1991).

[15] From (5f) the price of the futures contract under the assumption that $\psi \equiv 1$ is $F_{lt} = F_{bt} = P_{bt}/P_{st}$, while the price of the forward contract is $P_{lt}/P_{st} = (P_{bt} - E(\mu))/P_{st}$. Thus, the futures price less the forward price is $E(\mu)/P_{st}$.

vations that provide better information. The work on principle-agent and signaling problems and the interaction with financial structure is a case in point. That work suggests that financial structure can serve as a signaling device that conveys information about possible states of nature and serves as a substitute for the "transactions costs" that would be required by individual investors in their attempts to ascertain that information by other methods. A second example is given in Fama (1985) where banks have access to inside information from handling the transactions activity of the firm. They are paid to convey that information either by a somewhat higher return on their holdings of the subordinated debt of the firm, or by the receipt of fees paid on (underutilized) lines of credit.

Financial market participants have also innovated to reduce transactions costs by reducing the expected cost of search for trading partners. A recent example of such a financial innovation that increases liquidity and thus reduces search costs for individual agents is the development of the high-yield, or junk, bond market. Despite how one views the other problems in this market, the fact that Drexel Burnham and other brokerage houses were willing to provide at least a limited secondary market in these securities undoubtedly added real value to the issuing firms. That the market failed to develop as much as some may have hoped represents a real cost to the individual investor.

The effects of search and information costs may help to explain the increase in the value of the firm that accompanies many of the unanticipated increases in dividend payments. Such announcements reduce information costs by signaling management's view of the longer-term profit opportunities of the firm, and thus an unanticipated increase in dividends leads to an increased valuation of the firm. Further, if there is an innovation that permits the firm to access capital markets even more cheaply than individual households, then increasing the payout rate reduces the effective cost to equity holders of obtaining liquid funds that would otherwise be acquired by selling equity in costly markets: increased dividend rates tilt the cash flow to households forward, reducing the likelihood of the asset holder being rationed in future idiosyncratic bad states. This and the signaling effect provide at least a partial explanation of why firms pay dividends despite the tax disadvantages of doing so.

Concluding remarks

In this paper I have argued that financial theory provides one method of assessing the value of the firm and the desirability of undertaking new investment. Critical to that financial theory is the assumption that markets are costless and perfectly competitive. This provides the neo-classical economist an observable measure of the demand price of capital that can be used to evaluate investment decisions. If the form of business is a proprietorship rather than a corporation, an observable demand price for capital is not available. Nonetheless, to the proprietor, if not the outside observer, there are a set of implicit prices with which she can conceptually make an identical type of investment decision. This decision is independent of financial structure in the limited sense that the owner is indifferent to the type of securities that yield her a given cash flow. It is not independent if the unavailability of outside funds to the firm indirectly constrains the feasible consumption patterns of the entrepreneur herself.

The availability of these funds is restricted most generally because of transactions costs broadly defined to include both search and informa-tion costs. Because of them, the owner is less able to diversify risk or to enjoy the flexibility of choosing the optimal consumption plan that would be available if capital markets were perfectly competitive and free of these transactions costs. There is thus an incentive for the proprietor to change to a corporate form if the setup costs of doing so do not outweigh the potential benefits.

In a world with costly financial markets, models based on the PCCM assumption would tend to result in actual risk premiums greater than predicted by the model, and, for securities in the same risk class, asset prices will be higher the more liquid (the lower are transactions costs in) the market. Recent evidence confirms that the consumption CAPM model implies risk premiums significantly below those that are actually observed, and data from the U.S. T-bill futures market indicate that T-bills of maturity as short as six months sell at a significant discount relative to what would be predicted if the PCCM assumption held true in the markets for these securities. This discount averaged over 35 basis points in a market where explicit buy–sell spreads plus brokerage fees averaged no more than 6 basis points, suggesting that unmeasured costs of exchange are substantially greater than "objective" measures would lead us to believe.

Violation of the fundamental assumption of PCCM does not require the economist to forsake the neoclassical theory of investment, although it will require more innovative methods to obtain an empirical measure of the cost of capital. To determine this measure, researchers would do well to look to theories of information and of market structure to provide some guidance. My conjecture is that, in doing so, the resulting implications will have a decidedly Keynesian flavor. For instance, I would envision that, in a model richer than the simple one developed here, incorporating transaction costs and/or rationing would imply that retained earnings will appear to be a significant determinant of investment, that investment would appear to be less stable a function of measured interest rates than it would with PCCM (since $E(\mu)$ and measured interest rates are not perfectly correlated), and that a case could be made for an interest-inelastic investment function in periods when the principle shocks to the economic system arise from shifting perceptions of future rationing (since $E(\mu)$ and measured interest rates on liquid assets are negatively related in equilibrium in the face of these innovations). Finally, the recognition of the influence of marketability, or liquidity, on decision making should renew interest in the effects of liquidity preference on economic activity. For instance, monetary policies that increase the stock of real cash balances and other liquid assets will, *ceteris paribus*, reduce the probability that proprietors will be affected by the borrowing constraints that impinge on the firm itself. As such, $E(\mu)$ will decrease, increasing the value of the firm and, ultimately, investment. No doubt there are a number of both Post Keynesians and Monetarists who would welcome the "rediscovery" of money by both financial and real business cycle theorists.

REFERENCES

Barsky, R.B. "Why Don't the Prices of Stocks and Bonds Move Together?" *American Economic Review*, 1989, *79*, 1132–1145.

Benninga, S., and Protopapadakis, A. "Leverage, Time Preference, and the 'Equity Premium Puzzle'." *Journal of Monetary Economics*, 1990, *25*, 49–58.

Fama, E. "The Effects of a Firm's Investment and Financing Decisions on the Welfare of Security Holders." *American Economic Review*, 1978, *68*, 272–284.

———. "What's Different about Banks." *Journal of Monetary Economics*, 1985, *15*, 29–39.

Fama, E., and MacBeth, J.D. "Risk, Return, and Equilibrium: Empirical Tests." *Journal of Political Economy*, 1973, *71*, 607–636.

Fried, J. "U.S. Treasury Bill Forward and Futures Prices." Unpublished manuscript, 1991.

Fried, J., and Howitt, P. "Credit Rationing and Implicit Contract Theory." *Journal of Money, Credit and Banking*, 1980, *12*, 471–487.

Gordon, M.J. "The Neoclassical and a Post Keynesian Theory of Investment." *Journal of Post Keynesian Economics*, 1992, *14* (4), 425–443. Chapter 1 of this volume.

Mehra, R., and Prescott, E.C. "The Equity Premium: A Puzzle." *Journal of Monetary Economics*, 1985, *15*, 145–161.

Miller, M.H., et al. "The Modigliani–Miller Propositions after Thirty Years." [And comments.] *Journal of Economic Perspectives*, 1988, *2*, 99–158.

Modigliani, F., and Miller, M. "The Cost of Capital, Corporation Finance and the Theory of Investment." *American Economic Review*, 1958, *48*, 261–297.

Ross, S.A. "The Determination of Financial Structure: The Incentive Signaling Approach." *Bell Journal of Economics*, 1977, *8*, 23–40.

Stiglitz, J., and Weiss, A. "Credit Rationing in Markets with Imperfect Information." *American Economic Review*, 1981, *71*, 393–421.

Weil, P. "The Equity Premium Puzzle and the Risk Free Rate Puzzle." *Journal of Monetary Economics*, 1989, *24*, 401–422.

4

Neoclassical and Keynesian approaches to the theory of investment

JAMES R. CROTTY

The main conclusion of Myron Gordon's essay is that all five of the core propositions of neoclassical investment theory he identifies are "false," a conclusion that raises a fascinating question: How can an economic theory based on universally false propositions dominate the economics profession?

The simplest and most compelling answer is ideological in character. Neoclassical theory is the concrete theoretical embodiment of a powerful, overarching "pre-analytic Vision" (to use Schumpeter's term) of capitalism as an economic way of life—a metatheoretical, intuitive grasp of the essential properties of an unregulated capitalist system that is overwhelmingly supportive of it. As such, it *must* be a theory of how markets efficiently coordinate the decisions of atomized agents, creating coherence and optimality where chaos might otherwise have been. Neoclassical investment theory has adopted the particular assumptions Gordon criticized because they are necessary for the construction of a theory of investment that can sustain the systemwide stability and optimality properties that are the hallmark of the neoclassical worldview.[1]

The author is Professor of Economics at the University of Massachusetts, Amherst. He would like to thank Jerry Epstein, Jon Goldstein, Peter Skott, and Douglas Vickers for helpful comments on an earlier draft of this paper.

[1] I do not mean to suggest that neoclassicists are oblivious to the existence of potential impediments to Pareto-optimal outcomes. My point, rather, is that a stable position of market-clearing general equilibrium is typically seen as the center of gravity of a competitive market economy, the point to which the system will be attracted in the absence of some contingent market failure. As such, competitive general equilibrium is the analytical and ideological heart of neoclassical theory, its short answer to the question, "What is a free market economy really like?" For this reason, investment models that fit comfortably within this system, such as Jorgenson's user cost model or Tobin's q theory, dominate models, such as the irreversible investment models discussed below, which do not. My comments in the following two sections are addressed primarily, though not exclusively, to such Vision-sustaining models.

In the remainder of this essay I discuss the relation between three core neoclassical assumptions and the Vision-sustaining properties of neoclassical investment theory. After explaining why these assumptions should be rejected, I speculate about the characteristics of an alternative Keynesian investment theory based on a more realistic assumption set. The critique offered here is sympathetic to but distinct from the one presented by Gordon.

Three core assumptions of neoclassical investment theory

The objective function of the enterprise

The separation of ownership and management in the modern corporation, a phenomenon that Keynes saw as the root of many of the problems of modern capitalism, created a principal agent problem that is difficult if not impossible to resolve. Neoclassical financial theorists have made acrobatic theoretical efforts to defang the principal agent problem so that the Pareto-efficiency properties of markets could escape unscarred from its grasp.[2] Unfortunately, the assumptions required to accomplish this task have no significant foundation in empirical or institutional reality. Stiglitz has accurately characterized the neoclassical principal agent literature as "the triumph of ideology over theory and fact" (1985, p. 134).

Neoclassical investment theory, on the other hand, fails even to acknowledge the existence of the problem. Virtually all neoclassical models of the enterprise investment decision begin with the unsupported assertion that the firm's objective *is* pursuit of the owners' objectives: the firm maximizes market value. Three points about the value maximization assumption are worthy of note. First, there is a great deal of empirical and institutional evidence that this assumption is false and virtually no *direct* empirical evidence that it is true.[3] Second, if this highly questionable assumption is rejected, it is not at all clear that a distinct neoclassical approach to the theory of the firm can be identified. In its absence, neoclassical theorists have no generally agreed upon method for choosing an enterprise objective function, for specifying the constraint set, or even for identifying the cost of financial capital. Third,

[2]See, for example, Fama (1980), Jensen and Meckling (1976), and Fama and Jensen (1983).

[3]See, for example, the reviews in the *Journal of Economic Literature* by Cyert and Hendrick (1972), Marris and Mueller (1980), and Williamson (1981) as well as the widely cited study of decision making in large industrial corporations by Donaldson and Lorsch (1983) and the discussion in Crotty (1990a).

if firms are partly independent or semiautonomous from their owners and can make investment decisions that run counter to shareholders' perceived interests, there is no wealth holder control of, or "sovereignty" over, the capital accumulation process and no mechanism to assure optimal coordination between the real and financial sectors of the economy. Thus, when management is semiautonomous, the real sector becomes semiautonomous as well, a result that is inconsistent with the neoclassical Vision.

In Crotty (1990a), I argued that the relevant non-neoclassical literature (managerial, behavioral, and institutional) characterizes top managers of large nonfinancial corporations as concerned with the long-term reproduction, growth, and safety of the firm itself. By achieving these objectives, managers assure their own status and security. The constraints they face derive in part from their desire to retain decision-making independence from financial market "constituents"—stockholders and creditors. For the "managerial" firm, dividends, like interest payments, are a cost of maintaining managerial decision-making autonomy, a constraint rather than an objective to be maximized. Thus, an acceptable investment theory requires the specification of the firm as a partially independent or semiautonomous economic agent with a preference function of its own.

This characterization of owners and managers is broadly consistent with Keynes' own view. Keynes theorized owners and managers as distinct agents with different objectives and planning horizons—the former seeking short-term capital gains, the latter the long-term viability and growth of the enterprise itself, and significantly different degrees of knowledge about the firm and its environment—the former are relatively ignorant, the latter are professionally well informed. Keynes also stressed the fact that, while owners hold liquid financial assets, firms accumulate relatively illiquid physical capital.

Neoclassical risk or Keynesian uncertainty?

In the first footnote in his essay, Gordon notes that Post Keynesians have "correctly" rejected the way in which neoclassical investment and financial theories represent agent knowledge of the future. He does not, however, carry this critique into the body of the paper and does not substitute an alternative Keynesian assumption about agent knowledge of the future in his suggested Keynesian investment model. Yet, as Gordon knows, the choice between neoclassical and Keynesian assumptions about knowledge of the future profoundly affects the character of both investment and financial theory.

Neoclassical theory does indeed adopt the untenable assumption that agents can assign numerical probabilities to all possible future economic states and, therefore, can associate a probability distribution of expected returns with every possible choice available to them. Stretching credulity still further, it adds the truly heroic assumption that agents are absolutely certain that these probability distributions are *knowledge*—the truth, the whole truth, and nothing but the truth about the future consequences of current agent choice. The universal adoption of this logically and empirically repugnant assumption can only be understood as "the triumph of ideology over theory and fact."

Keynes' views about uncertainty have been explored at great length by Shackle, Vickers, Davidson, and others. For Keynes, the information needed to make an optimal investment decision—the future net revenues that will be generated by each potential investment project—does not exist and therefore cannot be known at the moment of choice. It is not "out there" for agents to find. For Keynes, the future is created by current and future agent decisions that are inherently unpredictable: "About these matters there is no scientific basis on which to form any calculable probability whatever. We simply do not know" (Keynes, 1937, p. 214). Nonetheless, firms and wealth holders *must* make investment and portfolio selection decisions; they cannot avoid the decision-making dilemma created by Keynesian uncertainty. "We do not know what the future holds. Nevertheless, as living and moving beings, we are forced to act" (Keynes, 1973, p. 124).

Thus, in a world of uncertainty there is an *empty space* in the logical chain linking agent characteristics and hard data to agent decisions. Neoclassical theories of rational choice are impotent in this environment because their very definition of rationality assumes that agents have complete and correct knowledge of the effects on outcomes of all possible rival courses of action. Where the information required to connect decision to outcome is incomplete and undependable, neoclassical theories have nothing—literally—to say.

Keynes, by way of contrast, outlined a solution to this problem: he adopted a theory of *conventional* decision making.[4] Keynes theorized an expectations formation process based on custom, habit, tradition,

---

[4]See Crotty (1991b) for an analysis of uncertainty, conventional decision making, and conditional stability in Keynesian macromodels.

rules of thumb, instinct, and other socially constituted conventions and practices.[5] He argued that in "normal" times at least, agents base their forecasts on conventional assumptions such as: (1) the future will look like the relevant past extrapolated ("modified only to the extent that we have more or less definite reasons for expecting a change" [Keynes, 1936, p. 148]); and (2) while individual agents understand themselves to be inescapably ignorant of the future, the collective or average opinion or the "conventional wisdom" is seen as reasonably or even scientifically well informed.

Conventional expectations formation creates or imagines the previously missing data needed to link rival choices to expected outcomes. More important, conventions create *confidence* that the expectations thus formed have a degree of meaningfulness or validity or truth-content sufficient to sustain an investment or portfolio decision of great moment for the agent. This creation of confidence in the meaningfulness of forecasts or in the "scientific" character of the conventional wisdom is essential to both the growth potential and the conditional stability of the economy. No rational management would undertake a large, risky investment project on the basis of an optimistic forecast in which it had little faith. In concert with the private and public institutional structures that guide economic activity and set bounds on expected future outcomes, *conventional decision making creates a significant degree of continuity, order, and conditional stability in a Keynesian model* in spite of the potential for chaos and perpetual instability seemingly inherent in the assumption of true uncertainty. It is simply not true, as Lucas has argued, that "in cases of uncertainty, economic reasoning will be of no value" (1981, p. 224).

On the other hand, social conventions are inherently "fragile" and "subject to sudden and violent changes" (Keynes, 1937, p. 215). On those occasions when the consensus forecast turns out to be disastrously mistaken, knowledge of the irreducible ignorance of even the collective wisdom will break through the conventional barriers we have constructed to conceal it from ourselves. At such times, confidence in the meaningfulness of the forecasting process will shatter, and key behavioral equations may become extremely unstable. These are the points of

---

[5] Such socially constituted conventions arise in part because human beings have a deep-seated psychological need to impose order and controllability on their environment when they are able and even to pretend to see order and predictability when it is not there. "Peace and comfort of mind," Keynes noted, "require that we should hide from ourselves how little we foresee" (1973, p. 124).

crisis and panic that have pride of place in Keynesian, Minskian, and Marxian theories of investment instability, but are prohibited by assumption in neoclassical investment theory because they are incompatible with its Vision.

Physical capital as a liquid asset: reversible investment

All neoclassical investment models that are demonstrably consistent with the overarching neoclassical Vision of a well-coordinated and efficient system of markets assume that long-lived capital assets have perfect or near perfect resale markets. Jorgenson's model and Tobin's q theory are the two most important examples. With perfect resale markets the neoclassical investment decision is as riskless and reversible as the decision to hire a worker.

The liquidity of capital finds reflection in the neoclassical concept of a user cost or a "rental price" for capital goods. Neoclassical firms are indifferent between owning and renting their capital: in either case they are paying only for capital "services." But renting capital goods is not a very risky business. If expectations turn out to be disappointed by the unfolding of events, the firm can always resell the goods or choose not to renew its rental agreement at the end of the period. With liquid capital, the beyond-first-period future is not particularly relevant, so neither is the degree of uncertainty. And when investment is reversible, financial commitments are reversible as well. Capital goods can always be resold to retire the debt that financed them and there is no "legacy of past [debt] contracts" to burden the accumulation process (Minsky, 1982, p. 63).

Thus, *the firm faces no sunk costs, no intertemporal profit trade-offs, and no irreversible debt burdens.*[6] With liquid capital goods, even the prospect of bankruptcy, which would be devastating to management, would be of slight concern to owners because it would cost them little. The assumption of reversibility robs uncertainty of its sting because it renders mistakes relatively costless.[7] How much effect can the unknowability of the future

[6]According to standard neoclassical theory, then, in the absence of adjustment costs, General Motors should invest its market value in Treasury bills whenever short-term interest rates exceed the profit rate in the auto industry, then sell the T-bills and buy or rent car-producing capital goods when the situation reverses itself.

[7]This reversibility property is not be altered by the assumption of gestation lags. With perfect resale markets, such lags have no effect on the speed or cost of disinvestment and a rational firm would take forward lags into account in its planning. Nor is it *qualitatively* affected by either moderate *or* relatively short-lived "costs of adjustment." Of course, if these costs were quite large, were attached to the *resale* of capital goods, and remained quite large for many years or even decades after a decision to disinvest, they would be equivalent to the assumption of irreversibility. But

have on the investment decision of a firm that can get its money back (minus one period's depreciation) if that decision turns sour?[8]

The modest mainstream literature dealing with irreversible investment that has emerged over the past decade is a welcome first step toward the development of a more realistic investment theory.[9] However, these investment models cannot yet serve as a foundation for the neoclassical Vision. For one thing, this literature formally demonstrates that irreversibility "undermines the theoretical foundation of standard neoclassical investment models" (Pindyck, 1991, p. 1110). For another, no one has yet analyzed the properties of an economic *system* incorporating an irreversible investment function (and the underutilized capital stock that would accompany it). Unless and until it can be shown that these models are consistent with the neoclassical Vision, they will remain at the margin of the neoclassical investment literature. Unfortunately, these models cannot yet make a major contribution to Keynesian macrotheory either because they are forced to rely on almost all of the standard, grossly unrealistic neoclassical efficient-markets assumptions in order to make the extraordinarily complex problems they construct analytically tractable.

Any model of the investment decision with a serious pretension to realism must assume with Keynes that capital accumulation is an inherently risky process because many capital goods are substantially industry-, firm-, and/or use-specific. Plant and equipment that is designed for a particular firm and a particular purpose, perhaps integrated in a larger system of production, suffers a significant loss of market value when it is produced and again when it is installed. The assumption of substantial illiquidity of capital goods is a *sine qua non* of Keynesian investment theory.

Implications of the assumption set for neoclassical investment theory

The combined effect of these assumptions helps give neoclassical investment theory its defining characteristics. The assumption that

---

this is not the standard specification of adjustment cost models. The convex adjustment cost literature "generally ignores the effects of irreversibility" (Pindyck, 1991, p. 1138). Just as time has been said to be a device to keep everything from happening at once, adjustment costs are an analytical device designed to keep the optimal capital stock from happening at once and make investment a continuous function of its determining variables.

[8]The user cost or rental price is also affected by prospective capital gains or losses on the resale of investment goods, but this effect is generally considered to be of little theoretical or empirical significance.

[9]See the survey of the irreversible investment literature in Pindyck (1991).

owners and managers are identical agents settles the otherwise conten-
tious problem of specifying a preference function for the firm itself.
Most important, it eliminates the embarrassing possibility that ownership and management will have conflicting objectives and conflicting
attitudes toward risk. It thus sustains the neoclassical Vision by helping
to assure the optimal coordination and synchronization of the real and
financial sectors.

In neoclassical financial theory, management concerns itself only with
the expected value of the distributions of expected future returns on
prospective investment projects, not with other moments. The discount
rate it applies to these expected returns does reflect perceived risk, but
it is risk as evaluated "from the [financial] investor's viewpoint" and
not from its own (Brealey and Myers, 1988, p. 188). In typical neoclassical macroeconomic investment models, on the other hand, the firm is
formally assumed to be risk-neutral. Risk enters the model through the
cost of capital, a variable that is determined in financial markets and is
thus exogenous to the firm. In either case, there is no role for an
autonomous enterprise preference function.

In the absence of managerial autonomy, the suppliers of financial
capital to the firm exercise sovereignty over the accumulation process.
They do have utility functions, of course, and are, in general, risk-averse.
It is their job to evaluate expected corporate cash flows with different
risk characteristics, decide on optimal leverage ratios, diversify portfolios so as to maximize expected utility and achieve risk-return efficiency, and determine the cost of capital to the enterprise. The enterprise
then passively implements the investment strategy its owners have
chosen. A necessary condition for the validity of the neoclassical
assertion that financial agents do their job optimally is the assumption
that they have perfect knowledge of the stochastic future. The conflation
of ownership and management and the neoclassical treatment of uncertainty thus help create the ethereal world of the Modigliani–Miller
theorem and of Gordon's propositions (3) and (4). Neither dividend
policy nor the degree of leverage of the firm has any effect on its
investment decision, a proposition that "holds under reasonably general
conditions" (Blanchard and Fischer, 1989, p. 295). There is no room for
Minsky's "financial fragility " hypothesis here.

The assumption of liquid physical capital or reversible investment
makes the central conclusions of neoclassical investment theory insensitive to the moderate relaxation of the other assumptions. With liquid
capital, it would make little difference to the character of investment

theory if the firm itself were risk-averse, because investment would not be very risky. And it would not matter much if the firm had less than complete information about future states of the economy, because with reversible investment and reversible debt, mistakes would be relatively costless.

Conversely, if capital were assumed to be substantially illiquid, the financial commitments associated with investment spending would be irreversible: mistakes would be costly and could be catastrophic. Under such conditions, the degree of managerial risk-aversion would matter. And, as the irreversible investment literature demonstrates, even the risk-neutral firm would be "highly sensitive to risk in various forms" (Pindyck, 1991, p. 1141). In an environment of Keynesian uncertainty, investment would be sensitive to changes in expectations and in the degree of confidence management placed in them. Instability in the expectations and confidence formation process would bring instability in investment spending in its wake.

In the next section I argue that the combined assumptions of illiquid capital, a semiautonomous firm, and Keynesian uncertainty are needed to construct an investment theory adequate to capture the essential characteristics of the world in which we actually live.

A Keynesian alternative

Gordon presents a formal model of what he calls the Keynesian theory of investment. We are less ambitious here, attempting only to sketch out the general characteristics of an investment theory based on the substitute core assumptions discussed in the previous sections.[10]

A realistic theory of investment should incorporate the assumption that the firm is a semiautonomous agent with a preference function of its own. We would expect the firm to pursue growth in size or market share and in profits—its *growth* objective—and avoid threats to its decision-making autonomy or its financial security—its *safety* objective. The existence of this safety objective makes the firm itself risk-averse.

Growth is attainable only through capital accumulation, but capital accumulation must be financed. Debt finance creates explicit, legally binding cash flow commitments to creditors. But even internal funding

[10] The discussion that follows abstracts from the effect of the firm's competitive environment and "strategic" considerations on the investment decision. See Crotty (1993) for an analysis of the effect of changes in the competitive environment on the enterprise investment decision. See Crotty and Goldstein (1992) for one attempt to construct a formal model of the enterprise investment decision along these lines.

and stock flotation create implicit cash flow commitments to shareholders. If commitments to stockholders cannot be met out of the future operating profits generated by invested capital, management may experience a threat to its decision-making autonomy; if commitments to creditors are not met, the firm might go bankrupt. In a Keynesian world, financial commitments, especially to creditors, are relatively certain while expected profits are not. With long-lived illiquid capital, the firm must form expectations of cash flows well into the future and must assess the quality of the expectations thus formed. But about such matters, "We simply do not know." When capital goods are illiquid and the future is unknowable, serious mistakes are possible and the financial commitments associated with them are irreversible. Thus, capital accumulation is simultaneously *necessary* and *dangerous* for the firm itself: necessary to achieve growth and defend its markets and its profits from aggressive competitors, and dangerous because disappointed expectations can make it difficult or even impossible for the firm to fulfill its financial commitments.

Were firms to undertake only those investment projects with very high expected profit rates and low risk, they might be able to improve their growth and safety prospects simultaneously. But, as the firm considers projects with decreasing expected profits and increasing risk, the higher expected growth that increased investment promises will be associated with greater financial burdens and decreased safety. Conversely, if the firm maximized safety, it would forgo growth opportunities. The essence of management's decision-making dilemma is that, at the margin, it confronts a *growth-safety trade-off.* Firms must seek a level of investment that achieves a satisfactory balance between their growth and safety objectives.

In a Keynesian model, then, investment will be determined by management's preference for growth relative to safety and those variables that affect the perceived relation between investment and growth and between investment and safety. For example, the expected profit rate has a powerful influence on investment because a higher profit rate will, by increasing expected profits per unit of investment and by raising expected profit flows relative to cash flow commitments to owners and creditors, increase both growth and safety simultaneously. On the other hand, increased financial leverage, higher interest rates, or a decrease in management's confidence in its ability to foresee future economic conditions will depress investment because they lower the safety level associated with every prospective investment project. The enterprise investment decision at a fixed point in time can be briefly characterized as follows: *Ceteris paribus, a managerial preference for growth relative to safety, a high expected profit rate, financial robustness, low interest rates, and a minimal sense of uncertainty all stimulate investment, and vice versa.*[11] Specifying the determinants of investment at a point in time, however, is but the first step in the construction of a dynamic investment theory. There are two potential endogenous sources of change in a Keynesian model: (1) conventional expectations and confidence formation; and (2) the effect that the investment decision in the aggregate might have on the value of its real sector determinants.

Keynes and Minsky have used the theory of conventional decision making to explain how and why financial market participants endogenously change their expectations and, therefore, their behavior over the course of a business cycle. But conventional decision making must be applied to the enterprise as well. Here, as in financial markets, realized outcomes can change the investment decision whether or not they are consistent with managerial expectations of them. Unexpected outcomes will change forecast values and could induce an alteration in the forecasting procedure and/or a decline in management's confidence in the validity of the forecasting process. But even the confirmation of expectations by events will alter the level of investment because it will raise confidence in the meaningfulness of forecasts. For example, the longer the realized profit rate is rising (or at least not falling), the more confidence management will place in its forecast that the profit rate is unlikely to fall during the relevant future. And the longer the existing debt–equity or interest–coverage ratio has been maintained without triggering a threat to financial security, the more likely it becomes that a more confident management will revise upward its estimate of the maximum degree of leverage that it is safe to accept. To paraphrase Shackle, investment is an inherently restless variable.

When the firm is either pessimistic about the future or has no confidence in its ability to make meaningful predictions, it will consider the accumulation of even modest amounts of debt-financed capital to be unsafe and will see even normal debt–equity ratios as dangerous, so investment will be depressed. Conversely, when management is upbeat about the future and confident that its optimism is well founded, the

---

[11] These results are formally derived in Crotty and Goldstein (1992). The relation between investment and confidence is in fact more complex than indicated in the text. While confidence in an optimistic forecast will raise investment, confidence in a pessimistic forecast will lower it.

growth objective will dominate and investment will accelerate. Boom euphoria will make even historically high debt–equity ratios seem unthreatening. Thus, safety is jointly constituted by objective variables such as recent profit rate trends and debt–equity ratios and by *subjective*, conventionally constituted variables such as maximum acceptable leverage, optimism (about future prospects), and confidence in the meaningfulness of expectations.

As Keynes, Minsky, and Marx emphasized, these subjective variables alone can create boom–bust cycles: the safety concerns that restrain the managerial firm's drive to invest ebb and flow in endogenous Keynes-Minsky-Marx cycles.[12] *Ceteris paribus*, so does investment spending. But, as Minsky has stressed, these endogenous cycles have across-cycle ratchet effects. Neither the high leverage of the boom nor the conservatism induced by crisis automatically evaporate at cycle's end. Rather, they continue to depress investment for an extended period.[13]

Of course, the determinants of safety are not the only endogenous sources of cyclical or secular instability. In Marxian real sector models and in some Keynesian-Kaleckian multiplier-accelerator models, an investment boom stimulated by a high rate of profit can initiate a chain of events that will eventually cause the profit rate to fall. In Marxian theory the rate of investment depends on the rate of profit, an endogenous variable whose value changes with changes in aggregate demand, cost-price relations, and technology. Movement in the determinants of the profit rate triggers change in the pace of investment that alters the state of the economy, and thus changes the rate of profit. In other words, investment is always responding to conditions that are altered by its response. As argued in Crotty (1990a), a theory of endogenous instability should have both real and financial sector roots.

An investment theory of this type has several noteworthy properties. First, though based on partly conflicting assumptions, it has much in common with Gordon's model: the firm itself is risk-averse; capital structures matter; the firm has an incentive to try to regulate its competitive environment—less intense competitive pressure raises the profit rate and makes the future more predictable; and, as formally demonstrated in Crotty and Goldstein (1992), a firm facing almost assured

[12]See Crotty (1985) for a discussion of the role of money, credit, uncertainty, and endogenous expectation and confidence formation in Marx's theory of accumulation and crisis.

[13]For example, capital accumulation in the 1990s may be severely burdened by financial burdens built up in the 1980s.

bankruptcy under existing conditions will "adopt a go-for-broke policy" (Gordon, 1992, p. 440).

Second, the theory is *institutionally specific and historically contingent*, as Keynes intended macrotheory to be.[14] The particular properties of a macromodel based on an investment theory of this sort would depend on the concrete specification of several functional relations and parameter values: management's degree of risk-aversion; the form and the stability of the expectations and confidence generating functions; the size and composition of the initial capital stock and the degree of enterprise leverage; the maximum level of indebtedness acceptable to management; and the impact of investment on the realized profit rate. Thus, the appropriate specification of the investment model and the dynamic properties of the macromodel would change with time and institutional circumstance.

Third, an investment theory of this kind would be more consistent with and reflective of the broad contours of the historical record than is the neoclassical investment model and could, therefore, help underpin a Keynesian alternative to the neoclassical Vision. As argued in Crotty (1991b), a macromodel based on conventional decision making will be stable much of the time: it will typically be characterized by relatively smooth, continuous, and orderly dynamics. However, from time to time a Keynesian model will exhibit endogenously generated bouts of disorder and instability, of economic crisis and financial panic, whenever the conventions that sustain the expectations-formation process crumble. And this is precisely what we find in the empirical record: cyclical patterns of investment spending and corporate leverage, significantly different average net rates of capital accumulation and average degrees of financial fragility in distinct secular periods, and recurrent though irregular bouts of instability and financial crises.

---

[14]Crotty (1990b) argues that the methodology used by Keynes to construct his macrotheory was institutionally specific and historically contingent.

REFERENCES

Blanchard, O., and Fischer, S. *Lectures on Macroeconomics*. Cambridge, MA: MIT Press, 1989.

Brealey, R., and Myers, S. *Principles of Corporate Finance*. New York: McGraw-Hill, 1988.

Crotty, J. "The Centrality of Money, Credit and Financial Intermediation in Marx's Crisis Theory." In *Rethinking Marxism*, S. Resnick and R. Wolff, eds. New York: Autonomedia, 1985.

————. "Owner-Manager Conflict and Financial Theories of Investment Instability: A Critical Assessment of Keynes, Tobin and Minsky." *Journal of Post Keynesian Economics,* Summer 1990a, *12* (4), 519–542.

————. "Keynes on the Stages of Development of the Capitalist Economy: The Institutional Foundation of Keynes's Methodology." *Journal of Economic Issues,* September 1990b, 761–780.

————. "Rethinking Marxian Investment Theory: Keynes-Minsky Instability, Competitive Regime Shifts and Coerced Investment." *Review of Radical Political Economics,* March 1993, 25 (1): 1–26.

————. "Are Keynesian Uncertainty and Macrotheory Incompatible? Conventional Decision Making, Institutional Structures, and Conditional Stability in Keynesian Macromodels." Working Paper 1991–17, University of Massachusetts, 1991b.

Crotty, J., and Goldstein, J. "Keynes-Minsky Instability and the Investment Decision of the Firm." Mimeo, University of Massachusetts, 1992.

Cyert, R., and Hendrick, C. "Theory of the Firm: Past, Present and Future; An Interpretation." *Journal of Economic Literature,* June 1972, 398–412.

Donaldson, G., and Lorsch, J. *Decision-Making at the Top: The Shaping of Strategic Direction.* New York: Basic Books, 1983.

Fama, F. "Agency Problems and the Theory of the Firm." *Journal of Political Economy,* April 1980, 288–307.

Fama, F., and Jensen, M. "Separation of Ownership and Control." *Journal of Law and Economics,* June 1983, 301–325.

Gordon, M.J. "The Neoclassical and a Post Keynesian Theory of Investment." *Journal of Post Keynesian Economics,* Summer 1992, *14* (4), 425–443. Chapter 1 of this volume.

Jensen, M., and Meckling, W. "Theory of the Firm: Managerial Behavior, Agency Costs and Ownership Structure." *Journal of Financial Economics,* October 1976, 305–360.

Keynes, J. *The General Theory of Employment, Interest and Money.* Cambridge: Cambridge University Press, 1972 [1936].

————. "The General Theory of Employment." *Quarterly Journal of Economics,* February 1937, 209–223.

————. *The Collected Writings of John Maynard Keynes. Volume 14. The General Theory and After: Part II.* London: Macmillan, 1973.

Lucas, R. *Studies in Business-Cycle Theory.* Cambridge, MA: MIT Press, 1981.

Marris, R., and Mueller, D. "The Corporation, Competition, and the Invisible Hand." *Journal of Economic Literature,* March 1980, 32–63.

Minsky, H. *Can "It" Happen Again?* Armonk, NY: M.E. Sharpe, 1982.

Pindyck, R. "Irreversibility, Uncertainty, and Investment." *Journal of Economic Literature,* September 1991, 1110–1148.

Stiglitz, J. "Credit Markets and Control of Capital." *Journal of Money, Credit, and Banking,* May 1985, 133–152.

Williamson, O. "The Modern Corporation: Origins, Evolution, Attributes." *Journal of Economic Literature,* December 1981, 1537–1568.

5

Is investing for the long term theory or just mumbo-jumbo?

PETER L. BERNSTEIN

What do we mean by "investing for the long term"? The aim of this paper is to demonstrate that "long term" is in the eye of the beholder.

For those investors infested with quarterly measurements, a year can be the long run and five years is just about the outer limit. For enthusiasts of the Dividend Discount model, the long run is the indefinite future. Most of us fall somewhere in between. Yet, each of us will define the long run with a different time span in mind, which means that yours will be appropriate for me only by coincidence. But no matter how we figure it, there is more to the long run than shutting your eyes and hoping that some great tidal force will bring your ships home safe, sound, and laden with just the right merchandise for the occasion.

I am going to approach the issue from two different viewpoints. First, we shall explore whether there really is such a thing as long run. Second, assuming that we can identify and define the long run, I shall try to demonstrate that moving from the short run to the long run transforms the investment process in ways that are far more profound than most people realize.

How long is the long run?

When people talk about the long run, they are really saying that they can distinguish between the signal and the noise. Yet, the world is a terribly noisy place. Discriminating between the main force and the perpetual swarm of peripheral events is one of the most baffling tasks that human beings must confront—and can never duck.

Do two unusually warm winters in a row signify the onset of global

The author is President of Peter L. Bernstein, Inc., and Founding Editor of *The Journal of Portfolio Management*.

warming, or are they a normal variation, to be succeeded by bitterly cold winters in the years following? When the championship baseball team loses three games in a row, is that the beginning of the end of their league dominance, or a brief interruption in their string of victories? When the stock market drops 10 percent, is that the start of a new bear market or just a correction in the ongoing bull market? Was October 1987 the beginning of the end, or the end of the beginning?

Those long-run investors who believe that they can distinguish signal from noise scorn the traders who are so busy chasing the wiggles and the ripples that they run the risk of losing the main trend. The watchwords of the true long-run investor are "regression to the mean." In the long run, everything will even out; main trends are identifiable; main trends dominate. This concept rules much active investment management. The very idea of "undervaluation" or "overvaluation" implies some identifiable norm to which values will revert. Other investors may choose to succumb to fads and whims and rumors, but investors who hang in there will win out in the long run.

Or will they? The lesson of history is that norms are never normal forever. Paradigm shifts belie blind faith in regression to the mean. This is precisely the problem with which Alan Greenspan is now wrestling: has the long and reliable relationship between M2 and nominal GNP finally crumbled, or is the current disturbance just an anomaly? Here is another. For 170 years, the highest quality long-term bonds in the United States yielded an average of 4.2 percent within a standard deviation of only a percentage point. In 1970, yields broke through the old upper limits and started heading for 7 percent. Investors stared: how could they decide whether this was a blip or a new era? And then there was the moment in the late 1950s when the dividend yield on stocks slipped below bond yields. Again, investors back then had no handy rules to tell them whether this totally unexpected development was a fundamental shift in market structure or just a temporary aberration that would soon correct itself, with the "normal" spread of stocks yields over bond yields reestablishing itself.

John Maynard Keynes, who knew a few things about investing, probability, and economics, took a dim view of the idea that you can look through the noise to find the signal. In a famous passage, he declared that:

> [T]he long run is a misleading guide to current affairs. In the long run, we are all dead. Economists set themselves too easy, too useless a task

if in the tempestuous seasons they can only tell us that when the storm is long past the ocean will be flat.

Keynes is suggesting that the tempestuous seasons are the norm. The ocean will never be flat soon enough to matter. In Keynes's philosophy, equilibrium and central values are myths, not the foundations on which we build our structures. We cannot escape the short run. These considerations explain why I asserted at the outset that the long run is in the eye of the beholder. The way you feel about the long run and the way you define it are ultimately gut issues. These issues are resolved more by the nature of your basic philosophy of life, or even how you feel when you get up each morning, than by rigorous intellectual analysis.

Those who believe in the permanence of tempestuous seasons will view life as a succession of short runs, where noise dominates signals and the frailty of the basic parameters makes normal too elusive a concept to worry about. These people are pessimists who see nothing in the future but clouds of uncertainty. They make decisions based only on the short distance ahead that they can see.

Those who live by regression to the mean spend their time entirely differently. They expect the storm to pass, so that one day the ocean will be flat. On that assumption, they can make the decision to ride out the storm. They are optimists who see the signals by which they will steer their ships toward that happy day when the sun shines through.

My own view of the matter is a mixture of these two approaches. Hard experience has taught me that chasing noise leads me to miss the main trend too often. At the same time, having lived through the bond yield/stock yield shift of the late 1950s and the breakthrough of bond yields into the stratosphere beyond 6 percent in the late 1960s—just to mention two such shattering events out of many—I look with suspicion at all main trends and all those means to which variables are supposed to regress. To me, the primary task in investing is to test and then retest some more the parameters and paradigms that appear to govern daily events. Betting against them is dangerous when they look solid, but accepting them without question is the most dangerous step of all.

The impact of the long run on investment management

It is a truism that investing for the long run is different from short-term trading. But I would argue that time is such a critical variable in the investment process that the differences between short- and long-term investing are far more profound than most people realize. The long-term game is so unlike the short-term game that you need a whole new set of rules when you are playing it. I shall mention three areas where this requirement applies.

1. Volatility

The first difference is in the impact of volatility. Volatility is noise. The short-term trader bets on the noise; the long-term investor listens to the signal. But the long-term investor who thinks that the main trend will even out volatility over time is in for a shock. Volatility is the central concern of all investors, but it matters more in the long run than in the short run.

Volatility matters, because it defines the uncertainty of the price at which an asset will be liquidated. The Ibbotson Associates data tell us that the expected total return on the S&P 500 for a one-year holding period is about 12.5 percent, but you should not be surprised if you come out somewhere between –8 percent and +32 percent, a spread of 4000 basis points. The range for individual stocks is much wider. So volatility appears to matter a lot if you are going to hold for only a year.

Stretch your holding period out from one year to ten years, and the range of the expected return narrows to between about +5 percent to +15 percent a year, a spread of only 1000 basis points and implying very little chance of loss over the ten-year period. Although volatility now seems much less troublesome than it did in the one-year horizon, and although the odds on losing money when you liquidate are now greatly reduced, do not be lulled by that relatively narrow range of annual rates of return. What matters is not the annual rate of return but the final liquidating value at the end of ten years. A dollar invested for ten years at 5 percent compounds to $1.63; at 15 percent, it compounds to $4.05. As a dollar invested for one year is likely to end up at the end of the year between $.92 and $1.28, the spread in liquidating value over one year is far narrower than the probable outcomes over a ten-year holding period, despite the greater standard deviation of short-run returns. So where is the uncertainty greater—in the short run or the long run? Talk about the ocean being flat! It could be very flat indeed.

2. Liquidity

When you buy something to make a few points, or even ten or twenty, eighths and quarters matter. Good execution counts for a lot. When you buy to hold for the long run, for years, even a few points on the price will not matter a great deal. Liquidity is a concern of the short-term investor and a minor matter for the long-term investor.

The point is obvious, but it receives too little attention. How much does pricing matter for assets that are not about to be liquidated? If you are a multibillion-dollar investment management organization that has no choice but to acquire and hold indefinitely Exxon and IBM and other major high-cap companies, what difference does the daily price fluctuation make? Why bother to watch their daily action? Throughout our financial system, many more assets are marked to market than is necessary, creating serious distortions as to the soundness of the institutions involved. Assets held for the long pull are simply not the same thing as assets that are to be liquidated in a matter of weeks or months.

3. Income

Investment income is a critically important link between the short and the long run. Income is also a dramatic illustration of the important principle of Hegelian dialectics that changes in quantity ultimately become changes in quality.

For the short-term trader, the dividend on a stock is a gauge to valuation, but the actual money income from the dividend is irrelevant. The trader's return will be dominated by price change, because prices tend to move in ranges that far exceed one year's income receipt. Now expand the time horizon. Income payments pile up over time, altering the character of the return structure. Investors who are able to reinvest income now begin to have the opposite desire from short-term traders: traders want prices to rise so they can sell, while investors reinvesting income are buyers and must want prices to *fall* while the buying process is going on.

In the case of bonds, this story is obvious. Current coupons being what they are, interest and interest-on-interest soon prevail over price change and, for long-maturity bonds, account for an overwhelming share of the total return.

The story in the stock market is similar in character, but few people take notice of it. If you had put a dollar in the stock market at the end of 1925 and just let it appreciate, spending all the income you received over those 66 years, you would have $30 today. If you ignored the price appreciation and simply piled up the sixty-five years' worth of dividends, without any reinvestment income, you would have a pile equal to $20. Not bad. In fact, given the starting period in 1925 and the intervening stock market crash of 1929 to 1932, your growing pile of dividends would have exceeded the market value of your portfolio for thirty-five years from 1930 to about 1965; the dividend pile fell behind the portfolio value by a meaningful amount only after 1982—fifty-seven years after your original purchase.

Let me go back to the end of 1925 for a moment, to give you the full flavor of what I am talking about. According to the Ibbotson Associates data, a dollar invested in the stock market at the end of 1925, with all dividends reinvested and no taxes and brokerage paid, would have grown to about $600 today, far above the $30 from appreciation alone. The difference of $570 comes from the receipt and reinvestment of that pile of income, swelling the total to the magnificent sum of $600. An investor who came into the market at the top in 1929 would have had to wait until 1953 before stock prices would have returned to what they cost to purchase. Yet, with income reinvested, break-even would have arrived in 1944, nine years sooner.

Therefore, the role of price in determining total return diminishes steadily in importance as we move from the short run to the long run. The mean annual income return since 1925 has been 4.7 percent a year with a standard deviation of only 1.2 percentage points. The annual appreciation return has averaged 7.1 percent, but with a standard deviation of *twenty* percentage points. These facts explain why the income turtle puts up such a good race against the appreciation hare. But they also help to explain why the standard deviation of returns tends to shrink with the passage of time.

Quite aside from the demonstration that volatility matters a lot more in the long run than conventional wisdom would lead us to believe, there is an additional and overwhelmingly important lesson here for investors. Do not simulate equity portfolio returns with the familiar long-term Ibbotson figure of 10 percent to 12 percent a year *unless the portfolio can accumulate and reinvest all the income that it earns.*

Investors who must pay taxes on their income or, even worse, are not in a position to accumulate and reinvest every penny of dividend income they receive cannot rely on the long run to bail them out of the inherent volatility of equity investments. There have been fifty-six ten-year rolling holding periods beginning with 1925–35. In nine of those cases—of which only three were in the 1930s—stock prices ended up below where they started. In another twelve cases, the increase in stock prices over ten years lagged the rise in the cost of living, so that the portfolio lost real value. This means that the market's price performance was negative one-third of the time in these ten-year holding periods even though, over the whole span of sixty-six years, prices rose thirtyfold, or 5.1 percent a year. Those are scary numbers without the precious support and smoothing of income accumulation. Equity investing is risky business, even in the long run.

Noises, signals, and tempestuous seasons

The long run in the popular view is a process that smooths the bumps, that cuts through the clutter, that captures the main trend. But if there is a moral to the story I have related here, it is that the long run is a complex, ambiguous, even elusive concept, better in theory than it often is in practice. We cannot escape those difficulties. They are part of life.

Despite the complexity, ambiguity, and elusiveness of the long run, there is another moral, and a useful one. Time matters. Quantitative changes become qualitative changes, and fundamental transformations take place as the time period lengthens. Although I am not sure where the short run ends and the long run begins, I do know that the character of my expected investment results are dependent on the length of the holding period. That, at least, is a beginning to wisdom.

6

Investment, capital, and finance: corporate and entrepreneurial theories of the firm

EDWARD E. WILLIAMS

The preceding thought-provoking articles by Gordon, Vickers, Fried, and Crotty illustrate the many similarities, and quite a few differences, in ideas on the theory of investment posited by economists who consider themselves Post Keynesians. The similarities are not surprising in light of the general disagreement between neoclassical and Post Keynesian investment theories. The differences, it seems to me, occur mostly when the Post Keynesians allow neoclassical precepts to enter into their basically non-neoclassical models.

In this article, I do not intend to critique each of the four papers in an attempt to ferret out Post Keynesian versus neoclassical notions. Indeed, this would be a waste of time because, as the divergence in the afore-mentioned essays illustrates, there really is no "party line" on what is and what is not truly Post Keynesian. Suffice it to say that, in my mind at least, all four of the theorists contributing to this discussion have substantial neoclassical elements in their arguments. Fortunately, this is not necessarily bad. My own recent work has focused on ways to reconcile neoclassical and Post Keynesian positions in an attempt to forge a realistic synthesis between the two and to illustrate that in many areas the two schools have never been as far apart as each has maintained (see Taylor and Williams, 1991–92). Many neoclassical scholars in financial economics have already come to understand that a rigid adherence to their competitive market, marginalist views is unrealistic,[1]

The author is Henry Gardiner Symonds Professor at the Jesse H. Jones Graduate School of Administration, Rice University, Houston, Texas.

[1] For years, the finance literature insisted that the financial capital markets were perfectly efficient. More recently, however, even the most extreme proponents of

and Post Keynesians have never completely given up on markets as a means of efficiently allocating resources.

Rather than criticize the work of Gordon/Vickers/Fried/Crotty, I prefer to build upon what they have already constructed. Gordon and Vickers, in particular, have long and distinguished records going back four decades, and even some of their earliest works (which are demonstrably neoclassical in persuasion) contain nuggets of wisdom that readily apply in a synthesized neoclassical/Post Keynesian world. Indeed, in the models proposed below there is a substantial intellectual debt not only to the recent work of Gordon and Vickers but to their earlier endeavors as well.

At the risk of being challenged as a neoclassical Trojan horse with Post Keynesian paint before I begin, I should point out the premises upon which I build my theories:

1. The future is uncertain (in the sense that Knight and Keynes used the term).

2. Production takes time and therefore, if production is to occur in a specialization economy, someone must make a contractual commitment in the present involving performance and payment in the uncertain future.

3. Economic decisions are made in the light of an unalterable past, while moving toward a perfidious future.

Of course, these are precisely the assumptions made by Davidson as he developed Post Keynesian monetary theory many years ago (Davidson, 1978, p. 7).

Corporate and entrepreneurial theories

Part of the problem in constructing theories of investment, capital, and finance is that there are really two very different types of enterprises to model. On the one hand, we find highly complex, institutionally driven, quasi-political entities which we call publicly held corporations. On the

---

market efficiency have recognized the existence of "puzzles" and "anomalies" that are inconsistent with perfect efficiency. There has even arisen a market microstructure subliterature that attempts to explain market "overpricing" and "underpricing" of financial assets. In a recent article in the *JPKE*, Professor Taylor and I argue that "salient features of the prevalent neoclassical, market microstructure asset pricing models that have been developed recently in the financial economics literature are related to earlier economic insights of Keynes and Hicks" (Taylor and Williams, 1991–92, p. 233).

other hand, we find more simple, noninstitutional, apolitical entities that Gordon (1992) and Fried (1992) designate as "proprietors." It is clear that it has been the neoclassical attempt to model the former in the same way as the latter that has caused Post Keynesians to complain about the lack of realism of neoclassical ideas about investment, capital, and finance. The neoclassical theory of the firm is really a theory of proprietors operating in competitive markets, whereas Post Keynesian theories generally examine the world of the large, publicly held corporation that by no means operates in competitive marketplaces.

In the work to follow, we shall develop two sets of models. One model will trace out a real-world theory of investment, capital, and finance as it applies to publicly held corporations. The second model will do the same for entrepreneurially owned and operated businesses. Interestingly, our entrepreneurial model will not precisely image the neoclassical world because the entrepreneurial firm is not really the small, homogeneous entity facing generally competitive markets envisaged by neoclassical writers (or the proprietorship proposed by Gordon and Fried). It is probably true that that firm does not exist, and much of the problem with the neoclassical theory of the firm is that it really does not fit precisely any real-world business.

A corporate theory of investment, capital, and finance

Any realistic theory of large, publicly held corporations must recognize and take into account several important characteristics of these entities. First, it has been clear for many years that the ownership and control of the large, publicly held corporation are separate and distinct from one another. This separation affects both the governance of the public corporation and the way it operates. Any model that fails to highlight this characteristic must be unrealistic and is destined to be a poor descriptor of the real world. Second, due to the separation and control issue, there are several layers of agents, which complicates the usual assumptions about the firm made by neoclassical researchers. Although many neoclassical theorists attempt to make their models work despite the separation problem, they can do so only by trivializing it. Finally, decisions made by the large, publicly held entity are decisions made under uncertainty (à la Knight and Keynes) and not under conditions of risk where probability and Bayesian approaches are operative.

We shall analyze each of these characteristics in some detail. Much of the work here has its origin in papers previously written by myself and other co-authors, particularly M.C. Findlay, formerly Professor of Finance at the University of Southern California and presently Chairman of Findlay, Phillips and Associates. This work goes back over a span of twenty years. As part of our attempt to provide a useful Post Keynesian corporate theory of investment, capital, and finance, we must first build a concise, yet fairly complete, version of the neoclassical model. This we shall do as a prelude to the construction of our Post Keynesian theory.

Separation of ownership and control [2]

A nontrivial theory of investment, capital, and finance must specifically recognize that the ownership and control of the large, publicly held corporation are separate. Berle and Means identified this salient feature of these entities sixty years ago in *The Modern Corporation and Private Property* (1932). Although the corporation finance literature continued until relatively recently to assume that the chief goal of these enterprises was to maximize the wealth position of the shareholders, it eventually dawned on scholars in that area that there was an internal inconsistency in assuming individual maximizing and at the same time that some individuals (i.e., managers) would automatically maximize someone else's wealth (i.e., stockholders) without market incentives to do so. As Gordon points out, "Prior to a paper by Jensen and Meckling (1976), the principal agent problem was ignored by most neoclassical financial economists" (1992, p. 429).[3] However, as Gordon further suggests, the neoclassical school proceeded to trivialize the problem.[4]

In legal terms, the large, publicly held corporation is really a group of contracting parties who join forces for multifarious reasons. These parties may be identified in general categories as: (1) the management of the firm, (2) the directors, (3) the firm's nonmanagement employees, (4) the suppliers of other factor inputs, and (5) the customers who buy from the enterprise. Notice that the stockholders are not mentioned as

---

[2] This section is adapted from Williams and Findlay (1983, 1984).

[3] Post Keynesians were quicker to see the fallacy inherent in the shareholder wealth maximization postulate. Professor Findlay and I treated the issue at length in 1972 in an early article in *Financial Management*, where we showed that the usual capital budgeting/cost of capital model then in use in finance was overdetermined precisely because the cost of equity capital could not be both a cost and a variable subject to maximization.

[4] Again, Post Keynesians were more attuned to the real-world conflicts. These conflicts could not be assumed away by positing competitive conditions, say, in the managerial labor market and/or competition in the market for corporate control to force managers to behave "optimally." See Williams and Findlay (1983, 1984).

one of the general categories. Actually, the stockholders (along with the bondholders, bankers, and other institutional investors) are a subpart of the suppliers category—not really different in character from those who lease land to the firm or who sell it raw materials. All of these parties have some form of contractual relationship with the firm that spells out what they will do for the enterprise and what they will get in return. Top managers will normally have a written contract stating that they will work exclusively for the company, devoting all their time and energies on behalf of the business. For this, they will receive salaries and perquisites. The directors contract (not necessarily in writing) to come to board meetings, elect officers, and approve major policies. Other contractors with the firm (employees, materials suppliers, customers, etc.) may or may not have explicit contracts with the enterprise, but there are always present implied contractual commitments. Bankers, bondholders, and other lenders will have a written contract (loan agreement, indenture, etc.) that is quite specific about what the firm must (and must not) do in consideration for the funds supplied. Only the stockholders are left with what amounts to a very weak, legally untenable contract. It is never written. It guarantees nothing. If the firm does well, there is no obligation on the part of the directors to pay the stockholders a dividend. If it does poorly, on the other hand, the stockholders usually lose the most.

Figure 1 illustrates the contractual relationships we have outlined above. The arrows demonstrate what is given to and what is received from the enterprise by each contracting party. The broken line between the shareholders and the enterprise indicates that shareholders may own stock directly, but the solid line passing through the financial institutions suggests the more significant role of intermediaries in the financing process. The addition of intermediation still further weakens the political position of the stockholders. The broken line from the shareholders and the financial institutions to the board of directors portrays the legal right of the shareholders to elect the board. This right may have more ceremonial than real value.

Agency layers[5]

Jensen and Meckling (1976) argue from a perspective similar to that above and agree that the firm is essentially a set of contracts among factors of production in which each factor is motivated by self-interest. Given a number of assumptions (including several quite restrictive

---

[5] This section is adapted from Williams and Findlay (1983).

Figure 1
The enterprise as a set of contracts

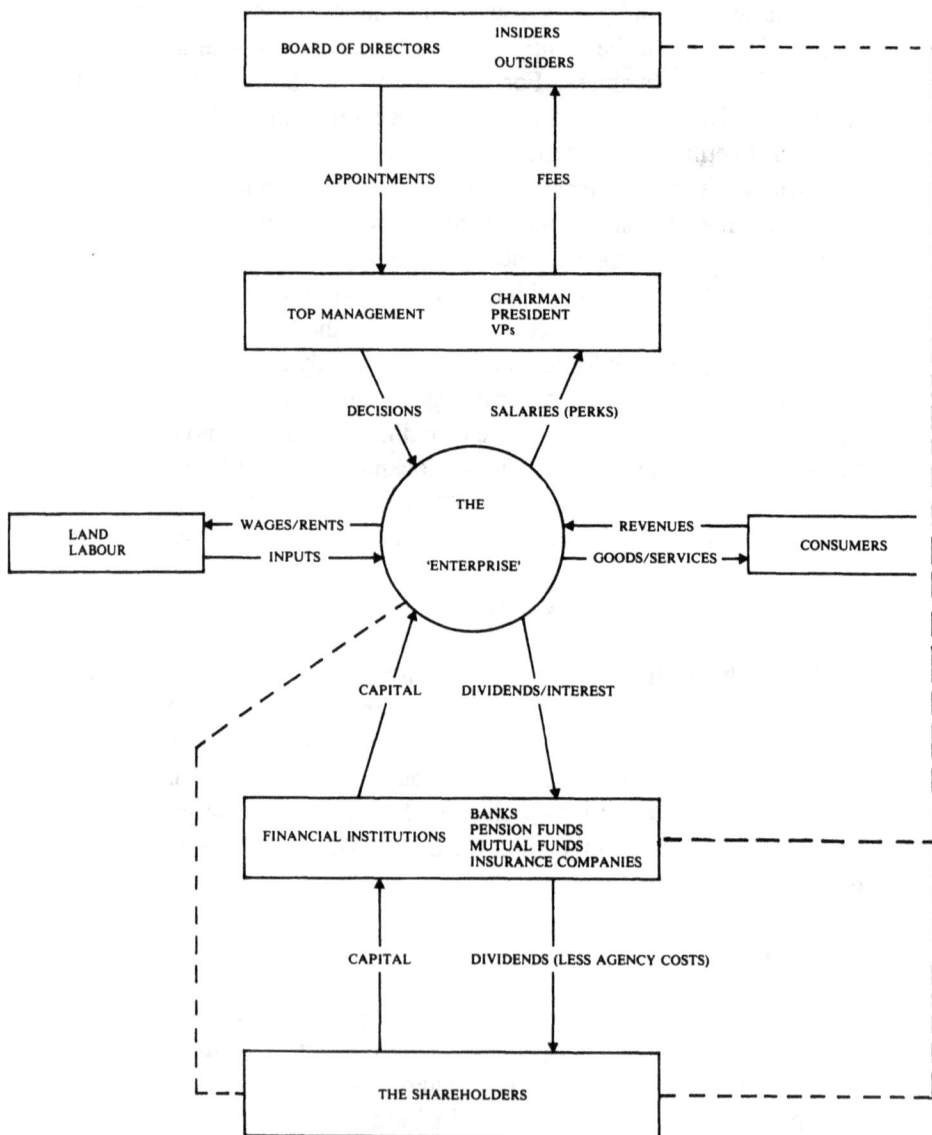

ones), they posit an entrepreneurial situation where the manager begins as the sole owner of the firm and then sells shares to outsiders. The outsiders realize that the manager will consume more perks and may have a tendency to shirk after the shares are sold, and this knowledge is reflected in a lower price for the shares. The reduction in value is the residual loss portion of agency costs and is borne by the manager. By incurring monitoring costs, equity holders can restrict the manager's consumption of perks, and, since the former owner bears these costs ultimately, there will be an incentive to minimize them. In general, both monitoring and bonding costs occur at levels to satisfy efficiency conditions, but they do not result in value maximization. The divergence between the actual value and the "idealized" value is the cost of agency or the cost of the separation of ownership and control. Fama (1980) maintains that managers rent a substantial fraction of their wealth (human capital) to a firm and that the rental rate is provided by the managerial labor market. These rates depend on the success or failure of the firm and, consequently, the manager has a strong stake in its success. A competitive managerial labor market will exert pressures on the firm to sort and compensate managers according to productivity. If a firm's reward system is not sensitive to productivity, existing managers will leave and new managers will not want to join the firm. Thus, it is the relative competitiveness of the managerial labor market that is the ultimate policing device to make the firm operate optimally.

In the papers mentioned above, the agency problem tends to vanish because of the competitive conditions that are presumed to exist in one or more markets. In the Jensen and Meckling article, it is a competitive capital market that serves to diminish the problem. In the Fama paper, a competitive managerial labor market serves this role. For those of us who are not convinced that either of these markets is highly competitive, however, the problem remains. Moreover, perfect competition in the market for agents is only a necessary condition for the neoclassical result to obtain. To the extent that there are monitoring costs or non-observabilities, an inferior (i.e., constrained optimal) solution will be obtained even with competition. A strict delineation of property rights over which the parties are to contract is also required. Neoclassical theory provides no real guidance for this delineation. Indeed, in terms of production value in frictionless markets, one distribution is as good as another by the criterion advanced and the issue degenerates to a legal question of the "appropriate" assignment of property rights.

Another complication in the agency framework is the growth of intermediation, which has led to an ever-increasing amount of shares and bonds being held indirectly by institutions, pension funds, and the like. These, in turn, are managed by agent/fiduciaries who have their own goals and cannot be perfectly monitored by the ultimate beneficiary. Hence, in the real world, we now have at least two (and generally more) levels of agency between the production plan and the supposed beneficiaries of the profits to be earned thereby. It should be clear that the presence of institutions complicates the beneficiary monitoring process and causes economic results for the large, publicly held corporations to diverge even further from the entrepreneurial model. Hence, we encounter a situation where: (1) information flows from the firm are basically controlled by the managers; (2) the first line of economic oversight, the board of directors, may or may not be effective, depending on the board; and (3) institutions often sign their proxies over to the managers or sell their stock when they are in disagreement with the way the corporation is being run (the so-called "Wall Street Rule"). Moreover, despite the Securities and Exchange Commission's (SEC) desire to improve the monitoring process in the United States, the tax laws actually discourage intermediaries from monitoring the firm,[6] while they encourage individuals to invest through intermediaries.[7] Furthermore, the tax laws discourage any monitoring of the intermediaries.[8]

Thus, we arrive at an even more revealing understanding of the actual position of the shareholder in an agency context. We might illustrate the condition as in figure 2. Notice that there are at least two agency layers between the production plan and the shareholders (the board and top managers), and there is frequently a third as well (the financial institutions). Monitoring just one layer to achieve a Pareto-efficient system has taxed the imagination of those who have ventured into this area thus far. Monitoring two or three will pose an even more difficult challenge for those who believe that both the capital and managerial labor markets are competitive.

[6] *Cf.* the maximum ownership restrictions and passive role required of mutual funds for tax exemption and the restrictions on equity ownership by many institutions (such as commercial banks).

[7] *Cf.* the deductibility of IRA and Keogh contributions, the tax-free compounding of life insurance values, and the various trust and qualified pension/profit sharing plan devices.

[8] *Cf.* the loss of deduction if any control can be shown and the big tax penalties often occurring if one takes money out of the intermediary system.

Figure 2
Layers of agents (fiduciaries) and the stockholding principals (beneficiaries)

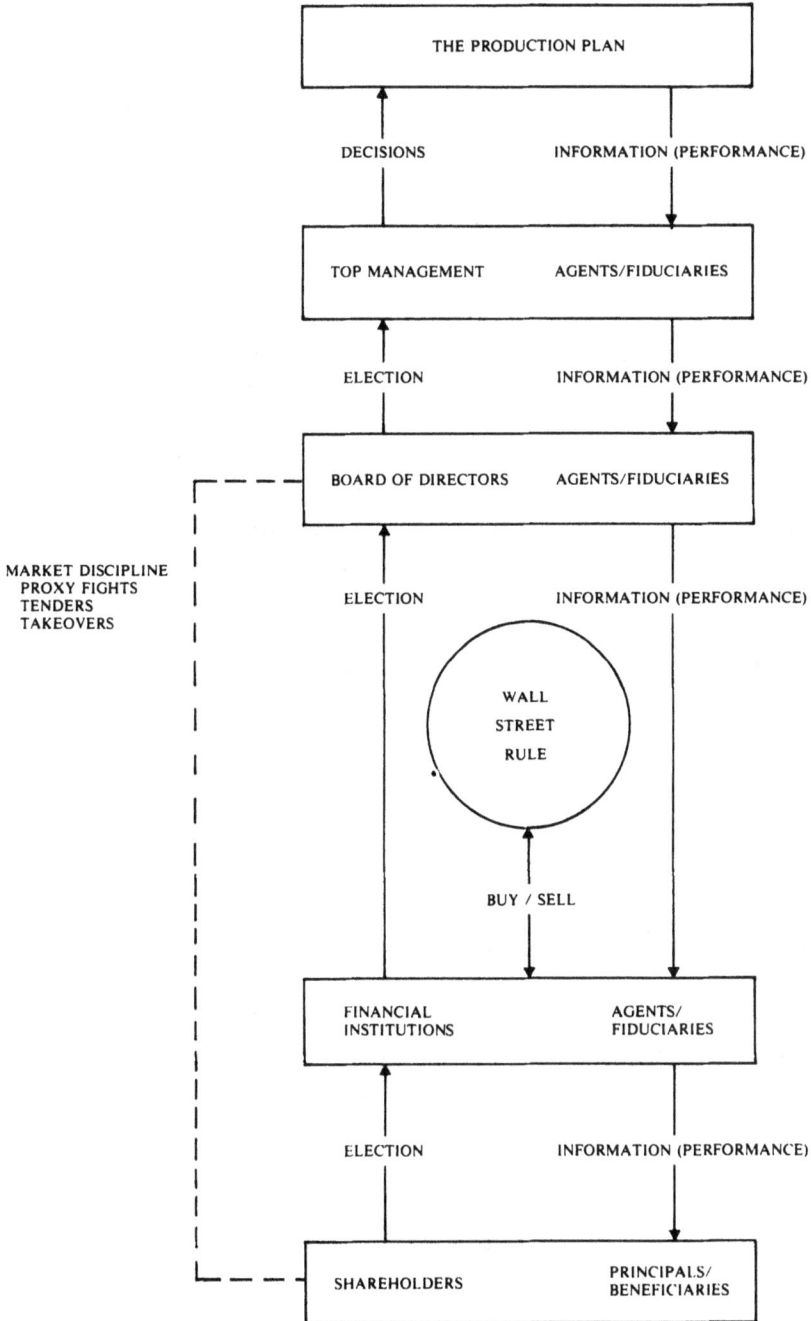

Agency and financial markets [9]

A major point about the difference between an agent and a principal has yet to be made, however. As a principal, if you place a bet and win, you take the money. If you lose, the croupier pulls it away. In the former case, you may wonder whether you were smart or lucky, and conversely in the latter case. The outcome of this examination of beliefs may determine whether you continue to play.[10] In any event, one fact may be determined unambiguously: for whatever reason, if any reason at all, you *did* win. If your agent is placing the bets, however, complications arise. You cannot observe the bets, the wheel, or the payoffs. You do not know what other, more favorable bets may have been available to him earlier. You cannot be sure, in the case of favorable results, how much is attributable to the skill of your agent (and, hence, subject to incentive rewards, à la neoclassical school) as opposed to luck, especially on a small sample, which is all we get this side of the "long run." In the case of unfavorable results, you cannot effectively distinguish between bad luck, stupidity, or venality (i.e., the agent pocketing most of the winnings). Finally, your notions of what constitutes a favorable outcome will generally be based on a comparison of the results of the dealings of other agents with their principals. These are very likely to be downward-biased in terms of what is actually attainable as a consequence.

The above makes one think of Keynes' beauty contest analogy in chapter 12 of the *General Theory*. A rational agent will perceive his reward to be based not on how well he does in fact, but rather on the perception of his principal. Furthermore, given the institutional rigidities discussed above, the major goal of the agent involves not being perceived as doing too well, for this might raise expectations to unfulfillable levels. Rather, the avoidance of the perception of doing very poorly becomes the objective. Obviously, if one is perceived as doing quite badly, this might induce an attempt to overcome the rigidities mentioned above on the part of the principal and cause him to terminate the services of the agent.

The theory of agency described above seems adequate to explain the behavior of the corporate "haves." This group includes the firms that generate sufficient cash flow (including debt capacity) to meet their needs, generate sufficient profits to maintain a share price high enough

---

[9] This section is adapted from Findlay and Williams (1981).

[10] Note from our discussion below that, under uncertainty, you can never really know whether you were smart or lucky.

to resist proxy fights and tender offers, and are large enough so that the difference between the two provides enough "slack" to satisfy the management. The "haves" also include the financial institutions that are large enough to meet their objectives from a percentage-of-assets fee and are sufficiently protected by tax penalties or transactions costs to maintain the level of assets under management with "normal" or even somewhat subnormal investment performance.[11] For the corporate "have-nots" to break into a game where most of the capital is already controlled by the "haves" is not an easy task. One approach involves obtaining an advantage from the government. Another involves raising the expectations of those holding noninstitutionalized funds. Yet another, at the firm level, involves convincing one institution that, if it does not buy your stock, others will, and they will earn extraordinary profits and make the aforementioned institution look bad. One thinks of "hot" issues and "one-decision" stocks, and the like as fitting this pattern. To the extent that several institutions can be convinced of this logic simultaneously, self-reinforcing expectations will exist for a time. Finally, at the institutional level, one gains business in the short run at least by taking large risks in order to "beat the market." This results in investment managers making sales pitches based on their quarterly performance in comparison with the market averages or, in Keynesian terms, musical chairs played at a gallop with half the remaining chairs removed each time the music stops!

In sum, those who expected an institutionalized market to be a better-informed, more stable estimator of "true value" and a force to compel corporations to reward stockholders properly were clearly naive. All of the game playing occasioned by adding another level of agency appears to have more than compensated for any gains in information, communication, and analysis. With the costs and difficulties of monitoring a multilevel agency system, which produces much of its own data and has strong compensation incentives for false signaling, it is not obvious that the financial markets as arbiters of rational capital allocation have progressed terribly far from Keynes' casino.

The basic neoclassical model [12]

Having examined several of the important characteristics of the large, publicly held corporation, we may now review the basic neoclassical

[11] See notes 6–8 above.

[12] This section is adapted from Williams and Findlay (1987).

investment/financing model to see how well it fits reality. A very simple depiction of that model is contained in figure 3.

All investment projects confronting the firm are arrayed in descending order of their internal rates of return in terms of the cumulative investment required to undertake them. The resulting function, shown as panel B in figure 3, is variously called the firm's MEC or MEI (i.e., marginal efficiency of capital or investment) curve. To be internally consistent, it is further necessary to assume that all projects on the MEC be of the same business risk (however measured) or else that the project rates of return be preadjusted to such a common level of risk. This level of business risk corresponds to the required return on an unlevered stream of this risk class, which is identified in panel A as ρ. To the extent that the employment of debt may lower (or raise) the cost of capital (K_o) from ρ, an optimal capital structure will exist for the firm such that the K_o function is U-shaped. The optimal structure is defined as the one(s) producing the minimum cost of capital; in panel A, K_o^* is found at $[D/(D + E)]^*$. Under the assumptions that the debt ratio is a sufficient measure of financial risk, that the business risk class of the firm does not vary, and thus that the demand for the firm's securities is perfectly elastic at current prices, the firm can raise (or return) all the capital it wishes at a point in time at K_o^* so long as it maintains the optimal capital structure. By further assuming the firm to be at this structure, it is implied that funds will be raised (or returned) in these proportions and that the structure is defined in terms of market values.

The model may be specified algebraically as follows:

(1) $$I_t^* = \Delta K_t^* + d_t K_t ;$$

(2) $$L_t^* = D_t / (D_t + E_t) ;$$

(3) $$K_t = D_t + E_t ;$$

(4) $$\Delta K_t^* = L_t^* \Delta K_t^* + (1 - L_t)^* \Delta K_t^* ;$$

(5) $$L_t^* = \Delta D_t / (\Delta D_t + \Delta E_t) ;$$

(6) $$\Delta E_t = \Pi_t - \phi_t ;$$

(7) $$L_t^* \Delta K_t^* = \Delta D_t - \delta_t$$

Figure 3

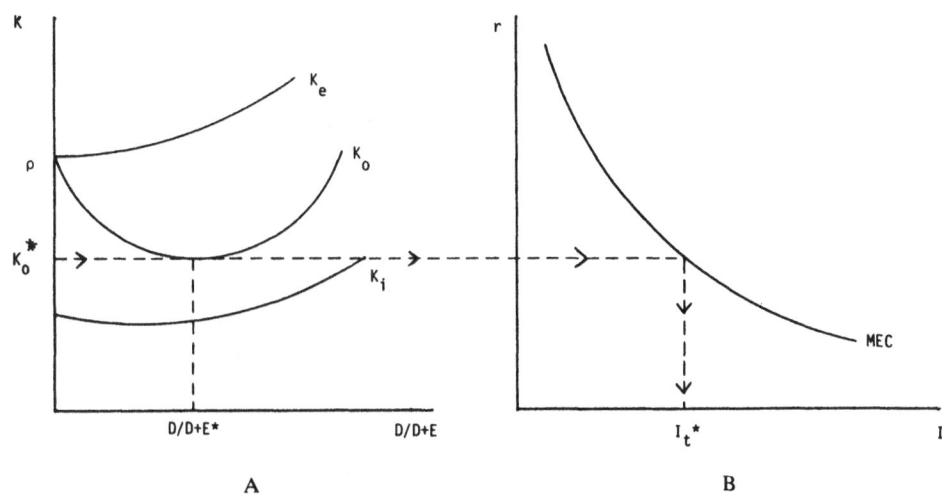

A

B

(8) $(1 - L_t^*) \, \Delta K_t^* = \Pi_t - \phi_t$;

(9) $I_t^* = \Delta D_t - \delta_t + \Pi_t - \phi_t + d_t \, K_t$;

where:

Π_t = the net income after tax of the firm at time t;
E_t = the volume of equity capital employed at time t;
D_t = the volume of debt capital employed at time t;
I_t = the gross investment flow made at time t;
d_t = the rate of depreciation (depletion, etc.) of the investment
          stock at period t;
K_t = the investment stock at period t;
ΔK_t = net investment at period t;
ΔD_t = gross debt sold at period t;
δ_t = the dollar amount of sinking fund and other debt retirements
          at period t;
$\phi_t > 0$ = dividends paid at period t;
$\phi_t < 0$ = new common stock sold at period t;
*   = optimal amounts.

A form of separation enters at this point. The K_o function has been defined to be independent of the shape of the MEC function; the only interrelationship (at the level of the firm) has been the assumed constancy of business risk along the MEC and its correspondence to the ρ intercept of the K_o function. Thus, assuming unlimited availability of funds at K_o^*, the firm may proceed to select all projects yielding at least this rate from the MEC function. The arrows from panel A to panel B reflect the application of standard net present value or internal rate of return selection rules to arrive at the optimal capital budget, I_t^*. Panel B is drawn to reflect the recommended practice of including all investment, including replacement expenditures, in the budgeting procedure. Hence, I_t^* depicts gross investment and will be non-negative. With standard simplifying assumptions, depreciation and the like may be deducted to arrive at net investment, ΔK_t^*. Depending upon whether plant is being expanded, replaced, or contracted, $\Delta K_t^* \geq 0$, or $\Delta K_t \leq 0$.

Suppose that expansion is occurring. Then ΔK_t^* must be raised in the optimal debt and equity proportions to validate the employment of K_o^*. To debt's share of ΔK_t^* must be added any maturing obligations, sinking fund payments, or the like, to arrive at the gross amount of debt to be raised. The equity component could be raised by earnings retention or new share issues. The existence of transaction costs would favor retentions; any personal tax effects regarding dividends would also increase the desirability of retentions. Hence, by this model, earnings would be retained to meet equity's share of ΔK_t^*. Any remaining earnings would be paid out; a shortfall would give rise to a new share issue. If, on the other hand, the firm were simply maintaining its plant, a steady-state result (popular in the economics literature) would occur. Debt would simply be rolled over and all earnings would be paid out. Finally, a reduction in plant would occur if $\Delta K_t^* < 0$. The debt would be retired over time and liquidating dividends would be paid to shareholders. Under these circumstances, figure 3 illustrates the basic points that depreciation "belongs" to both stock- and bondholders and has a "cost" of the cost of capital (i.e., the opportunity forgone by reinvesting funds represented by the depreciation allowance is a proportional shrinking of the capital structure at a saving of K_o).

We may consider a numerical example.
Let:

$$\Pi = 100;$$
$$E_t = 750;$$
$$D_t = 250;$$
$$d_t = 0.10;$$

K_t = 1,000;

ΔD_t = unknown;

δ_t = 50;

ϕ_t = unknown.

If the optimal I_t^* where K_o intersects the MEC is 500, we would find:

(1′) $500 = 400 + (0.10)(1,000);$

(2′) $0.25 = 250 \,/\, 1,000;$

(3′) $1,000 = 250 + 750;$

(4′) $400 = (0.25)\,(400) + (0.75)\,(400);$

(5′) $0.25 = \Delta D_t \,/\, (\Delta D_t + \Delta E_t);$

(6′) $\Delta E_t = 100 - \phi_t;$

(7′) $100 = \Delta D_t - 50;$

(8′) $300 = 100 - \phi_t;$

(9′) $500 = 150 - 50 + 100 - \phi_t + 100;$

$$\phi_t = -200.$$

Thus, our model would indicate the firm should sell new shares equal to 200. The gross investment of 500 would be broken down into 400 new investment and 100 replacement. The gross investment would be financed by 100 of net new debt (150 less 50 to be paid off), 100 of retained earnings, 200 of new stock sold, and 100 of depreciation cash flow. The new investment stock would be: $1,000 - 100 + 500 = 1,400$. The new debt structure would be: $250 - 50 + 150 = 350$; and the new equity structure would be: $750 + 100 + 200 = 1,050$. Of course, L would remain at: $350 \,/\, (350 + 1,050) = 0.25$.

Extensions of the neoclassical model [13]

The basic model developed in the preceding section has not changed

[13] This section is adapted from Williams and Findlay (1987).

much in over twenty years, although extensions to it have been made in several respects. For the last decade or more, a renewed debate has emerged over whether the return on shares varies with dividend yield (i.e., whether a tax penalty exists). The issue has yet to be resolved. By favoring retentions (primarily on transaction cost grounds), the simple model is not inconsistent with either side of the debate. Litzenberger and Ramaswamy (1979, 1980) would favor retentions, while Miller and Scholes (1978, 1982) would be indifferent, on tax grounds; both would favor retentions on transaction cost grounds. If dividends are penalized in the market, however, a broader conceptual problem arises. If it is possible to retain everything forever or to cash the firm out in tax-favored ways, dividends should not be observed. If it is not possible, then retentions will subsequently appear as dividends. The market's tax circumstances, among other things, will determine the discount rate applied to those dividends over time. A firm with superior tax-sheltering ability will find its cost of equity lower relative to available project yields. The conditions under which separate required returns on dividends and retentions could exist in equilibrium are unclear, however. In the simple model, small or no dividends are a good signal of plentiful investment opportunities. Some papers (Bhattacharya, 1979; Kalay, 1980) have made a case for large dividends as a good signal. This issue is also unresolved. A major problem with placing great reliance on signaling stories is that they undermine the information assumptions about capital market equilibrium required to justify the selection and use of a discount rate in the first place.

The basic model does not place much reliance upon the assumed shape of the K_o function in panel A of figure 3. This has been the source of much debate, however. The first argument for the interior minimum illustrated was probably the conventional (or straw man) view first suggested by Modigliani and Miller (1958). They contended that some people felt shareholders paid little attention to small amounts of debt (i.e., K_e virtually horizontal at first) and became very alarmed at large amounts (i.e., K_e approaching vertical at large debt structures). This would imply a U- or V-shaped K_o function. Of course, Modigliani and Miller then presented their famous theory that, in the absence of taxes, the K_o function would be horizontal and everywhere equal to the cost of equity capital. They then (1963) added corporate taxes and obtained the corner solution of the all debt structure being optimal. The interior optimum returned to favor as part of the consensus of the early to mid-1970s (see, e.g., Kraus and Litzenberger, 1983). Tax effects were felt to cause an initial decline in K_o. Costly bankruptcy effects were felt to become dominant at some point, causing the curve to rise. Hence, an interior optimum was implied. Miller dismissed the consensus view as "horse and rabbit stew" in his 1976 American Finance Association address (Miller, 1977). By adding personal as well as corporate taxes and moving to a more general equilibrium mode of analysis, he demonstrated that there could be an optimal capital structure for the economy as a whole based upon tax effects but that one structure would be as good as another for any given firm. Hence, the horizontal K_o curve reappeared. De Angelo and Masulis (1980) extended Miller's analysis to allow for alternative and competing sources of tax shelters to firms. They demonstrated that the value a given firm would place on the interest tax shield of debt would depend upon income variability, past profits, and other (e.g., depreciation, tax credits) tax shields. Thus, the amount of debt that could be employed as a tax advantage would vary from firm to firm. Hence, even in Miller's framework, individual-firm optimal structures could exist, and for the third time the interior optimum, depicted in panel A, reappeared.

The basic model also does not place great reliance upon the shape of the MEC in panel B. It has been noted (Findlay and Williams, 1979; Williams and Findlay, 1979) that a downward-sloping MEC curve (i.e., positive NPV projects) may represent a violation of the one-price law in the project market. In the absence of legislated barriers to entry, this assumption is difficult to reconcile with the notions of symmetric information and free entry to the financial capital market. Taking this view to the limit, the MEC would be flat and coincident with K_o^* in panel B at first. At some point, it would then decline (to depict infeasible projects).

The various equilibrium asset pricing models (APMs) that have been developed over the past two decades actually constitute neoclassical "bells and whistles" added to the basic model. With respect to panel B, the hurdle rate for a given project would depend upon its relative risk with respect to the particular APM chosen. With respect to panel A, Miller's arguments suggest that securities (e.g., bonds) with less desirable personal tax consequences would have higher relative market returns than those (e.g., shares) with more desirable consequences. Unfortunately, empirical evidence (e.g., Blume and Friend, 1973) suggests exactly the opposite on this point. With respect to the stock market, the theoretical critique of Roll (1977) and the empirical ambiguities of the "anomalies" literature have raised serious questions regarding the capital asset pricing model (CAPM). The asset pricing theory (APT; Ross, 1976), its apparent successor, is far less parsimonious and has already been found to be subject to similar anomalies (e.g., Reinganum, 1981a, 1981b). When applied to capital budgeting, the problems multiply. The major text applications of the CAPM are essentially pedagogic exercises. No effort is made to suggest how the numbers might be estimated. The more sophisticated treatments (Bogue and Roll, 1974; Myers and Turnbull, 1977) are theoretical and do not attempt to provide numbers. The "pure play" example (a similar single project firm, where market betas may be estimated) is so rare as to be of very limited use. The "accounting beta" example (Beaver, Kettler, and Scholes, 1970; Breen and Lerner, 1973), even on existing firms, provided such bad fits that it was apparently abandoned. The various simulation and decision tree models (Hertz, 1964; Magee, 1964) which are to be found in the "practical" chapters on capital budgeting in texts provide, at best, a multiperiod variance of project return without any reference to market correlation. In sum, the theoretically required period-by-period covariance of return between a project that has never before existed and one or more marketwide factors is a datum that appears almost philosophically incapable of estimation or measurement.

Uncertainty [14]

Given the problems outlined above, any real-world (e.g., Post Keynesian) theorist would have severe reservations about the basic neoclassical investment/financing model. However, the biggest problem with the model lies with its assumptions about risk and uncertainty. The model is essentially reduced to certainty equivalence terms by means of constructing probability distributions around the exogenous variables and determining covariance matrices among those variables. The difficulties associated with constructing covariance matrices, of course, is what caused neoclassical theorists to conceive of the asset pricing models in the first place. Unfortunately, the core analytical problem confronting any model that relies on probability theory for a solution is far more serious than those outlined above regarding asset pricing models. Literally, if one cannot construct the distribution (knowing all possible outcomes and the probabilities associated with each outcome), the whole model comes apart.

[14] This section is adapted from Findlay and Williams (1985, 1986) and Williams and Findlay (1986).

The neoclassical world is essentially a world of certainty to which lotteries have been added. Individuals determine courses of action to maximize the utility of their available consumption vector, which, with perfect markets, is the equivalent of maximizing the utility of wealth. This ensues directly from the certainty model. Lotteries are then added and priced in terms of the (certain) alternative forgone, given the relative risk aversion of market participants. Unfortunately, several problems of logic can be found in this theory. Risk and certainty cannot coexist; in a certain world, the outcomes of all lotteries are known. In a world of risk, there are no certainties (e.g., no part of an integrated Walrasian system is in equilibrium until all of it is—if X and Y are interdependent, one cannot be deterministic if the other is stochastic). Given this choice, one sees clearly that certainty is not descriptive of even a part of the real world. There is literally no way to guarantee oneself a consumption vector over time. Even hoarding is subject to the political risk that the property will be confiscated (cf. Findlay and Williams, 1981).

In modern economies, however, individuals generally deal in contracts. Political risk and economic risk (e.g., a crop failure), however, would enter the picture even if there were complete futures markets in commodities. Needless to say, such markets are far from complete. Moreover, men deal in money contracts, which further adds the risks of inflation and default to the equation. Thus, a consumption vector cannot be guaranteed ex ante, and there are numerous risks (uncertainties) between any notion of wealth and the ex post consumption vector experienced. Wealth may be viewed as the certain current market value of the risky lotteries one holds. However, the associated consumption vector is a certainty only to the extent that one is prepared to consume everything today (i.e., a scalar) or else that a certain medium exists to transfer wealth forward in time (which cannot be the case if there is no certainty). Otherwise, wealth itself is a lottery in consumption. If it is held in money, its payoffs are relatively immune to most risks but highly sensitive to inflation and related political risks.

The notion of current wealth as a certainty is such a crucial foundation of the conventional wisdom that the points just made bear repetition. Suppose an individual is able to put all his or her wealth, in cash, in the center of the table. In what sense is that sum a certainty? Clearly (in the absence of robbery), the individual could consume it all now and then die. If the person wished to go on living, however, he or she would need to carry the sum forward (say, invested in government bonds), and might not be sure for how long (say, with annuities), or what this sum would buy (say, with commodities contracts). In our effort to convert current wealth into a certain stream of consumption, we have constructed a complex series of contracts (some of which may not even exist) and still we cannot be absolutely sure of performance. Hence, *certainty is not an available course of action, nor can it play a role in setting opportunity costs for risky courses of action.* This modest insight would appear to wreak havoc on the neoclassical framework. The notion of moving from a certain current wealth to ever riskier lotteries is destroyed. All one can do is swap one set of lotteries for another. Without the grounding in certainty, it is not clear which set of lotteries is "riskier," what constitutes "risk aversion," or, in the limit, what "risk" means.

Along these lines we might consider the literature of financial economics. Here the risk-adjusted discount rate/certainty equivalent models and the early capital asset pricing models (which employed a riskless rate) clearly represented certainty masquerading as risk. Indeed, if the assumptions of the latter were met (i.e., stationary distributions and zero serial correlation of security returns) and society had a sufficiently long horizon (including bequest motives), it has never been clear why the central limit theorem could not be invoked intertemporally to imply risk-neutral market pricing in the first place. The question arises, however, as to whether the more recent literature really addresses true risk. Beginning with Fischer Black's zero-beta version of the capital asset pricing model (1972) and continuing into the arbitrage pricing model (Ross, 1976), a world of no riskless asset has been posited. Although this more recent literature would escape some of our criticisms, problems remain. In the first place, although it may not be obvious, most of this literature "cheats" by invoking the law of large numbers or central limit theorem at key points to eliminate unwanted risk from the discussion. Thus, any risk not dealt with by beta (in the CAPM), the factors (in the APT), or the hedge portfolio in the option pricing model (OPM), is presumed to be eliminated by diversification in portfolios of sufficient size and no longer worthy of consideration. Nevertheless, in the world of risk that we envisage, substantial residual risk would still need to be borne. Second, a theory of choice (utility theory) among risky alternatives, in the absence of a certain alternative, remains to be developed. As discussed above, the current model, which opts for the certain consumption stream unless sufficient premiums are offered to induce the undertaking of risk, is simply not operational in a world where there is no attainable certain consumption stream. The current wealth endowment could be defined only in terms of a standard risk, not a certainty (at least with respect to future consumption, which is the ultimate object of interest). This standard could be expected to change if the world became a more (or less) risky place. Other problems arise once we acknowledge that wealth is only a set of lottery tickets and that all one can do is swap one set for another set. Risk would not be an unambiguous, monotonic concept; as discussed above, money is a low-risk asset in some senses, but very high-risk in others (such as inflation and other forms of political risk). For everyone wishing to hold a less-than-standard risk, there must be those prepared to hold more. Rules for swapping lotteries would probably be complex. Finally, there is the problem of assumed stationarity. Although zero-sum games among individuals can, with the appropriate political structure, be made stationary, such games with nature tend to break down over time. Harvests are hard to predict, such that only proportional shares are assured of exactly exhausting the product (i.e., only limited numbers of fixed claims can be issued). This implies that it would be difficult for many individuals to hold significantly less than standard risk portfolios and that during either very good or very bad years the political system may break down to allow recontracting on the terms of existing lotteries (Findlay and Williams, 1981). Such possibilities introduce fundamental uncertainty into the model. Hence, while models under true risk could be derived, it is not clear how robust they would be.

Rational expectations [15]

Neoclassical models have attempted to avoid some of the problems outlined above by injecting "rational expectations" assumptions into the argument. The theory of rational expectations states that economic agents do not make systematic mistakes in forming expectations about future events. Thus, even if probability distributions cannot be identified, decision makers can develop expectations about the likely outcome of events. Moreover, they can often be *wrong*. If they are rational, however, they will not be systematically wrong. Over the past two decades, the rational expectations literature has developed extensively. Since Muth's original paper (1961), a number of theoretical and empirical treatises have appeared. Over time, their proponents admitted that economic agents would make mistakes, but that "error learning" would occur (adaptive expectations) that would return an economy to its

[15] This section is adapted from Findlay and Williams (1985, 1986) and Williams and Findlay (1986).

long-run equilibrium path. Alternatively, economic actors would behave *as if* they had complete knowledge of the parameters of the real
world. Thus, we could deal with any expected changes in probability
over time by setting up a series of conditional probability distributions
and solving the implied problems for the optimal path. Ultimately, even
if the prior beliefs are diffuse, neoclassical doctrine holds that Bayesian
adjustments cause the posterior beliefs to become compact after relatively few iterations of the experiment.

The assumption of a stable process is at the heart of the neoclassical
position. The importance of this assumption to economic measurement
is by Ross (1978, p. 890n):

> This view is based upon a Bayesian argument that eventually with diffuse
> priors, the ex post observational data will swamp the priors and produce
> similar posteriors. Even with random news received idiosyncratically
> there would not be persistent differences in any one direction for any one
> agent. Unfortunately, this intuition is based on the assumption that the
> economic data follows a stationary process and this need not be the case
> when intertemporal prices are generated as a sequence of temporary
> equilibria. Jordan . . . (1976) has produced a counter example of this sort
> in which posteriori distributions do not settle down to any nice path.
> Without stationarity though, or some explicit model of nonstationarity,
> econometrics itself is in jeopardy and this seems too tragic to take
> seriously.

In the minds of most Post Keynesians, not only are econometrics "in
jeopardy" in a world of continuous disequilibrium; economic theory
itself is in troublesome waters. Thus, it becomes very important to the
neoclassicists *not* to admit the possibility of the existence of a decision
environment that is nonstationary.

The role of long-term expectations [16]

Post Keynesians readily concede the existence of a world "with con-
stantly changing and unpredictable expectations driving the system
onward through calendar time" (Davidson, 1978, p. 378). Nevertheless,
as Keynes noted, inevitable disappointment and surprise seldom lead to
violent alterations in the state of expectations (where the elasticity of
expectations is equal to or greater than unity). The reason for this is
provided by Davidson (1978, pp. 385–386):

[16] This section is adapted from Findlay and Williams (1985, 1986) and Williams
and Findlay (1986).

Recognizing the mercurial possibility of the economic system, man has, over time, devised certain institutions and rules of the game, which as long as they are operational, avoid such catastrophes by providing a foundation for a conventionality of belief in the stability of the system and hence in the quasi-stability of the state of expectations. It is the existence of spot and forward markets, money, and concurrent seratim time-length money (forward) contracts and their enforceability, as well as the expectations that these institutions will continue to operate with continuity of "orderliness" for the foreseeable future, which limits the magnitude of E_e and keeps real world economic fluctuations in bounds.

Thus, in macroeconomic analysis, institutional arrangements are recognized to have been created to assure sufficient "stickiness" in expectational behavior to prevent great instability.

The microeconomic theory on which Keynes based his "great instability" observation, however, has not been developed nearly so extensively as has been the case for the decision maker in the neoclassical world. Nevertheless, it is the possibility of rapid shifts that lends import to the microeconomic foundation of the decision-theoretic framework. To Post Keynesians, the recent introduction of neoclassical policies (e.g., indexing) has enhanced the prospects for an increasingly unstable environment. Hence, it seems clear that one may be less able to rely on "contractual stickiness" than was true in the past. Moreover, and it is likely that some Post Keynesians will disagree here, the institution of the forward contract *may not* be sufficient to guarantee stability in any event. Unfortunately, as rights and duties can be expressed only in terms of the ex ante set of states, *no ironclad* (i.e., perfect) *contract can, even in principle, be written.* In a world where one cannot know all possible outcomes, one cannot contract away all (or even most) of the uncertainty of the future. This implies that even if markets are complete in the Arrow–Debreu sense ex ante, they cannot be complete ex post. This further implies that a totally riskless security cannot even exist in theory. Thus, contracts on some ex post states will not exist and some state-dependent contracts will not be enforceable on their original terms.

It is important to note the distinction between the view that it is impossible to write a perfect contract under uncertainty and the neoclassical position that it is very costly to do so under risk (see Jensen and Meckling, 1976, p. 340). True, the perfect contract does not exist in either instance; but, since probabilities are known in the latter case, those covenants omitted cover the least likely cases (i.e., a cutoff where the marginal expected value of loss equals the marginal cost of contracting).

In the former case, however, nobody knows whether the contract deficiencies are significant or not. In other words, under risk one is omitting outliers that may, in fact, occur; under uncertainty, one may be omitting the ex post interquartile range for all one knows. Consequently, an unambiguous normative theory in an uncertain world cannot exist for the simple reason that the ex post set may contain outcomes preferable to all of those in the ex ante set upon which decisions were based. This means that we can never know ex ante whether we made the "right" decision (in the neoclassical sense of picking the preferred probability distribution or "urn" from which nature is to draw an outcome or "ball"). Moreover, as we observe only a limited portion of the ex post set (which, in turn, is at least partially a function of the ex ante decisions made), we can never know ex post whether we made the "best" decision and can only vaguely discern (usually by comparison with the experience of others) whether we even made a "good" decision.

We must distinguish here between *fact* and *belief.* A normative model requires some version of fact (e.g., true distributions) to make much sense. A positive model, on the other hand, can often function on belief alone. There are several points to be made. First, from beliefs alone we can develop positive models that do not depend for their accuracy upon whether the beliefs are correct (or, for that matter, whether "correct" has meaning in this context). For example, if everyone is confident about the future (both in the sense of feeling that we can predict an outcome accurately and that the outcome so predicted is favorable), economic actors will tend to consume more and to hire more labor and capital than if everyone is pessimistic (that is, feeling unable to predict the future, predicting an unfavorable future, or both). Second, widely held beliefs are self-reinforcing. In the example above, the pattern of behavior people would follow if they were confident would be much more likely to result in a favorable future outcome than would a pessimistic behavior pattern. It should be clear, however, that the impact of a failure of expectations is greatest when the expectations are most strongly held.

This sort of analysis gives insight into the ultimately important question of the decision time path. To be sure, "the time duration between the enacting of decisions based on ex ante expectations and the resulting ex post outcome [remains] 'incapable of being made precise' " (Davidson, 1978, p. 381). Nevertheless, it *does* become possible to get some inkling of what *may* happen to the future state of expectations based upon their present level. If a "surprise" occurs (an impossibility by definition in rational expectations models), expectations will shift. Without getting into the issue of whether "surprise begets surprise," we can say that, if the "impossible" continues to occur after a shift in expectation, there should be yet another movement in the decision function. If yet further surprise develops, a more dramatic shift would occur. Finally, in a completely chaotic world, the function would collapse, nothing would evoke further surprise, and economic activity would come to a standstill.

A Post Keynesian Model [17]

From the above one is left with a recognition that, in general, the world is an uncertain place in which equilibrium is undefined—other than in the temporary sense of markets clearing at a point in time. This crucial observation, along with the institutional analysis provided earlier in this paper provides the background for the real-world theory of investment, capital, and finance which we shall construct below. In building our model, we shall make several assumptions (in addition to the three listed at the beginning of this article):

1. *Uncertainty is bounded.* Welfare, bankruptcy laws, laws against human bondage, and the like cause points near the origin of a Von Neumann–Morgenstern utility function to be unattainable in modern societies. Thus, it is possible for individuals to take courses of action with positive probabilities of ruin in a world where this is cushioned. In like manner, social recontracting will occur (e.g., price controls on oil after OPEC) prior to infinite wealth being achieved. However, the bounds for a given individual can be quite far apart and the intervening range undefined.

2. *Many political and social arrangements exist to moderate uncertainty.* Financial institutions may also tend to bound uncertainty. The simple neoclassical models cannot explain the institutions' existence, while the more complex models rely on information and transactions costs. An alternative view would be that these represent the first line of defense for socializing the impacts of uncertainty, with government as the fallback defense. In an uncertain world, subsequent events can change the rules of the game. This does provide a role for government beyond confusing price signals in Walrasian markets.

[17] This section is adapted from Findlay and Williams (1985) and Williams and Findlay (1987).

3. *Uncertainty cannot be perfectly hedged.* No matter how much wealth one possesses or in what form it is held, there is always the possibility of losing it. Even gold in a Swiss vault could be confiscated at some point. Furthermore, given that one must live in physical space, all of which is controlled by government, one must worry about one's neighbor as well as about nature.

4. *Social arrangements can be manipulated.* In an uncertain world with redistribution, one can increase one's slice of the pie more easily by appropriating someone else's than by helping to make a bigger pie. Hence, the search for, and role of, power should be appreciated. It is further likely that all possible social outcomes are Pareto-optimal, and that this criterion is useless and should be abandoned. If we add the possibility of changing (manipulated) tastes, all social welfare criteria seem useless.

5. *Conventions, stickiness, and indivisibilities play a role.* A true world of static equilibrium would be as unpleasant as a perfectly competitive one. Nobody really wants to be the victim of instantaneous, and possibly quite large, adjustments. The Keynesian convention of liquidity, for example, allows us to sleep at night with our IBM holdings, even though we have no idea what they are really worth, because we all agree (absent the unlikely event of significant news) that the market will be prepared to pay about the same for them tomorrow as it did today. These conventions also allow firms to undertake uncertain production processes with fundamental indivisibilities without great fear of total ruin. Mistakes are not fun, but they are rarely fatal because everybody makes them and free entry ex post is made difficult by institutional forces. The latter provides an argument for regulation, trade restrictions, and other forms of entry barriers.

6. *Although individuals can adjust their positions quickly, society cannot.* This fundamental fact is ignored by perfect market models which implicitly put the entire capital stock at the margin. The result is wealth and present value computations which only apply so long as nobody attempts to realize them. It is neither possible nor desirable that society "cash out." At the individual level, there must be a buyer for every seller; many of these computations are made for assets that have no market anyway.

7. *Individuals lie and engage in self-delusion.* Finance has historically been an endeavor in which the great fortunes were made by violating laws prior to their enactment. A world where "we simply do not know" is a world where skill and luck are very difficult to differentiate on

small samples, even ex post. Indeed, with sufficient uncertainty, the ex ante conceptual distinction between the concepts is not terribly clear. Hence, there is a natural tendency, in dealing with others or even one's self, to attribute good outcomes to skill and poor outcomes to luck. Thus, it may be that firms simply do what they do: some of it works and some of it does not, and managers grab for credit and shift blame as best they can.

In a microfinancial context, we would argue that real-world decision makers do, in fact, form expectations about the future and that recent experience is probably the most important determinant of those expectations. Nevertheless, few financial executives calculate intricate probability distributions about the variables on which they have to decide. Despite the fact that probability analysis has been taught for at least three decades in the more prestigious graduate business schools, the use of such in an actual decision-making environment has never caught on. The reason for this is not difficult to discern if, as was argued above, the world is characterized by fundamental uncertainty and not risk. Thus, we would not know what future outcomes are possible, much less the relative probabilities of these outcomes. Computing means and variances (much less, covariances) for distributions that may not exist, or that are highly unstable, is a fruitless way to cope with the gains associated with making successful (correct? lucky?) decisions or the losses accompanying unsuccessful ones. In the real world, it would appear that decision makers actually "hedge their bets." Among the larger enterprises, the really major decisions are typically made by committees. In this way, the "collective judgment" of a number of executives is brought to bear on problems. Politically speaking, this makes it unnecessary for any one executive to be held accountable for "bad" choices. This may be a proper way to socialize the personal risk associated with having to make such choices, particularly if there is no way to be "right" anyway (as was suggested above may be the case). For the enterprise as a collective entity, choices are made in a fashion so as to minimize the danger of jeopardizing its existence. Substantial commitments that could bankrupt the firm are avoided even though the subjective thoughts about the potential payoffs might be quite positive. This, of course, makes the larger companies increasingly conservative and their activities at the margin, at least, less significant.

The role of liquidity in financial decision making is also important. Although it may be impossible to determine all possible outcomes of a decision and assign probabilities to each, the financial executive usually knows how much cash he or she will have to commit to implement a decision (new product line, replacement of given plant, etc.). If funds have to be expended over time, of course, this may be an uncertain amount, but there is always a boundary on the expenditure. One can simply abandon the decision if it becomes "too expensive" over time. On the return side, if the investment turns out to be a winner, positive cash flows are accepted and the decision makers congratulate themselves on having made a "good decision." If a lemon ensues, no permanent harm has been done since only funds that the firm could lose without jeopardizing itself have been committed. Much of what we maintain about decision theory in general applies to specific financial choices as well. If the future is highly uncertain, much modern capital budgeting analysis simply does not work. It is a waste of time to attach discount rates to projected cash flows when neither the proper rates nor flows can be known with any certitude. Practicing financial managers have known this for years and, despite admonitions from professors about their backwardness, they have continued to use such supposedly erroneous techniques as the payback method since it provides really significant information (i.e., how much cash do we have to spend on a capital project and when do we expect to get it back?).

Similar observations could be made about key financing decisions, and a number of the institutional arrangements that neoclassical theory has such difficulty explaining (or must refer to as "neutral mutations") can be at least understood if one abandons probabilistic/discounting approaches. For most firms, the optimal capital structure, optimal dividend payment arguments are irrelevant, and attempts to equate the marginal returns on investment with the marginal costs of capital are nonsensical. Large firms borrow when they can do so with impunity and without risking the life of the enterprise. Equity capital is raised when bull markets are raging and funds are available without significant dilution. Earnings are retained as a general policy, and dividends are paid *only* when it is fairly certain that future payments can be maintained.

We describe the above in a positive sense, and also in a normative sense for those in such a system. It is considered to be a fair depiction of financial decision making in the real world. Furthermore, it seems to work. If the world is a highly uncertain place, and we believe that it is, large entities are advised to hedge their bets with liquidity and not take foolish gambles. Collective decision making should be engaged in since it really makes no sense to hold any one individual responsible for things over which he or she probably has little control. All of these issues carry over into decision making within the firm. There they are joined by some additional serious estimation problems (e.g., it is not clear that even single betas for projects have ever been satisfactorily estimated, while the notion of estimating multiple betas for projects to apply the APT boggles the mind). The approach we recommend begins with certain theorems which we shall call "stylized facts." These stylized facts have been observed to be consistent with the behavior of real-world corporate managers and boards of directors, and they come from the conclusions of scholarly empirical investigations or from studies of the way certain economic actors (i.e., managers and directors) actually make decisions. In many cases, the "facts" are at odds with what has been generally accepted as "good theory" in the finance literature. Nevertheless, it should be remembered that what we propose is a positive model. The so-called rational maximization assumptions of neoclassical economics may be violated in such a model, but then there has developed an extensive behavioral literature in economics (which will not be recited here) that suggests that any number of goals (besides share price maximization or profit maximization) may be adopted, and adopted successfully, by firms that operate in less than perfectly competitive environments. We outline the stylized facts as follows:

1. Real-world firms operate in a continuum of calendar time. At any one point in time, they must make decisions that will be influenced by other decisions that were made in the past. For example, the ABC Co. at January 1, 1994, may find itself in the widget business, with plant and equipment of a certain size, age, and efficiency, with a given supplier and customer base, with a given liquidity posture, and with specific creditors and stockholders who were attracted to the firm for a variety of reasons. On January 2, 1994, ABC cannot become XYZ in a totally different business with another asset/liability inheritance and with a new set of client-creditor/investors. Only with the passage of time can ABC change to become XYZ. This, the Walrasian assumption of having the entire asset/liability stock of the nation "on the block" every day for repricing (along with goods and factors whose prices are also "sticky"), is at odds with reality.

2. Firms set policies based on numerous goals that are consistent with the desires and needs of the numerous clienteles that they serve (customers, suppliers, employees, creditors, stockholders, etc.). Hence, "the firm is essentially a *socio-political* institution. Legally

speaking, it is really a large group of contracting parties who join forces for multifarious reasons" (Williams and Findlay, 1983, p. 41).

3. Past history strongly influences management attitudes about future choices. Nevertheless, although decision makers may employ probability (Bayesian) approaches on occasion to address specific problems that lend themselves to repeat experimental solutions, they do not use these techniques exclusively (or even primarily) as a means for dealing with any substantial risk. Firms often face conditions of fundamental uncertainty (where probability distributions cannot be determined), and must employ other approaches to make decisions. Contractual commitments are often employed as an uncertainty-reducing device under these circumstances.

4. Many firms hope to offer their shareholders (including managers holding options) an opportunity for capital gains rather than dividends, although some firms have carved out a niche for themselves as high payout firms. In any case, however, dividends are not set as a residual, nor do firms omit them prior to new share issues (or at any other time if they can avoid it). One of the most robust empirical findings of finance is that firms set dividends as though by some sort of share adjustment model. This result was first explicitly stated in Lintner's survey (1956) and has been confirmed in Fama's various empirical studies (1968; Fama and Babiak, 1968). Observation also indicates that setting the dividend is one of the major items on the agenda of directors' meetings.

5. Firms have target debt ratios, generally expressed in book value terms. Since the end of World War II, book value debt ratios have been far more stable than their market value counterparts. Because of changes in market conditions, short-term debt and leasing have become more prominent at the expense of long-term debt, but a comprehensive, book value liability ratio will demonstrate surprising stability. Executives tend to think in these terms. So do their commercial bankers and investment bankers. Rating agencies and loan agreements operate in book value terms. Any effort to stabilize a market value debt ratio would involve issuing additional shares in bear markets and repurchasing them in bull markets. Even with a modest belief in efficiency, this "reverse" portfolio balancing rule for capital structure seems bizarre. Target debt ratios may vary with the cash flow and liquidity position of the firm (*cf.* Donaldson, 1971a, 1971b) and the basic attitude of management toward risk.

6. Firms budget capital from a centralized authority in terms of set time intervals (e.g., quarterly or annually). The fully decentralized, continuous time capital budgeting (i.e., accept any project, anywhere in the firm, at any time yielding more than K_o) contemplated in the texts is never observed for projects of any size. Furthermore, most firms invariably deem themselves in a rationing environment, much to the chagrin of theorists. Firms continue to use payback and accounting return capital budgeting techniques (cf. Hoskins and Mumey, 1979) and they are loath to specify a hurdle rate.

7. Major firms rarely issue new common shares.

Given the above "stylized facts," we may posit a model that is a reversed view of figure 3, represented as figure 4.

We assume the firm is at a point in calendar time and has earned net income for the previous period. Such income is determined by the average rate of return (r^A) earned on the firm's previous asset investment (K_t) less payments to creditors and corporate income taxes. In the light of this income and previous payouts, the board of directors sets a tentative dividend. From such, a provisional value for retained earnings may be determined. Given a previously established target debt to equity ratio, $L^T = D / (D+E)$, which might or might not represent an optimal capital structure but would be expressed in book values and would reflect the liquidity posture of the firm and its attitude toward risk, retained earnings will provide additional debt capacity. Together, these figures will provide net investment. Adding back depreciation, a gross investment fund is obtained. Projects are then selected until this fund is exhausted. The selection may be made project by project (i.e., along the MEC) or by alternative overall budgets (i.e., along the AEC). Firms generally do not determine either the MEC or the AEC using probabilistic future cash flows as in the neoclassical model. Rather, the MEC arrays projects by means of accounting rates of return or payout periods.

If the process ends here, a result similar to hard rationing is obtained. The procedure presents two guides to further action, however. One is the overall or average return on the investment budget, r^A The other is a marginal shadow price on the budget constraint, r^M. If r^M seems "high" (relative to a notion of K_o or "experience") and there is some slack in r^A, an incentive may exist to undertake more projects. After an analysis of project postponability, another iteration in the process may be initiated. In this case, a result similar to soft rationing is obtained. One or more budget constraints must be relaxed. Observation suggests that a

Figure 4

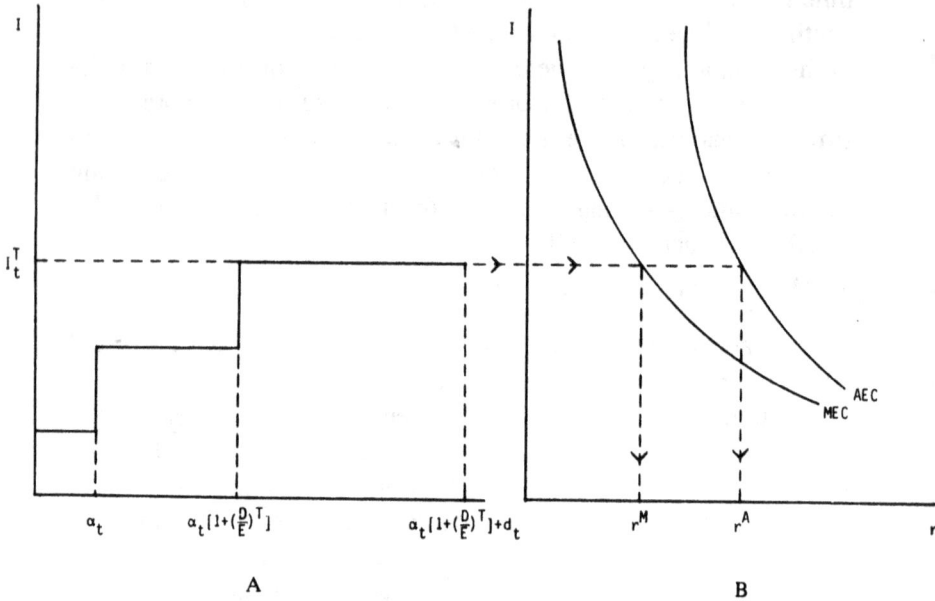

A   B

"temporary" relaxation of the target debt ratio is typically the candidate chosen. The process in figure 4 is then repeated. If more funds are required, the next choice would probably be an asset liquidation (e.g., sale of marketable securities, a divestiture, or perhaps a sale-leaseback), followed by a (rare) new share issue, with the idea of a dividend cut bringing up the rear. The model would appear as follows:

$$(10) \qquad I_t = \alpha_t + (D/E_t)^T \alpha_t + d_t K_t ;$$

$$(11) \qquad \alpha_t = (r_t^A K_t - i_t D_t) (1 - C_t) - \phi_t ;$$

$$(12) \qquad (D/E_t)^T \alpha_t = \Delta D_t - \delta_t ;$$

$$(13) \qquad I_t = (r_t^A K_t - i_t D_t) (1 - C_t) - \phi_t ;$$
$$+ \Delta D_t = \delta_t + d_t K_t.$$

where:

I_t = the gross investment at period t;

α_t = earnings retained at period t;

$r_t^A K_t$ = income earned at period t, expressed as the average return on the firm's investment stock (r^A) times the stock (K_t);

i_t = average coupon (interest) rates on the corporation's indebted-
          ness at period t ;
C_t = the corporation's average rate of taxation at period t ;
ϕ_t = dividends paid at period t ;
D_t = the book value of the firm's debt at time t ;
E_t = the book value of the firm's equity at time t ;
ΔD_t = gross debt sold at period t ;
d_t = the rate of depreciation (depletion, etc.) of the investment
          stock at period t ;
δ_t = the dollar amount of sinking fund and other debt retirements
          at period t ;
T = targeted amounts.

If, on the other hand, the r's are "too low" on the first iteration, a reverse procedure can be implemented. In the short run, marketable securities can be purchased or some debt can be retired (especially if it is selling at a discount and will boost earnings). If the situation persists, however, either a merger campaign or a higher dividend payment may be required to prevent the firm from becoming a target itself (by virtue of a low return, high liquidity, or both). Although an MEC was employed for convenience in figure 4, an IRR ranking is not envisioned, nor, for that matter, is project-by-project selection. Any ordinal scheme such as payback or accounting return, or pure whim of management would do. What also will not work is net present value, as nowhere in the analysis has a value for K_o been specified.[18] The normative model, however, does emerge as a special case. If the target debt ratio happens to be the optimal one (assuming such exists), if relaxations in the funds constraint maintain this ratio, and if the process iterates until r^M converges (from above or below) upon K_o, then the two models become observationally equivalent. It is perhaps useful in this regard to contemplate how special a case the standard textbook normative model is.

The model presented here is, in some sense, a rationing model. Yet it does not depict the standard ill-justified introduction of a funds constraint into an assumed perfect market, neoclassical value-maximizing process. It is, rather, more in the spirit of advancing Weingartner's suggestion that rationing be viewed as a planning process to the point

---

[18] To the extent that some firms purport to use their historic book return (a version of r^A) as a cutoff rate (i.e., r^M), some support is provided for the notion that the actual MEC may be a good bit steeper than its depiction in figure 4. See Williams and Findlay (1979).

of proposing a rationing approach as the central paradigm. Viewed another way, a quantity adjustment approach has been advanced as an alternative to the pure price adjustments in the valuation approach. Aside from the greater descriptive validity of the model, several other advantages obtain. Budgeting is a special case of rationing. Approaches based upon the former must introduce rather awkward digressions (e.g., market imperfections, programming techniques) to explain the latter. Starting from the other direction, budgeting is dealt with rather quickly. Another advantage, given the difficulty of its estimation, is that the cost of capital has no central role to play in the model presented. The target debt ratio may minimize it and investment may proceed until r^M equals it, but neither of these conditions is necessary. The model works quite well in a world where nobody knows or cares what his or her cost of capital might be (i.e., the real world other than for public utilities which have quite different reasons for producing those data). A notional value of K_o may be employed, but only to consider if r^M may provide an overlooked opportunity.[19]

An entrepreneurial theory of investment, capital, and finance

As is the case for the large, publicly held corporation, it is equally true that any realistic theory of the entrepreneurial firm must take into account the important characteristics of these entities. Clearly, for the entrepreneurial firm, there is no separation of ownership and control. Hence, all of the agency issues addressed above disappear (until, of course, the entrepreneurial firm decides to go public—but at this point it makes the transition to being publicly held). Like those for the publicly held entities, decisions of the entrepreneurial firm are also made under pure uncertainty. Although there are some occasions where, due to the existence of large data bases and the repetition of experiments, the long-existing entity (which is also typically large and publicly held) may be able to use probabilistic approaches and Bayesian analysis (as discussed above), this is almost never true for the entrepreneurial concern. New enterprises usually have the least data with which to work of all businesses, and other entrepreneurial endeavors usually do not have the resources to put together requisite data bases. Although these entities may prepare business plans with elaborate projections and forecasts, there is rarely a solid foundation for these numbers (see Williams and

---

[19] Real-world estimated values for K_o are probably highly influenced by K_i with K_e having little meaning to the practicing financial manager.

Manzo, 1983). Thus, entrepreneurial firms are like their large, publicly held corporate cousins in that they too face a world of fundamental uncertainty. They are unlike the publicly held institutions in that there are no agency issues to obscure the production plan from the beneficiaries of those plans (i.e., the entrepreneurs).

Psychology and entrepreneurs [20]

Whereas certain sociopolitical issues influence the structure and decision making of the publicly held entity (see above), it is probably true that the psychological make-up of the entrepreneur may be more important to the entrepreneurial firm. Fortunately, this is one area where quite credible and applicable academic work has been done (practically all by psychologists and sociologists). Much of the early scholarly research in entrepreneurship was centered on the sociopsychological characteristics of entrepreneurs. From Collins and Moore (1964) onward, researchers have been probing into the psyche of those individuals who decide to start a business of their own. The early view that "entrepreneurs are men who have failed in the traditional and highly structured roles available to them in society" (Collins and Moore, 1964, p. 243) has been displaced in the literature with the view that most founders of new enterprises "had experienced a generally higher than average level of success in their previous employment" (Liles, 1974, p. 3) and in fact were quite capable of functioning in a structured environment. It is also generally accepted that at both the individual and the societal level needs are far more complex than those simple requirements typically envisioned by economic models. Work by Maslow (1954), McGregor (1960), Boyatzis (1972), Winter (1973), McClelland (1975, 1976), and others have identified the need for achievement (n-achievement), the need for affiliation (n-affiliation), the need for autonomy (n-autonomy), and the need for power (n-power) as the driving forces behind human behavior.

A striking conclusion of much of the sociopsychological research is that monetary reward is only of secondary importance in motivating individuals. One observer has attempted to synthesize man's needs in a so-called "money motive," but this is a rather different phenomenon from the one generally contemplated in economic models (Wiseman, 1974). Indeed, it turns out that people have ambivalent attitudes about money. Anal types continue to amass it for no other reason than for its collection value, but others are actually repelled even by the discussion

---

[20] This section is adapted from Williams (1981) and Williams (1983).

of monetary matters—at least when applied to themselves. In discussing the achievement motive, McClelland found that high achievers were not much influenced by monetary reward except as a score-keeping device. Lower achievers, on the other hand, might be motivated by money and might be encouraged to work harder for financial incentives. Perhaps most significant of all the conclusions, however, is the general indictment by psychologists of the rationality postulate generally assumed in economic models. As McClelland has put it (1976, p. 38):

> [Freud] destroyed forever (except, perhaps in the minds of economic theorists) the notion that motives are rational or can be rationally inferred from action. By concentrating his attention on notable irrationalities in behavior—slips of the tongue, forgetting of well-known facts, dreams, accidents, neurotic symptoms—he demonstrated over and over again that motives "are not what they seem." In fact they might be just the opposite. It could no longer be safely assumed that a man walks across the street just to get to the other side. He might, in fact, want just the opposite—to enter a tavern on this side, a desire revealed indirectly by his exaggerated avoidance behavior. [See also Williams and Findlay, 1981]

Thus, it appears that any model attempting to explain entrepreneurial behavior which postulates maximizing profit, wealth, or some such monetarily-oriented objective, will fail to capture the essential determinants. Many entrepreneurs appear to be irrational and even quixotic, and pecuniarily maximization models do not handle well this sort of behavior. To be sure, many of the great economists of the past have recognized that irrational (non-economic) motives might dominate the entrepreneurial decision-making process. Schumpeter (1934), for example, argued frequently that such motives as the desire to found a private dynasty, the will to conquer in competitive battle, or the sheer joy of creation could rule the judgments of the entrepreneur. Keynes, of course, argued frequently that animal spirits might be far more important than perhaps any other factor in explaining the stock market or even real investment activity. In the neoclassical competitive models, however, the entrepreneur is a sterile eunuch, a puppet manipulated by the invisible hand. In the condition of competitive equilibrium envisaged by these models, the entrepreneur does nothing. He does not create, he does not innovate, he merely reacts. It is fortunate for human progress that the entrepreneur of the real world does not behave in the fashion envisaged by neoclassical economic theory.[21]

[21] See Kirzner (1973).

Economics and entrepreneurs [22]

One might be pardoned for thinking that there is an extensive literature on the role of the entrepreneur in economic theory. Unfortunately, there is not. As Professor Baumol has observed (1968, p. 64):

> The entrepreneur is at the same time one of the most intriguing and one of the most elusive characters in the cast that constitutes the subject of economic analysis. He has long been recognized as the apex of the hierarchy that determines the behavior of the firm and thereby bears a heavy responsibility for the vitality of the free enterprise society. In the writings of the classical economist his appearance was frequent, though he remained a shadowy entity without clearly defined form and function. Only Schumpeter and, to some degree, Professor Knight succeeded in infusing him with life and in assigning to him a specific area of activity to any extent commensurate with his acknowledged importance.
> In more recent years, while the facts have apparently underscored the significance of his role, he has at the same time virtually disappeared from theoretical literature. And, as we will see, while some recent theoretical writings seem at first glance to offer a convenient place for an analysis of his activities, closer inspection indicates that on this score matters have not really improved substantially.

Baumol goes on to discuss *why* economic theory has failed to develop an illuminating formal analysis of entrepreneurship (principally because economic models are essentially mechanistic and automatic and "call for no display of entrepreneurial initiative" (p. 68), and he maintains that such analysis is not likely to be forthcoming in the foreseeable future. Nevertheless, he argues, "If we are interested in explaining . . . the 'really big dissimilarities in economic life,' we must be prepared to concern ourselves with entrepreneurship" (p. 65). Among those "really big dissimilarities" are those associated with economic development. Baumol tells us (pp. 65–66):

> It has long been recognized that the entrepreneurial function is a vital component in the process of economic growth. Recent empirical evidence and the lessons of experience both seem to confirm this view. For example, some empirical studies on the nature of the production function have concluded that capital accumulation and expansion of the labor force leave unexplained a very substantial proportion of the historical growth of the nation's output. Thus, in a well-known paper, Solow has suggested on the basis of American data for the period 1909–49 that

[22] This section is adapted from Williams (1981) and Williams (1983).

"gross output per man-hour doubled over the interval, with 87.5% of the increase attributable to technical change and the remaining 12.5% to increase in the use of capital." But any such innovation, whether it is purely technological or it consists in a modification in the way in which any industry is organized, will require entrepreneurial initiative in its introduction. Thus we are led to suspect that by ignoring the entrepreneur we are prevented from accounting fully for a very substantial proportion of our historic growth.

Baumol concludes (p. 71):

> In a growth-conscious world I remain convinced that encouragement of the entrepreneur is the key to the stimulation of growth. The view that this must await the slow and undependable process of change in social and psychological climate is a counsel of despair for which there is little justification. Such a conclusion is analogous to an argument that all we can do to reduce spending in an inflationary period is to hope for a revival of the Protestant ethic and the attendant acceptance by the general public of the virtues of thrift! Surely we have learned to do better than that, in effect by producing a movement along the relevant functional paths rather than undertaking the more heroic task involved in shifting the relationships. This is precisely why I have just advocated more careful study of the rewards of entrepreneurship. Without awaiting a change in the entrepreneurial drive exhibited in our society, we can try to learn how one can stimulate the volume and intensity of entrepreneurial activity, thus making the most of what is permitted by current mores and attitudes. If the theory succeeds in no more than showing us something about how that can be done, it will have accomplished very much indeed.

Although Baumol's conclusion is grounded more in intuition than in rigorous economic theory, it does not differ from the findings of the economic historians who have analyzed the role of the entrepreneur in the development of the United States. There is a more complete literature in this area (see Cole, 1968; Soltow, 1968; and Giacalone, 1968), although "business history has not yet created a satisfactory general hypothesis of the role of entrepreneurship" (Soltow, p. 90). One economist who believes that an axiomatic-theoretic approach to entrepreneurship may be adopted is Leibenstein, yet his views are quite compatible with Baumol's. Leibenstein maintains (1968, pp. 77–78):

> Although there is no universally accepted theory of development, we can point to two important elements in the process: (1) Per capita income growth requires shifts from less productive to more productive techniques per worker, the creation or adoption of new commodities, new

materials, new markets, new organizational forms, the creation of new skills, and the accumulation of new knowledge. (2) Part of the process is the interaction between the creation of economic capacity and the related creation of demand so that some rough balance between capacity growth and demand growth takes place. The entrepreneur as a gap-filler and input-completer is probably the prime mover of the capacity creation part of these elements of the growth process.

We now know that development is not simply a process of physical and human capital accumulation in the usual sense. If that were all that were involved, then development would simply be a function of the willingness to save. Experience has shown that this is not the case. The work of Solow and others [has] shown that growth cannot be explained by the contributions of the increase in standard inputs. The work of Chenery and Strout emphasizes that the degree of capital absorption can be a significant constraint to growth in developing countries. The existence of and need for gap-filling and input-completing capacities could explain why standard inputs do not account for all outputs and why capital absorption should be a problem. Economic planning experience in many countries reveals that there is frequently a considerable divergence between plan targets and results. This divergence may be partly explained by the fact that entrepreneurship is not a normal input whose contribution can be readily determined, predicted, planned for, or controlled.

Thus, even though we may not have a good economic theory of entrepreneurship, few could argue with the proposition that entrepreneurship is an essential determinant of economic development. Moreover, it is very likely to be the case that entrepreneurship is far more important than other variables (such as the rate of saving, the capital stock of society at a point in time, etc.). This conclusion has some incredibly important implications because, unlike other economic factors, the supply of entrepreneurship can be limitless. Entrepreneurial activity involves creation and innovation, and the creative process may be fostered. It is altogether possible that creativity can even be taught (à la de Bono; 1976). If this is in fact the case, then there can be no logical limits to economic growth. The usual bane of the economist, natural resources, becomes fundamentally unimportant because entrepreneurial talent should be able to find better and better techniques that require fewer and fewer resources. Given the natural conservation laws of physics, it might even be argued that resources are *not* an essential requirement for economic growth! Unfortunately, in the past, economists have spent most of their time worrying about the scarcity phenomenon (scarce capital, scarce savings, etc.) when they really should be concentrating on the abundance of entrepreneurial talent that exists in the world. To be sure, this takes economists out of the comfortable world of the "Robbinsian economizer." But it is perhaps overdue that economists start thinking about the issues that determine 87.5 percent of the growth rate rather than the 12.5 percent that they can deal with mechanically.

An entrepreneurial model [23]

Despite the fact that there really is no good or well-developed economic theory of entrepreneurship, we shall construct an investment/financing model for the entrepreneurial firm. Although this model is rigorous and assumes maximizing behavior, there is still room for entrepreneurial whim and fancy to play a role if the entrepreneur so wishes. A model similar to the one we shall develop was posed by Vickers (1968) almost twenty-five years ago for the publicly held entity. This model was further refined by myself and R.B. Siok (1972), allowing for a simultaneous solution, providing for a correct interpretation of the "marginal productivity (efficiency) of money capital,"[24] and positing a firm producing a products with n inputs or factors of production. However, both of these models (Vickers' and mine) still focused on the large, publicly held entity. After many years of reflection, it seems to me that these models are far more useful for the entrepreneurial firm than for the publicly held corporation, and they are adapted here for that entity.

We begin with an entrepreneur who wishes to maximize his wealth position as follows:

(14)

$$\omega = \frac{1}{\rho(E, V)} [p(Q)f(X, Y) - \gamma_1 X - \gamma_2 Y - r(E, V)V] - E,$$

subject to:

(15)
$$E + V = g(Q) + \lambda X + \beta Y,$$

---

[23] This section is adapted from Williams and Siok (1972) and Findlay and Williams (1979).

[24] The debate over the "marginal productivity (efficiency) of money capital" is provided by Williams and Siok (1972) with a response by Vickers (1974).

where:

ω = the owner's net value of the firm;

ρ = the owner's opportunity capitalization rate;

r = the average rate of return expected from outside venture capital;

E = the amount of owner's capital invested in the firm (optmized where ω max);

V = the amount of venture capital employed by the firm (optimized where ω max);

p = the unit selling price of the firm's product;

Q = the quantity of output of the product produced (optimized where ω max);

X, Y = input factors of production;

γ_1, γ_2 = the unit factor costs of inputs X and Y respectively;

$g(Q)$ = a net working capital requirement;

λ, β = money capital requirement coefficients of X and Y respectively.

Within equation (14), it is assumed that ρ and r are functionally dependent on E and V (the amounts of owner and venture equity employed by the firm) and that p is a function of Q, which in turn is a function of X and Y. This, of course, implies that the entrepreneur is not operating in a competitive product market, which is the usual assumption microeconomists make about new firms. Instead, we are suggesting that the *purpose* of the entrepreneurial enterprise is to differentiate its product or service and, hence, that it faces a negatively sloped demand curve. An approach to maximizing ω while providing a completely simultaneous solution to X, Y, E, and V is worked out in Williams and Siok (1972), and the result is an intraequilibrium position for the firm. The mathematics need not be replicated here even though our focus is much different from that in Williams and Siok (1972). The method is the usual Lagrangian process which differentiates ω partially with respect to each decision variable (X, Y, E, and V), sets the results equal to zero, and constrains the solutions with equation (15).

The one-product firm envisaged in equation (14) may be generalized to encompass the production of a products using n inputs such that for all:

(16)
$$i\,(i = 1, n),\ \sum_{j=1}^{a} \overline{X}_{ij} = X_i.$$

The constrained owner's valuation function becomes:

(17)
$$\omega = \frac{1}{\rho(E, V)} \left[\sum_{i=1}^{a} p_i(Q_i) f_i(\overline{X}_{1i}, ..., \overline{X}_{ni}) - \sum_{j=1}^{n} \gamma_j X_j - r(E, V) V \right] - E,$$

subject to:

(18)
$$E + V = \sum_{j=1}^{a} g_i(Q_i) + \sum_{j=1}^{n} \lambda_j X_j,$$

where:

Q_i, i $= 1, a$ is the ith product produced by the firm;
X_j, j $= 1, n$ is the nth input factor;
X_{ji} $=$ the amount of input j used in producing Q_i;
λ_i, i $= 1, n$ is the investment needed per unit of X_i;
γ_i, i $= 1, n$ is the unit cost of input i;
$g_i(Q_i) =$ the net working capital requirement for output i;
$p_i(Q_i) =$ the gross revenue per unit of output i sold at price p_i;
$f_i, (X_{1i}, X_{ni}) =$ the production function for output i.

In this instance, ω is differentiated partially with respect to each $\overline{X}_{ij}$, E, and V; the results are set equal to zero and equation (18) is employed to constrain the solution to find optimal values for each variable. It is also possible to add a time dimension by superscripting each p_i, Q_i, X_j, X_{ji}, λ_i, and γ_i over time. The resulting series of cash flows, less the appropriate venture capital return, can then be discounted at ρ to obtain the net ownership value of the firm. Of course, this process must be done bearing in mind the caveats set out earlier about uncertainty. The projected future cash flows would be rough estimates at best, and would clearly not be generated by probabilistic methods.

The model described in equations (14) through (18) ignores taxes. This is not because taxes are unimportant in the real world. Rather, the means of handling the taxation issue would depend on the legal form of enterprise adopted by the entrepreneur. Were the entrepreneur to operate as a corporation and elect (or be required) to be taxed according to Subchapter C of the Internal Revenue Code, the business entity itself would be subject to tax before any distributions were made to the entrepreneur (or the venture capitalist). Were the entrepreneur to operate as a sole proprietorship or partnership, or be able to elect Subchapter S status, or be able to become a limited liability company,[25] then the business entity would not be taxed. Instead, the owners of the business would be taxed directly and one layer of taxation would be avoided. Since taxation clouds the issues at stake here, we have avoided the subject. Suffice it to say that not only do taxes in general affect value, but the way the business entity is legally structured will also affect its value.

The model of equations (14) through (18) also considers but does not fully develop the role of the venture capitalist in the entrepreneurial setting. More work on this subject by the author will be forthcoming in the future, although it should be noted that a literature in this area is developing (see Amit, Glosten, and Muller, 1990). Debt financing is also ignored in our entrepreneurial model. Although the debt /equity trade-off and optimal debt to equity ratios feature in the publicly held model, debt is not really an option for the entrepreneur. To the extent that the entrepreneur borrows money, he or she must personally guarantee payment. As such, this is really a form of disguised equity capital. Similarly, although the venture capitalist's investment may take the form of debt (say, for tax reasons), it also remains essentially a form of equity capital. Finally, the model does not formally deal with entrepreneurial whim and fancy. Variables designed to take into account the noneconomic but nevertheless important entrepreneurial characteristics discussed above will have to be incorporated into any complete investment/financing model of the entrepreneurial firm.

Summary and conclusions

The impetus for this essay was a series of articles by Gordon, Vickers, Fried, and Crotty on the theory of business investment that originally appeared in the *Journal of Post Keynesian Economics*. Rather than provide a critique of what I consider to be "correct" or "incorrect" theory and analysis in these articles, I have chosen instead to build upon the spirit of what these writers have done. My paper carefully distinguishes between corporate and entrepreneurial theories of the firm and constructs a real-world model for each. In the arena of the publicly held corporation, we first note the importance of the issue of the separation

[25] Only a few states presently allow companies to be legally structured as limited liability companies.

of ownership and control in these enterprises. From this, we identify agency layers and discuss the role of agency in financial markets. The basic neoclassical model with appropriate recent extensions is then reviewed. It is noted that the neoclassical model is essentially a certainty model with bells and whistles attached that simply cannot apply to the real world, that is, the world where fundamental uncertainty exists and where expectations may not always be perfectly "rational." Given our critique of the neoclassical model, we build a Post Keynesian investment/financing model for the large, publicly held corporation. This model utilizes assumptions and stylized facts that are apparent from real-world observation and is almost a reverse reflection of the neoclassical theory.

The second part of the paper describes an entrepreneurial theory of the firm. The theory is based on psychological as well as economic factors, although the actual investment/financing model constructed does not take the psychological factors into account. A refined version of this effort (to be forthcoming) will hopefully do this. It is noted that there is no really good economic theory of entrepreneurship, although the model proposed should be useful in developing such a theory.

REFERENCES

Amit, R.; Glosten, L.R.; and Muller, E. "Does Venture Capital Foster the Most Promising Entrepreneurial Firms?" *California Management Review*, Spring 1990, 102–111.

Baumol, W.J. "Entrepreneurship in Economic Theory." *American Economic Review*, May 1968, 64–71.

Beaver, W.; Kettler, P.; and Scholes, M. "The Association between Market Determined and Determined Risk Measures." *The Accounting Review*, October 1970, 654–682.

Berle, A.A., and Means, G.C. *The Modern Corporation and Private Property*. New York: Macmillan, 1932.

Bhattacharya, S. "Imperfect Information, Dividend Policy, and the 'Bird in the Hand' Fallacy." *The Bell Journal of Economics*, Spring 1979, 259–270.

Black F. "Capital Market Equilibrium with Restricted Borrowing." *Journal of Business*, July 1972, 444–455.

Blume, M., and Friend, I. "A New Look at the Capital Asset Pricing Model." *Journal of Finance*, March 1973, 19–33.

Bogue, M., and Roll, R. "Capital Budgeting of Risky Projects with 'Imperfect' Markets for Physical Capital." *Journal of Finance*, May 1974, 601–613.

Boyatzis, R.E. *A Two-Factor Theory of Affiliation Motivation*. Dissertation, Harvard University, 1972.

Breen, W., and Lerner, E. "Corporate Financial Structures and Market Measures of Risk and Return." *Journal of Finance*, May 1973, 339–352.

Cole, A.H. "The Entrepreneur: Introductory Remarks." *American Economic Review*, May 1968, 60–63.

Collins, O.F., and Moore, D.G., with Unwalla, D.B. *The Enterprising Man*. Michigan State University Business Studies, East Lansing, 1964.

Crotty, J.R. "Neoclassical and Keynesian Approaches to the Theory of Investment." *Journal of Post Keynesian Economics*, Summer 1992, *14* (4), 483–496. Chapter 4 of this volume.

Davidson, P. *Money and the Real World*, 2d ed. New York: John Wiley, 1978.

De Angelo, H., and Masulis, R. "Optimal Capital Structure Under Corporate and Personal Taxation." *Journal of Financial Economics*, March 1980, 3–29.

de Bono, E. *Lateral Thinking*. New York: Harper and Row, 1976.

Donaldson, G. *Corporate Debt Capacity*. Homewood, IL: Richard D. Irwin, 1971a.

―――. *Strategy for Financial Mobility*. Homewood, IL: Richard D. Irwin, 1971b.

Fama, E. "The Empirical Relationships between the Dividend and Investment Decisions of Firms." *American Economic Review*, June 1974, 304–318.

―――. "Agency Problems and the Theory of the Firm." *Journal of Political Economy*, April 1980.

Fama, E., and Babiak, H. "Dividend Policy: An Empirical Analysis." *Journal of the American Statistical Association*, December 1968, 1132–1161.

Findlay, M.C., and Williams, E.E. "Capital Allocation and the Nature of Ownership Equities." *Financial Management*, Summer 1972, 68–72.

―――. "Owners' Surplus, Market Equilibrium, and the Marginal Efficiency of Capital." *Journal of Business Finance and Accounting*, Spring 1979, 17–36.

―――. "A Positivist Evaluation of the New Finance." *Financial Management*, Summer 1980, 7–17.

―――. "Financial Theory and Political Reality under Fundamental Uncertainty." *Journal of Post Keynesian Economics*, Summer 1981, 528–544.

―――. "A Post Keynesian View of Modern Financial Economics: In Search of Alternative Paradigms." *Journal of Business Finance and Accounting*, Spring 1985, 1–18.

―――. "Better Betas Didn't Help the Boat People." *Journal of Portfolio Management*, Fall 1986, 4–9.

Fried, J. "Financial Theory and the Theory of Investment." *Journal of Post Keynesian Economics*, Summer 1992, *14* (4), 465–481. Chapter 3 of this volume.

Giacalone, J.A. "Entrepreneurial Theory and American Business History: A Survey." *Review of Social Economy*, September 1968, 156–167.

Gordon, M.J. "The Neoclassical and a Post Keynesian Theory of Investment." *Journal of Post Keynesian Economics*, Summer 1992, *14* (4), 425–443. Chapter 1 of this volume.

Hertz, D. "Risk Analysis in Capital Investment." *Harvard Business Review*, January–February 1964, 95–106.

Hoskins, C., and Mumey, G. "Payback: A Maligned Method of Asset Ranking." *Engineering Economist*, Fall 1979, 53–65.

Jensen, M., and Meckling, W.H. "Theory of the Firm: Managerial Behavior, Agency

Costs, and Ownership Structure." *Journal of Financial Economics*, October 1976, 305–360.

Kalay, A. "Signaling, Information Content, and the Reluctance to Cut Dividends." *Journal of Financial and Quantitative Analysis*, November 1980, 855–870.

Keynes, J.M. *General Theory of Employment, Interest, and Money*. New York: Harcourt, 1936.

Kirzner, I. *Competition and Entrepreneurship*. Chicago: University of Chicago Press, 1973.

Kraus, A., and Litzenberger, R. "A State Preference Model of Optimal Financial Leverage." *Journal of Finance*, September 1983, 911–922.

Leibenstein, H. "Entrepreneurship and Development." *American Economic Review*, May 1968, 72–83.

Liles, P. *New Business Ventures and the Entrepreneur*. Homewood, IL: Richard D. Irwin, 1974.

Lintner, J. "Distribution of Incomes of Corporations among Dividends, Retained Earnings, and Taxes." *American Economic Review*, May 1956, 97–113.

Litzenberger, R., and Ramaswamy, K. "The Effect of Personal Taxes and Dividends and Capital Asset Prices: Theory and Empirical Evidence." *Journal of Financial Economics*, June 1979, 163–195.

———. "Dividends, Short Selling Restrictions, Tax-Induced Investor Clienteles and Market Equilibrium." *Journal of Finance*, May 1980, 469–482.

Magee, M. "How to Use Decision Trees in Capital Investment." *Harvard Business Review*, September–October 1964, 79–96.

Maslow, A.H. *Motivation and Personality*. New York: Harper and Row 1954.

McClelland, D.C. *Power: The Inner Experience*. New York: Irvington Publishers, 1975.

———. *The Achieving Society*, rev. ed. New York: Irvington Publishers, 1976.

McClelland, D.C.; Atkinson, J.W.; Clark, R.A.; and Lowell, E.L. *The Achievement Motive*, rev. ed. New York: Irvington Publishers, 1976.

McGregor, D. *The Human Side of Enterprise*. New York: McGraw-Hill, 1960.

Miller, M. "Debt and Taxes." *Journal of Finance*, May 1977, 261–276.

Miller, M., and Scholes, M. "Dividends and Taxes." *Journal of Financial Economics*, December 1978, 333–364.

———. "Dividends and Taxes: Some Empirical Evidence." *Journal of Political Economy*, December 1982, 1018–1041.

Modigliani, F., and Miller, M. "The Cost of Capital, Corporation Finance and the Theory of Investment." *American Economic Review*, June 1958, 261–297.

———. "Corporate Income Taxes and the Cost of Capital." *American Economic Review*, June 1963, 433–443.

Muth, J.F. "Rational Expectations and the Theory of Price Movements." *Econometrica*, July 1961, 315–335.

Myers, S., and Turnbull, S. "Capital Budgeting and the Capital Asset Pricing Model: Good News and Bad News." *Journal of Finance*, May 1977, 321–332.

Reinganum, M. "The Arbitrage Pricing Theory: Some Empirical Results." *Journal of Finance*, May 1981a, 313–321.

———. "A New Empirical Perspective on the CAPM." *Journal of Financial and Quantitative Analysis*, November 1981b, 439–462.

Roll, R. "A Critique of the Asset Pricing Theory's Tests: Part I. On Past and Potential Testability of the Theory." *Journal of Financial Economics*, March 1977, 129–176.

Ross, S. "The Arbitrage Theory of Capital Asset Pricing." *Journal of Economic Theory*, December 1976, 341–360.

———. "The Current Status of the Capital Asset Pricing Model." *Journal of Finance*, June 1978, 885–901.

Schumpeter, J. *The Theory of Economic Development*. Cambridge, MA: Harvard University Press, 1934.

Solow, R.M. "Technical Change and the Aggregate Production Function." *Review of Economics and Statistics*, August 1957, 312–320.

Soltow, J.H. "The Entrepreneur in Economic History." *American Economic Review*, May 1968, 84–92.

Taylor, W.M., and Williams, E.E. "Market Microstructure and Post Keynesian Theory." *Journal of Post Keynesian Economics*, Winter 1991–92, *14* (2), 233–247.

Vickers, D. *The Theory of the Firm: Production, Capital, and Finance*. New York: McGraw-Hill, 1968.

———. "Disequilibrium Structures and Financing Decisions in the Firm." *Journal of Business Finance and Accounting*, Autumn 1974, 375–387.

———. "The Investment Function: Five Propositions in Response to Professor Gordon." *Journal of Post Keynesian Economics*, Summer 1992, *14* (4), 445–464. Chapter 2 of this volume.

Weingartner, M. "Capital Rationing: Authors in Search of a Plot." *Journal of Finance*, December 1977.

Williams, E.E. "Cost of Capital Functions and the Firm's Optimal Level of Gearing." *Journal of Business Finance*, Summer 1972, 78–83.

———. "Innovation, Entrepreneurship and Brain Functioning." In K. Vesper (ed.), *Frontiers of Entrepreneurship Research*. Wellesley, MA: Center for Entrepreneurial Studies, 1981.

———. "Entrepreneurship, Innovation, and Economic Growth." *Technovation*, February 1983, 3–15.

Williams, E.E., and Findlay, M.C. "Capital Budgeting, Cost of Capital, and Ex-Ante Static Equilibrium." *Journal of Business Finance and Accounting*, Winter 1979, 281–299.

———. "A Reconsideration of the Rationality Postulate: 'Right Hemisphere Thinking' in Economics." *American Journal of Economics and Sociology*, January 1981, 17–36.

———. "Is Common Stock Obsolete?" *Abacus*, June 1983, 39–55.

———. "Corporate Governance: A Problem of Hierarchies and Self Interest." *American Journal of Economics and Sociology*, January 1984, 19–36.

———. "Risk and the Role of Failed Expectations in an Uncertain World." *Journal of Post Keynesian Economics*, Fall 1986, 32–46.

———. "Toward a Positive Theory of Corporate Financial Policy." *Abacus*, September 1987, 107–121.

Williams, E.E., and Manzo, S. *Business Planning for the Entrepreneur*. New York: Van Nostrand, 1983.

Williams, E.E., and Siok, R.B. "The Marginal Productivity of Money Capital, Simultaneous Solutions, and the Optimal Structure of the Firm." *Journal of Business Finance*, Winter 1972, 53–57.

Winter, D.G. *The Power Motive*. New York: The Free Press, 1973.

Wiseman, T. *The Money Motive*. New York: Random House, 1974.

7

On the Keynesian investment function and the investment function(s) of Keynes

ROBERT S. CHIRINKO

This essay represents an initial exploration by the author of the world of Post Keynesian thought as it pertains to investment in business fixed capital.[1] Two striking findings emerge from these first readings. A number of important ideas that have been common currency for some time in the Post Keynesian literature—interactions between the real and financial sectors of the aggregate economy, problems of imperfect information among economic agents, and the general need to consider historic relations in economic analysis—are now receiving attention in mainstream journals.[2] Bernanke and Blinder (1988) have based their recent analysis of the "credit view" of aggregate fluctuations on an extended IS-LM framework where both schedules shift in response to monetary injections and credit shocks. Stiglitz (1992) has developed a vast body of microeconomic analysis in which "information is spread

The author is a Visiting Associate Professor at the University of Illinois (Champaign/Urbana), and a Visiting Scholar at the Federal Reserve Bank of Kansas City. He gratefully acknowledges the comments and suggestions from Steven Fazzari, John Golob, Bryon Higgins, and seminar participants at the Federal Reserve Bank of Kansas City. All errors, omissions, and conclusions remain the sole responsibility of the author. The views expressed herein do not necessarily reflect those of the Federal Reserve Bank of Kansas City nor of the Federal Reserve System.

[1] Formulating an appropriate definition of Post Keynesian thought would involve an essay in and of itself. The body of work that the author has in mind has been developed by, among many others, the editors of and contributors to the *Journal of Post Keynesian Economics*, papers cited in the survey article of Eichner and Kregel (1975), and contributors to recent conference volumes in honor of Alfred Eichner (Milberg, 1992) and Hyman Minsky (Fazzari and Papadimitriou, 1992).

[2] As with the Post Keynesian label, what constitutes "mainstream" research is highly debatable, but the vast majority of articles published in the *American Economic Review*, the *Journal of Political Economy*, and the *Quarterly Journal of Economics*, as well as more technical journals, would be representative.

disparately throughout the economy; there is limited transferability of information; and financial institutions, including banks, play a central role in the allocation process" (p. 278). Blanchard and Summers (1986) have explained the stubbornly high levels of European unemployment in terms of hysteresis, which makes "long-run equilibrium depend on history" (p. 71). Despite the Post Keynesian literature's prescient emphasis on these dynamic elements, the author is surprised by the largely static mode of analysis, which, while illustrative, is nonetheless incomplete. Many articles focus on steady states (despite a strong commitment to the fundamentally changing nature of the economic system over time), use informal arguments to describe movements thereto, analyze expectations in a similarly informal manner, and rely on two-dimensional diagrams, all of which provide only indirect treatments of the essential dynamics. The coarseness of the analytic tools does not do justice to the richness of the ideas under discussion.

Intending to arbitrage the profitable opportunities created by the autarky between mainstream and Keynesian/Post Keynesian approaches, this study brings to bear the dynamic tools employed in the former to some issues discussed in the latter. With the central role played by dynamics in capital accumulation, the investment function is a particularly appropriate place to conduct such an exploration. The proposed amalgamation may be troubling to some because it is based on, *inter alia*, a well-behaved production function, factor returns that depend on marginal products, a partial equilibrium model of a single firm, and a well-defined capital aggregate. These and other difficulties notwithstanding, the intent here is to begin to build bridges between the dynamic models in Post Keynesian thought and the dynamic models used in the mainstream, not to resolve all of the troublesome issues that have been highlighted in the Post Keynesian literature. The essay seeks to demonstrate some of the benefits that can be forthcoming from a more formal treatment of dynamics.

The absence of formal dynamic analysis has led to a substantial discrepancy between the Keynesian investment function and the investment function of Keynes. In his classic book, Leijonhufvud (1968) made a critical distinction between the then current Keynesian aggregate model—analyzed largely in terms of comparative statics—and the model reflecting the dynamic elements in Keynes' writings. As suggested by the title of this paper, a similar distinction applies to investment behavior. The standard view of the Keynesian investment function is one in which quantity variables (e.g., sales, liquidity, lagged invest-

THE KEYNESIAN INVESTMENT FUNCTION 133

ment) dominate price variables (e.g., interest rates, relative factor prices) as determinants of investment spending. As will be argued throughout, that view misrepresents the investment function of Keynes, which should be defined in terms of the Keynesian dynamics that impinge on the firm in making investment decisions. When these ideas are placed in a formal framework that properly analyzes the relevant dynamics, the relative importance of quantity versus price variables becomes a delicate matter. In some versions of the investment function of Keynes, only price variables appear; when other dynamics affect the firm, quantity variables reemerge. Analyses based on static concepts and informal models are inadequate for extracting these subtle implications and hence in uncovering the fundamental aspects of investment behavior.

Our inquiry begins in section 1 with a very simple optimization problem that will permit comparisons to be drawn among the Jorgensonian investment function, the Keynesian investment function, and the investment functions of Keynes. The conditions characterizing optimal behavior are related to the investment model developed by Dale Jorgenson and his various collaborators that has formed the basis for a substantial amount of empirical knowledge about the determinants of investment. As with any pioneering effort, this model has been subject to a number of criticisms, and those that pertain to dynamics are discussed. Some of these concerns can be addressed by introducing elements consistent with Keynes' views of the important dynamics governing investment decisions. Sections 2 through 4 expand the formal framework to incorporate these elements and derive three of the investment functions of Keynes. In light of these results, section 5 discusses several issues raised in the symposium papers reproduced as chapters 1 through 4 of this volume, and argues that the gulf between Post Keynesian and mainstream approaches is more apparent than real.

Apart from drawing connections between Post Keynesian and mainstream approaches, the exploratory analysis undertaken here impacts the proper formulation and evaluation of econometric investment equations. With a variety of specifications to choose from, how is one to decide which is most appropriate? Which Keynesian or non-Keynesian elements underlying these investment functions are essential for understanding the investment decision? This study closes with some thoughts on how to discriminate between these competing views, arguing that a better understanding will be achieved by pursuing a disciplined discourse in which all of the constraints impinging on the firm are considered explicitly in a formal optimization problem and in which econometric investment specifications used to examine the data are determined by the conditions characterizing optimal behavior.

1. The Keynesian investment function

> [I]n Keynes and Kalecki, investment in fixed capital primarily depends on a firm's demand expectations relative to its existing capacity and its ability to generate investment funding through internal cash flow and external debt financing. [Fazzari and Mott, 1986–87, p. 171]

> The Keynesian view of the equilibrating process has interest rates playing a smaller role than changes in output, because investment demand is thought to be relatively insensitive to interest rates, being dominated instead by producers' expectations of future demand for their products. [Coen and Eisner, 1987, p. 981]

There is widespread agreement that the defining characteristic of the Keynesian investment function is the dominance of quantity variables over price variables as determinants of investment spending. This view is represented by the above quotations, and has been largely confirmed on the econometric battlefield with models that bear a family resemblance to that pioneered by Dale Jorgenson and his numerous collaborators.[3] This section examines a very simple optimization problem (transformed to facilitate the computation of the first-order conditions), discusses the conditions characterizing optimal behavior, and relates these conditions to the Keynesian/Jorgenson investment function. This specification has been subjected to a number of criticisms, some of which have been emphasized in the Post Keynesian literature. To account for these criticisms, extended versions of the optimization problem can be developed, and they will serve as the basis for the investment functions of Keynes discussed in sections 2 through 4. It should be kept in mind that, rather than capturing all of the relevant aspects of the environment in which firms operate, the models developed in this essay are intended to connect ideas found in various literatures to an effective, though ultimately more complicated, analytic apparatus.

---

[3] That Jorgenson's model is frequently labeled as the "neoclassical" model of investment is unfortunate, especially since it has been an appropriate vehicle for assessing Keynesian implications. While not an inappropriate label, "neoclassical" refers in this case to the model's explicit statement of the benefits and costs of acquiring a marginal unit of capital.

A model of an optimizing firm

We begin by assuming that the firm chooses inputs to maximize the discounted sum of expected cash flows, which is equivalent to maximizing its market value.[4] The firm is a price-taker in both its input and output markets, and is further constrained by production and accumulation technologies. Output (Y_t) is determined by labor (L_t) and capital (K_t); hence the production technology is $Y_t = F [L_t, K_t]$.[5] The price of output is the numeraire; the relative prices of labor and investment are represented by p^L_t and p^I_t, respectively, and are constant in a given period. No adjustments are made for taxes, nor are inventories accumulated. To emphasize the fundamentally forward-looking nature of the firm's decision problem, we introduce an expectations operator, $E_t\{.\}$, where the subscript indicates that expectations are based on information available to the firm at the beginning of period t. These considerations lead to the following equation for the value of the firm's equity at the beginning of period t, equivalent to the value at the end of period $t-1$ (V_{t-1}):

(1a)
$$V_{t-1} = E_t\left\{ \sum_{s=t}^{\infty} R_{t,s}\left\{ F [L_s, K_s] - p^L_s L_s - p^I_s I_s \right\}\right\},$$

(1b)
$$R_{t,s} \equiv \prod_{u=t}^{s} (1 + r_u)^{-1},$$

where $R_{t,s}$ is the discount factor between periods t and s, and r_u is the discount rate in period u. Apart from the production technology and fixed prices, the firm is also constrained by an accumulation technology defining the stock of existing capital as a weighted sum of past investments. If capital depreciates at a geometric rate (δ), then the weights follow a declining geometric pattern, and capital is accumulated as follows:

---

[4] It is important to note that, with this maximand, the firm is uninterested in the higher moments of the stream of cash flows and its correlation with the owners' consumption path. Furthermore, potential conflicts among shareholders, bondholders, and managers are ignored. These considerations can be incorporated in more complex models of the firm.

[5] With no loss in analytic insights but much saving in notation, we assume that production is affected by the end-of-period capital stock.

(2)
$$K_t = \sum_{-\infty}^{s=t} (1-\delta)^{t-s+1} I_s \,.$$

The Lagrangian for the maximization of V_{t-1} subject to the capital accumulation constraint (2) is written as:

(3)
$$LG_t = E_t \{ \sum_{s=t}^{\infty} R_{t,s} \{F\,[L_s, K_s] - p_s^L L_s - p_s^I I_s$$
$$- \lambda_s \,[K_s - \sum_{-\infty}^{u=s} (1-\delta)^{s-u+1)} I_u \,]\}\}$$

A convenient transformation

In developing the first-order conditions associated with equation (3), it proves very convenient to rearrange the accumulation constraint in two steps. We begin by isolating those factors that affect current decisions and those that are predetermined, though not necessarily constant, from time t onward:

(4a)
$$\lambda_s \sum_{-\infty}^{u=s} (1-\delta)^{s-u+1} I_u = \lambda_s \sum_{t}^{u=s} (1-\delta)^{s-u+1} I_u + \lambda_s \sum_{-\infty}^{u=t-1} (1-\delta)^{s-u+1} I_u$$

(4b)
$$= \lambda_s \sum_{t}^{u=s} (1-\delta)^{s-u+1} I_u + \lambda_s K_{t,s} \,,$$

where the expectations operator has been omitted for notational convenience. The latter term in (4a) defines $K_{t,s}$; note that the u index never exceeds t, and hence $K_{t,s}$ is not affected by decisions taken during the planning period. The former term can be discounted, summed, and transformed as follows:

(5a)
$$\sum_{s=t}^{\infty} R_{t,s} \lambda_s \sum_{t}^{u=s} (1-\delta)^{s-u+1} I_u =$$

(5b)
$$\sum_{s=t}^{\infty} R_{t,s} I_s \sum_{u=s}^{\infty} (R_{s,u}/R_{s,s}) (1-\delta)^{u-s+1} \lambda_u =$$

(5c)
$$\sum_{s=t}^{\infty} R_{t,s} \, \Lambda_s \, I_s \, ,$$

(5d)
$$\Lambda_s \equiv \sum_{u=s}^{\infty} (R_{s,u}/R_{s,s}) \, (1-\delta)^{u-s+1} \, \lambda_u \, ,$$

where Λ_s is the shadow price for fixed capital. With (4) and (5), the accumulation constraint in (3) can be rewritten as:

(6)
$$\lambda_s \sum_{-\infty}^{u=s} (1-\delta)^{s-u+1} \, I_u \, = \, \Lambda_s \, I_s + \lambda_s \, K_{t,s} \, ,$$

and the Lagrangian for this optimization problem takes the following relatively benign form,

(7)
$$LG_t = E_t \bigg\{ \sum_{s=t}^{\infty} R_{t,s} \big\{ F \, [L_s, K_s] - p_s^L L_s - p_s^I I_s - \lambda_s \, K_s + \Lambda_s \, I_s + \lambda_s \, K_{t,s} \big\} \bigg\}.$$

Conditions characterizing optimal behavior

The conditions characterizing optimal behavior in period t by a profit-maximizing firm are obtained by differentiating (7) with respect to the flow and stock variables[6]:

(8a)
$$L_t : \quad p_t^L = F_L \, [L_t, K_t] \, ,$$

(8b)
$$K_t : \quad \lambda_t = F_K \, [L_t, K_t] \, ,$$

(8c)
$$I_t : \quad \Lambda_t = p_t^I \, .$$

---

[6] The necessity of these conditions for an optimum has been established by Kleindorfer, Kleindorfer, and Thompson (1977) and Weitzman and Schmidt (1971). In addition, there is a transversality condition that describes the limiting behavior of the value of the capital stock and that enters equation (7) implicitly by ensuring that the sum defining Λ_s converges. It is assumed throughout that the firm's optimal investment policy always results in interior solutions; hence complementary slackness conditions can be ignored.

(8d)

$$\Lambda_t \equiv E_t \left\{ \sum_{s=t}^{\infty} (R_{t,s}/R_{t,t})\,(1-\delta)^{s-t+1}\,\lambda_s \right\}.$$

Equation (8a) is the familiar marginal productivity condition for a variable input. In (8b), the "spot" shadow price of capital (λ_t) equals the one-period marginal product. Owing to capital's durability, these marginal benefits are accumulated over the useful life of capital, as represented in (8d) by Λ_t (which is equation (5d) rewritten with an expectations operator). The marginal acquisition cost equals the purchase price of a new unit of capital (p^I_t), and the requisite equality along an optimal accumulation path is given by equation (8c). The information provided by equation (8), as well as the related conditions that will be based on an expanded set of constraints, determines all of the investment specifications considered in this article.

The Keynesian/Jorgensonian investment equation

The investment equation developed in this section is based on a demand for capital and, with the addition of dynamics, a demand for investment.[7] The *demand for capital* follows directly from equations (8a–d) when expectations are static; in this case, the infinite sum in (8d) can be solved analytically, and $\Lambda_t = \lambda_t / (r_t + \delta)$.[8] Using equations (8b) and (8c) and maintaining that the production function has a constant elasticity of substitution (σ) between capital and variable inputs, we obtain the following well-known relation between the desired (or optimal) stock of capital (K^*_t), the level of output, and the user cost (or rental price) of capital (C_t):

(9a)
$$K^*_t = \zeta\, Y_t\, C_t^{-\sigma}\,;$$

(9b)
$$C_t = p^I_t\,(r_t + \delta)\,,$$

---

[7] See Jorgenson (1963) and Hall and Jorgenson (1967) for the original development, and Chirinko (1993, section II and the appendix) for a more extended discussion and references.

[8] Static expectations are defined as follows: $E_t\{x_s\} = x_t$, for all $s \geq t$, where $x_s = \{\lambda_s, r_s\}$. Owing to timing assumptions that become important only in discrete time models, the expression for Λ_t should be multiplied by $(1-\delta)/(1+r)$. The adjustment term reflects assumptions about the period during which new capital begins to depreciate and when cash flows are received.

where ζ is the CES distribution parameter. Equation (9a) highlights the dependence of the desired capital stock on a quantity variable (Y_t) and a set of price variables $(p^I_t$ and $r_t)$ combined in the user cost.[9]

Absent any dynamic considerations, the firm would achieve K^*_t instantaneously.[10] Dynamics enter when specifying the *demand for the flow of investment*, which is divided between replacement and net components. In the present model, the translation from a stock demand to a flow demand depends on depreciation and delivery lags.[11] Capital is assumed to depreciate geometrically at a constant mechanistic rate (δ); hence, replacement investment (I^r_t) is proportional to the capital stock available at the beginning of the period,

$$(10) \qquad I^r_t/K_{t-1} = \delta .$$

Net investment (I^n_t) is defined as the arithmetic difference between the capital stocks in periods t and $t-1$, and is determined by a distributed lag of new orders (O_t), which equal, in a given period, the change in the desired capital stock. To link net investment to new orders, the former is specified in terms of the relative change in the capital stock determined by the weighted geometric mean of relative changes in the desired capital stock:

$$(11) \qquad I^n_t/K_{t-1} + 1.0 = K_t/K_{t-1} = \prod_{j=0}^{J} (K^*_{t-j}/K^*_{t-j-1})^{\mu_j} ,$$

$$\prod_{j=0}^{J} ((\Delta K^*_{t-j}/K^*_{t-j-1}) + 1.0)^{\mu_j} ,$$

$$\prod_{j=0}^{J} ((O_{t-j}/K^*_{t-j-1}) + 1.0)^{\mu_j} ,$$

[9] Taxes are an important element omitted in this derivation of C_t. If the firm faces an investment tax credit (m_t), tax depreciation allowances with a present discounted value of z_t, and a business income tax rate (t_t), then equation (9b) would be multiplied by $(1-m_t-z_t)/(1-t_t)$.

[10] See, among others, Haavelmo (1960, ch. 29 and pp. 215–216), Witte (1963), and Jorgenson (1967). When any K^*_t can be achieved instantaneously, the firm does not need to take a deep look into the future, and static expectations are fully consistent with forward-looking optimal behavior.

[11] In addition to these dynamics, the specification of the investment function can also depend on expenditure and gestation lags (assumed here to be degenerate), vintage effects (assumed here to be absent; i.e., capital is putty–putty), or adjustment costs with changing the capital stock (considered in sections 2 and 3).

where the μ's represent the delivery lag distribution extending for $J+1$ periods.[12] Taking logs of equation (11), using the approximation $\ln(1+x) \approx x$, substituting equation (9) for the $(\Delta K^* / K^*)$'s, using equation (10) for replacement investment, and appending a stochastic error (u_t), we obtain the Jorgensonian investment equation,

(12)

$$ I_t / K_{t-1} = I_t^r / K_{t-1} + I_t^n / K_{t-1} $$

$$ = \delta + \sum_{j=0}^{J} \mu_j \, (\Delta Y_{t-j} / Y_{t-j}) - \sigma \sum_{j=0}^{J} \mu_j \, (\Delta C_{t-j} / C_{t-j}) + u_t \,. $$

In Jorgenson's work, σ was always assumed to be unity, although alternative values are also consistent with his model. When $\sigma = 0$, equation (12) reduces to the flexible accelerator and, if delivery lags are absent, the simple accelerator.

There are two important extensions that are relevant for understanding the empirical results with variants of equation (12). First, it has been frequently argued that a measure of liquidity (LIQ_t) should enter the model to account for short-term finance constraints that affect the timing of investment along the transition path between steady states. While LIQ_t does not influence K^*_t, it will have a positive effect, perhaps distributed over several periods, on investment expenditures. Second, in the presence of nonstatic expectations and delivery lags, the terms in (9a) would be distributed over current and future periods and interpreted as expected values. Assuming that expectations of the output and user cost terms are based on extrapolations of their past values, we obtain an extended version of the Keynesian/Jorgensonian investment equation[13]:

---

[12] The geometric adjustment process is employed in equation (11) because, since I_t and ΔY_t have pronounced trends, it is preferable to specify the investment equation so that all variables are in the same units. The standard practice is to replace the weighted geometric mean of relative changes equation (11) by the weighted arithmetic mean of arithmetic changes: $I^n_t = \Sigma \mu_j \Delta K^*_{t-j}$, $j=0,J$. Differences between estimated investment equations based on arithmetic and logarithmic versions of equation (11) are surprisingly modest (Eisner and Nadiri, 1970, table I).

[13] Since equation (13) depends on nonstatic expectations, it is plagued by an inconsistent treatment of delivery lags in the optimization problem. See n. 16.

(13)
$$I_t/K_{t-1} = \delta + \sum_{j=0}^{J_Y} \alpha_j (\Delta Y_{t-j}/Y_{t-j}) - \sum_{j=0}^{J_c} \beta_j (\Delta C_{t-j}/C_{t-j})$$
$$+ \sum_{j=0}^{J_L} \gamma_j (\Delta LIQ_{t-j}/LIQ_{t-j}) + u_t .$$

In this more general specification, the estimated distributed lag coefficients (α's, β's, γ's) represent an amalgam of technology, delivery lag, and expectation parameters.[14] The Keynesian conclusion—that investment spending is determined chiefly by quantity variables—follows from the statistical and economic importance of the α's and γ's relative to the β's.

Caveats and concerns

Given their central role in empirical investment studies, equations (12) and (13) have been subjected to a number of criticisms concerning key elements underlying the derivation. Three are important for the current essay, and they will be discussed sequentially: restrictions on expectations, consistency of the theoretical model, and the role of finance.

Expectations play a crucial role in investment decisions. Static or extrapolative expectations have been assumed in deriving equations (12) and (13), respectively. While easy to implement empirically, these expectation schemes are totally at odds with the fundamentally forward-looking nature of capital accumulation, and lead to some serious difficulties. First, such extrapolations treat all changes, perhaps brought about by monetary or tax policies (which affect p'_t in equation (9b)), as though they were permanent. For example, the change in the investment tax credit in 1966 that was announced to be temporary would have the same impact on the expected user cost as permanent changes. Second, preannounced changes in tax parameters would have no immediate effect in the Jorgensonian model, yet firms would be expected to alter their plans so as to benefit from the anticipated future policy. Such a scenario was presented by the phase-in provisions for depreciation allowances in the 1981 tax act's 10–5–3 program, where firms had an incentive to delay current investment in anticipation of more generous tax write-offs in later years (which were eventually rescinded). Similar

---

[14] Since the length of the distributed lags need not be equal, the assumption of extrapolative expectations in this derivation provides a justification for the differing lag lengths (J_Y, J_C) for output and user cost frequently found in empirical work.

incentives existed in the latter part of 1992 concerning an anticipated reinstatement of the investment tax credit under the Clinton administration. Third, firms form their expectations based on whatever information is available, and the assumption that firms use a single lag with invariant parameters may be restrictive. These parameters reflect basic characteristics of the economy that may themselves be subject to change. For example, the forecasting rules for interest rates before 1979, when they were targeted by the Federal Reserve, may have changed radically after the October 1979 policy switch to monetary aggregates and the reversal in October 1982. A fourth and related point is that, by utilizing a univariate autoregression for the expected user cost, we are constraining all of the variables embedded in C_t to have the same set of expectation parameters. Yet it is doubtful that expected rates of interest and taxation possess similar time-series properties. The ramification of unstable expectations from whatever source is that the investment function will be unstable over time. These concerns about the modeling of expectations are usually referred to as the "Lucas Critique."[15] Clearly, forward-looking expectations are an essential element regardless of one's school of thought, and need to be incorporated in any model that purports to be an investment function of Keynes.

A second set of criticisms of the Keynesian/Jorgensonian model pertains to the *consistency* of the theoretical model, and there have been two specific problems. First, the profit-maximizing firm chooses the capital stock, other factors of production, and output simultaneously. Equations (9), (12), or (13) do not usually recognize these interactions nor the dependence of the optimal level of output

---

[15] In his critique of the prevailing practice for quantifying the effects of alternative policies, Robert Lucas argues that, in formulating plans, economic agents necessarily look into the future, and thus the decision rules guiding their actions depend on parameters describing the expectations of future variables, as well as parameters of taste and technology. Lucas views economic policy as the selection of rules that generate paths of policy variables, rather than the selection of arbitrary paths. Thus, "any change in policy will systematically alter the structure of econometric models" (Lucas, 1976, p. 126), and the estimated coefficients in (the then current) consumption, wage/price, or investment models could not be considered structural, that is, invariant to alternative policy regimes. The important and damning implication for policy analysis is that these econometric relations will prove unstable in precisely those situations in which they are called upon to analyze proposed policies. In light of this Lucas Critique, quantitative policy analysis can proceed only if the econometric specification permits the expectation parameters, which will vary with alternative policies, to be identified separately from technology parameters, which are invariant to policy changes.

on the user cost.[16] Second, the development of equation (13) was based on an inharmonious treatment of delivery lags. The optimal capital stock equation (9) was derived under the assumption that delivery of capital goods was immediate, but the net investment equation (11) was based on a delivery lag distribution. In this formulation, the investment path may not be optimal. However, under static expectations (as assumed by Jorgenson), the model is consistent because the benefits and costs of acquiring capital are expected to be the same at any point in time, hence independent of any delivery lag. Nonetheless, once this implausible expectations assumption is removed, the above derivation becomes questionable. Incorporating dynamics that allow for a gradual transition between steady states consistent with forward-looking behavior will be undertaken in sections 2 and 3.

The *role of finance* represents a third concern with the investment models developed in this section. While liquidity enters the extended version of the Keynesian/Jorgensonian investment equation, liquidity constraints and financial factors have been considered in an ad hoc manner. This treatment reflects the schizophrenia in the investment literature concerning the role of financial structure and liquidity constraints. Liquidity variables have generally been included frequently as regressors in econometric studies, and have generally proven quite significant. However, the theoretical basis for inserting variables representing finance constraints has been largely absent and, in light of the well-known theorem of Modigliani and Miller (1958), such a development was discouraged. Recent mainstream work has begun to close this gap between theoretical implications and empirical regularities, and the implications of some of these developments on the investment function of Keynes will be assessed in section 4.

A number of the problems with equations (12) and (13) have been highlighted in the Post Keynesian literature, but the analytic apparatus

---

[16] Coen (1969) has noted that the problem is that Y_t in equation (9a), (12), or (13) needs to be replaced by Y^*_t, where the latter is the optimal output level. With non-static expectations and impediments to immediately incrementing the capital stock (e.g., delivery lags), Y^*_t will in general differ from Y_t. A consistent model of optimal capital accumulation with output as an argument can be developed by assuming that the firm is minimizing costs subject to an exogenous level of output, a cosntraint compatible with a Keynesian view of the macroeconomy in which the firm is buffeted by substantial demand shocks. The resulting expression for K^*_t would differ somewhat from equation (9a), but would not alter the key points pertaining to equation (12) or equation (13) (Coen, 1969, n. 12). We nonetheless proceed with the profit-maximization-cum-output model because of its prominence in the literature.

used in these studies has not been sufficient for extracting the implications for investment behavior. Building on these criticisms, we develop in sections 2 through 4 investment equations consistent with the dynamic elements found in the *General Theory*. The investment function of Keynes is not one that necessarily relies on sales and finance variables as key determinants, but rather one that emphasizes the important dynamic elements found in Keynes' writings.

2. The investment function of Keynes—internal adjustment costs

> [D]aily revaluations of the Stock Exchange, . . . inevitably exert a decisive influence on the rate of current investment. For there is no sense in building up a new enterprise at a cost greater than that at which a similar existing enterprise can be purchased; whilst there is an inducement to spend on a new project what may seem an extravagant sum, if it can be floated off on the Stock Exchange at an immediate profit. [Keynes, 1936, p. 151]

In this section, we are interested in uncovering those assumptions that lead to an investment function consistent with the view stated above and in addressing the criticisms concerning expectations and consistency. Returning to the optimization problem (7), which contains a general set of forward-looking expectations,[17] we introduce transitional dynamics with the assumption that, in varying its capital stock, the firm faces adjustment costs. These were proposed by Eisner and Strotz (1963), and may represent either external costs (considered in section 3) or internal costs, which represent lost output from disruptions to the existing production process (as new capital goods are "broken in" and workers retrained), additional labor for "bolting down" new capital, or a wedge between the quantities of purchased and installed capital. A crucial assumption is that these costs increase at an increasing rate. Convexity forces the firm to think seriously about the future, as too rapid accumu-

---

[17] The use of the rational expectations operator, $E_t\{.\}$, has been questioned by Davidson (1982–83). In his analysis, a significant role for history affects the stochastic process governing expectations, creating a nonergodic process and the fundamental uncertainty that characterizes many Post Keynesian studies. In the models presented in this paper, however, $E_t\{.\}$ simply refers to the firm's "best guesses" based on available information, "guesses" that are formed notwithstanding the properties or existence of an underlying stochastic process. Nonetheless, nonergodicity may cause difficulties in the econometric application of the investment functions considered here. See section 5 for a related discussion.

lation of capital will prove costly. Alternatively, too little accumulation results in forgone profits. Internal adjustment costs are also assumed to be affected (negatively) by the scale of the firm, as measured by its capital stock, and are represented in equation (7) by subtracting $G\,[I_t,K_t]$, which is increasing in I_t, decreasing in K_t, and valued by the price of forgone output.

The introduction of internal adjustment costs leads to two minor modifications of the conditions characterizing firm behavior:

(14a) $$L_t:\ p_t^L = F_L\,[L_t,K_t]\;;$$

(14b) $$K_t:\ \lambda_t = F_K\,[L_t,K_t] - G_K\,[I_t,K_t]\;;$$

(14c) $$I_t:\ \Lambda_t = p_t^I + G_I\,[I_t,K_t]\;.$$

In equation (14b), the definition of the marginal product of capital is altered slightly to account for the effects of size on lowering adjustment costs. More importantly, the marginal costs of investment are now the sum of purchase costs and the sunk adjustment costs associated with investing. Since the sunk costs cannot be recovered, they make capital an illiquid asset and force the firm to look ahead when investing.

Three additional steps are needed to relate investment to equity markets. First, $G\,[.]$ is assumed to be quadratic in gross investment and homogeneous of degree one in I_t and K_t:

(15) $$G\,[I_t,K_t] = (\alpha/2)\,(I_t^2/K_t)\;.$$

Second, the relation between financial market data and investment spending, as suggested in the quotation at the beginning of this section and subsequently developed by Brainard and Tobin (1968) and Tobin (1969, 1978), has been labeled the Q model. In this theory, Q is defined as the difference between the financial value of the firm (V_{t-1}, adjusted for the timing of cash flows by $R_{t,t}$) and the replacement cost of its existing capital stock ($p_t^I K_t$), normalized by the capital stock,

(16) $$Q_{t-1} \equiv (V_{t-1}/R_{t,t} - p_t^I K_{t-1})/K_{t-1}\;.$$

Third, the conditions characterizing firm behavior can be manipulated to yield the following Q investment specification[18]:

---

[18] The formal conditions needed to derive equation (17) have been established by Hayashi (1982): (1) product and factor markets are competitive; (2) production and

(17) $$I_t / K_t = (1 / \alpha) Q_{t-1} + u_t,$$

where u_t is an error term. Whenever Q_{t-1} is positive, the firm has an incentive to change its capital stock, but its actions are tempered by the convex adjustment cost technology. As the adjustment cost function becomes steeper, α becomes larger, and investment responds more slowly. Given Q_{t-1}, we have a great deal of information about future conditions of supply and demand affecting investment without having to make specific assumptions about expectations formation. The latter is an enormously important feature of this model because the general difficulty (impossibility?) in specifying stable functions for expectations is a prominent criticism in the Post Keynesian literature (see Davidson, 1978, especially chap. 16, part 1). Owing to its derivation directly from an optimization problem, equation (17) recognizes explicitly the dynamics due to expectations and technology, isolates their separate influences, and is theoretically consistent.[19] Although the firm is affected by adjustment costs and the state of current and expected future demand, quantity variables are conspicuously absent in this version of the investment function of Keynes.

3. The investment function of Keynes— rising supply price of capital goods

> If there is an increased investment in any given type of capital during any period of time, the marginal efficiency of that type of capital will diminish . . . partly because, as a rule, pressure on the facilities for producing that type of capital will cause its supply price to increase . . . [this factor is] usually more important in producing equilibrium in the short run. [Keynes, 1936, p. 136]

The investment function of Keynes, equation (17), is often criticized because of its reliance on *convex* internal adjustment costs, a property that seems implausible in a number of circumstances. Given the installation of the first of ten pieces of equipment, are the disruptions associ-

---

adjustment cost technologies are linear homogeneous; (3) capital is homogeneous; and (4) investment decisions are largely separate from other real and financial decisions. (Conditions 1 and 2 can be relaxed within the Q framework [Chirinko and Fazzari, 1988]; condition 4 is examined in section 4.) The derivation of equation (17) is obtained by multiplying the first-order conditions by the arguments with which they are differentiated, summing them together, using Euler's Theorem on Homogeneous Functions, discounting by $R_{t,s}$, summing over s from t to ∞, and rearranging to obtain $V_{t-1} = E_t \{ \Sigma R_{t,s} (\lambda_s K_s - \Lambda_s I_s) \}$, $s = t, \infty$). Using equation (6), $V_{t-1} = E_t \{ \Sigma R_{t,s} \lambda_s K_{t,s} \}$, which can be rewritten with equation (5) as $V_{t-1} = E_t \{ \Lambda_t K_{t-1} \}$, leading directly to equations (16) and (17) in the text.

[19] A further advantage of the formal approach for econometric work is that the error term can follow explicitly from the theory.

ated with the second, or tenth, installation likely to be more extensive than those associated with with the first? For a wide variety of circumstances, the answer is likely to be no, hence rejecting the convexity assumption essential for generating smooth transitional dynamics. An alternative and more plausible assumption is to posit a rising supply price of capital goods (i.e., external adjustment costs) that were also introduced formally by Eisner and Strotz (1963) and, per the above quotation, are very much in the spirit of Keynes' short-run analysis.[20] Such an assumption describes in a reasonable way the behavior of a monopsonistic firm or the collective behavior of a set of competitive firms, which, while having no effect individually on factor markets, anticipate a rising supply price because all firms react to similar demand stimuli.

The rising supply price is incorporated into the basic model, equation (7), by allowing the relative price of investment goods to depend positively on investment, $p'_t[I_t]$, and leads to only one modification to the conditions characterizing firm behavior developed in section 1:

(18a) $$L_t : \quad p_t^L = F_L[L_t, K_t];$$

(18b) $$K_t : \quad \lambda_t = F_K[L_t, K_t];$$

(18c) $$I_t : \quad \Lambda_t = p_t^I(1 + \beta);$$

(18d) $$\beta \equiv (dp_t^I[I_t]/p_t^I)/(dI_t/I_t) \geq 0.$$

As shown in equation (18c), the rising supply schedule of capital goods increases the marginal cost of investing by the supply elasticity, β, defined in equation (18d).

Paralleling the derivation in section 2 (see n. 18), we obtain the following investment specification:

(19a)

$$I_t/K_{t-1} = (1/\beta)(Q'_{t-1} - \beta) - E_t\left\{\sum_{s=t+1}^{\infty}(R_{t,s}/R_{t,t})(p_s^I I_s/p_t^I K_{t-1})\right\} + u_t,$$

(19b)

---

[20] See Mussa (1977) for further discussion of external and internal adjustment costs, and Rothschild (1971) for a critical examination of the convexity assumption in the latter formulation.

$$Q'_{t-1} \equiv (V_{t-1}/R_{t,t} - p_t^I K_{t-1})/p_t^I K_{t-1}.$$

Relative to the equation in section 2, there is a minor change in the definition of Q'_{t-1}, which is now divided by the relative price of investment goods and stated in equation (19a) as a deviation from β, and a somewhat more important change in that the coefficient on the Q variable is now the inverse of the supply elasticity. Of much more consequence, this specification now contains a long distributed *lead* of expected future investment expenditures, relative to the replacement value of the current capital stock.[21]

To understand the intuition underlying this model, consider the following reformulation of the information in equations (19a–b) as the difference between the marginal (Λ_t) and average valuations ($(V_{t-1}/R_{t,t})/K_{t-1}$) of capital,

(20)
$$\Lambda_t - (V_{t-1}/R_{t,t})/K_{t-1} = -\beta E_t \left\{ \sum_{s=t}^{\infty} (R_{t,s}/R_{t,t}) p_s^I I_s/K_{t-1}) \right\} \leq 0.$$

When $\beta = 0$, the wedge between marginal and average valuations disappears, and there is no impediment for the firm in obtaining any capital stock instantaneously. With an imperfectly competitive factor market, the marginal valuation of capital is less than its average valuation by the discounted sum, which represents the extra costs due to the discrepancy between upward-sloping and perfectly horizontal supply schedules. Thus, the substitution of external for internal adjustment costs results in a major change in specification. In contrast to equation (17), quantity variables enter this version of the investment function of Keynes.

4. The investment function of Keynes—finance constraints

> [A] second type of risk is relevant which we may call the lender's risk. This may be due either to moral hazard . . . or to the possible insufficiency of the margin of security . . . [Lender's risk] is a pure addition to the cost of investment which would not exist if the borrower and the lender were the same person. [Keynes, 1936, p. 144]

A principal theme in much Post Keynesian analysis is the critical role of liquidity in affecting the investment decision. As indicated in the

---

[21] If the discount rate, r_t, is assumed constant, then $R_{t,s}/R_{t,t} = (1+r)^{-(s-t)}$, and the distributed lead declines geometrically.

above quotation and emphasized in much recent mainstream literature, information problems between borrowers and lenders create an impediment to investing that may vary cyclically and be a major contributor to economic fluctuations.[22] But to what extent do finance constraints influence investment spending when the firm is optimizing? How do finance constraints interact with forward-looking behavior by the firm? Do these constraints imply that investment is sensitive to the stock of liquid assets, the flow of liquidity or availability of internal funds, both, or neither? While the modeling of finance constraints is itself a delicate matter and subject to a number of representations, this section considers a rather simple set of financial market frictions that capture some of the primary ideas discussed in both mainstream and Post Keynesian literatures.

The key idea in many studies is that there exists a differential between the costs of internal and external finance, a differential that would vanish "if the borrower and the lender were the same person." In this model, the former equals the firm's discount rate (r_t). The rate on external finance (i_t) may be sensitive to real and financial decisions because of actual and expected costs arising from financial distress that reduce payouts to creditors. In the extreme case of bankruptcy, there will be direct costs with settling claims and, more importantly, indirect costs associated with managing a company that is being reorganized or liquidated. Ceteris paribus, the smaller the stock of liquid assets and the larger the stock of external liabilities on the balance sheet, the higher the premium required by suppliers of financial capital. Given the hierarchical structure of claims on the firm's resources, agency considerations will tempt managers to pass up projects with positive net present values, adopt payout policies unfavorable to bondholders, or undertake adventurous, all-or-nothing investment policies (Jensen and Meckling, 1976; Myers, 1977). These problems become particularly acute when the firm is in distressed circumstances, and are thus related to balance sheet variables (Bernanke and Gertler, 1989; Gertler and Hubbard, 1988). The cost of external finance will be raised by information asymmetries between the firm and suppliers of financial capital, and will be sensitive to the structure of the balance sheet (Leland and Pyle, 1977; Myers and Majluf, 1984; Fazzari, 1992). Lastly, adverse selection

---

[22] See the surveys by Gertler (1988) and Stiglitz (1992) and the papers collected in Hubbard (1990) for some of the references to the mainstream literature, and the papers contained in Fazzari and Papadimitriou (1992) for a discussion of and references to the Post Keynesian perspective.

problems that affect lenders in credit markets may be partially resolved by collateralizable assets.[23] In light of these considerations, the cost of external finance is related generally to the flow of new external finance (b_t) and the stocks of external finance (B_t) and liquid assets (W_t), as well as exogenous characteristics (X_t) that may fluctuate through time:

(21)
$$i_t = i\,[b_t\,,B_t\,,W_t:r_t\,,X_t\,]\,,$$
$$\quad\; +\;\; +\;\; -\;\; +\;\; ?$$

where the signs below the arguments in $i[.]$ indicate the anticipated effects.

For expositional simplicity, we assume that $i[.]$ is homogeneous of degree zero in all arguments, although the model can be analyzed with more general assumptions. This simplifying assumption has the additional advantage of removing the effects of firm size on i_t, thus allowing for a focus on information problems as the critical factor raising the cost of external finance above that of internal finance. Of course, many of the factors influencing external finance are omitted in equation (21) (e.g., the effects of K_t as collateral), but could be incorporated in a more elaborate model. Rather than represent a large number of interactions, equation (21) is meant to capture in a tractable and plausible manner the relations among observable variables, information problems, and the differential between the costs of internal and external finance stemming from problems of asymmetric information.

A final element in this model is the identity linking investment in fixed capital $(p_t^I I_t)$ to the flow of external funds (b_t) and internal funds, where the latter equals retained earnings (e_t) less additions to the stock of liquid assets (w_t):

(22)
$$p_t^I I_t = b_t + (e_t - w_t)\,.$$

The conditions characterizing optimal behavior are computed by augmenting equation (7) with the following terms and additional constraints on the stocks of external finance and liquid assets, and thus yield the following Lagrangian:

[23] Adverse selection problems have been emphasized by Stiglitz and Weiss (1981). Bester (1985) has shown how collateral can resolve the information problems in the Stiglitz–Weiss model.

(23)
$$LG_t = E_t \{ \sum_{s=t}^{\infty} R_{t,s} \{ F[L_s,K_s] - p_s^L L_s - p_s^I I_s$$

$$- i[b_s,B_s,W_s:r_s,X_s] B_s + b_s + j_s W_s - w_s$$

$$- \lambda_s K_s + \Lambda_s I_s + \lambda_s K_{t,s}$$

$$+ \varphi_s B_s - \Phi_s b_s - \varphi_s B_{t,s}$$

$$- \psi_s W_s + \Psi_s w_s + \psi_s W_{t,s} \} \} .$$

where j_s is the exogenous interest rate on liquid assets, and Φ_s and Ψ_s are defined analogously to equation (8d) with $\delta = 0$. The conditions characterizing optimal behavior are obtained by differentiating equation (23) with respect to the flow and stock variables,

(24a)
$$L_t: \quad p_t^L = F_L[L_t,K_t] \, ;$$

(24b)
$$K_t: \quad \lambda_t = F_K[L_t,K_t] \, ;$$

(24c)
$$I_t: \quad \Lambda_t = p_t^I \, ;$$

(24d)
$$B_t: \quad \varphi_t = i_t + i_B[b_t,B_t,W_t:r_t,X_t] B_t \, ;$$

(24e)
$$b_t: \quad \Phi_t = 1 - i_b[b_t,B_t,W_t:r_t,X_t] B_t \, ;$$

(24f)
$$W_t: \quad \psi_t = j_t - i_W[b_t,B_t,W_t:r_t,X_t] B_t \, ;$$

(24g)
$$w_t: \quad \Psi_t = 1 \, .$$

The costs and benefits of marginal variations in real and financial variables are defined by Λ_t, Φ_t, and Ψ_t (see equation (8d)) and the first-order conditions (equation (24)), which constrain them to be equal along an optimal path. For external liabilities, marginal costs *in a given period* are defined by φt (equation (24d)), and depend on the external financing rate (i_t) and the deleterious effect on external finance costs ($i_B[.]$). The marginal costs are accumulated over the planning horizon, are represented by Φ_t, and are equated to marginal benefits, defined by equation (24e) as the proceeds of the issue less the sunk flotation costs associated with $i_b[.]$.

For liquid assets, marginal benefits *in a given period* are defined by ψ_t (equation (24f)), and depend on the interest rate (j_t) and the salutary effect on external finance costs $(i_W[.])$. The marginal benefits are accumulated over the planning horizon, are represented by Ψ_t, and are equated to marginal costs, defined by equation (24g) as the purchase cost. In contrast to external liabilities, there are no sunk costs with acquiring liquid assets.

We examine two variants of this finance constraints model. First, assume that the rate on external finance is sensitive to liquid assets and outstanding liabilities, but is insensitive to the amount of new debt issued. In this case, we obtain the following surprising result in which investment is absent:

(25a) $$0 = Q''_{t-1} + u_t.$$

(25b) $$Q''_{t-1} \equiv (V_{t-1}/R_{t,t} + B_{t-1} - W_{t-1} - p_t^I K_{t-1})/K_{t-1}.$$

Even though finance constraints impinge on the firm, equation (25a) contains only Q''_{t-1}, which is a forward-looking variable capturing the ramifications of all of the firm's decisions. Not only does Q''_{t-1} represent profitable opportunities in physical investment, but it also capitalizes the impact of finance constraints. As defined in equation (25b), Q''_{t-1} is the net financial value of the firm less the replacement value of its assets and liabilities. Differences between these two valuations are due only to the sunk costs already incurred when bringing physical or financial capital inside the firm. When new debt issues do not lead to any additional capital market frictions, the sunk costs vanish. With Q''_{t-1} as a regressor and linear homogeneity in the external financing technology, there is no scope for investment nor liquidity variables in the Q investment equation. Since there are no transitional dynamics impeding the firm, any desired level of capital can be attained instantaneously (see n. 10 for the Jorgensonian model), and Q''_{t-1} will equal zero (apart from random fluctuations due to the error term).

The second variant of the liquidity model recognizes the possibility that the rate of external finance is affected by b_t. Following the specification of adjustment cost technology, we assume that cost of external finance is quadratic in b_t, which is stated relative to B_t, and separable from the other arguments,

(26) $\quad i\,[b_t\,,B_t\,,W_t:r_t\,,X_t\,] \;=\; (\gamma/2)\,b_t^2/B_t^2 + f\,[B_t\,,W_t:r_t\,,X_t\,]$.

With these assumptions (which can be thought of as second-order approximations to more complicated functions), we obtain the following investment specification[24]:

(27a) $\qquad\qquad I_t/K_{t-1} \;=\; (1/\gamma)\,Q''_{t-1} + LIQ_t + u_t\;;$

(27b) $\qquad\qquad LIQ_t \;\equiv\; (e_t - w_t\,)/p_t^I K_{t-1}\,,$

where LIQ_t is the flow of net internal finance.[25]

A comparison of equations (25) and (27) indicates the substantial differences that can occur with a seemingly small change in the underlying assumptions. In the former model without sunk costs, we are unable to obtain an investment function. Thus, information problems do not necessarily lead to a relation between investment and a measure of liquidity in this version of the investment function of Keynes. Alternatively, when sunk costs affect financing, liquidity enters equation (27) by lowering external finance requirements and the associated sunk costs and, ceteris paribus, has a positive effect on investment. Quantity variables reemerge in this version of the investment function of Keynes.

5. Perspectives on the symposium

The "neoclassical" investment model found in mainstream work has been subjected to much searching criticism in the Post Keynesian literature, most recently in the symposium papers appearing earlier in this volume.

[24] Note that the coefficient on LIQ_t is constrained to be unity. By combining finance constraints with the dynamics from one of the other models, unconstrained coefficients would appear on all regressors.

[25] In equation (27a), Q''_{t-1} should be multiplied by (B_t/B_{t-1}) because of a timing convention. If the stock of external finance affected i_t in equation (21) at the beginning of the period (i.e., entered with a lag), then the correction vanishes. While this timing convention is more plausible, it has not been used here because it introduces additional notation in equation (24).

While the definition of the "neoclassical" model varies greatly,[26] the formal framework that is the basis for the models developed in sections 2 through 4 would most certainly be classified as "neoclassical." Nonetheless, I believe that there is very little distance between this framework and the challenges raised by Gordon, Vickers, Fried, and Crotty. To draw out these connections in a manageable way, I focus on only four of the central issues presumably separating "neoclassical"/mainstream from Post Keynesian approaches.

Financial decisions

A great deal of concern has been expressed about the lack of attention given financing issues in mainstream models. The fourth point raised by Gordon focuses on the sensitivity of the value of the firm to dividend policy, which determines whether internal or external funds will be used to finance investment. Gordon notes that "transaction costs involved in a new share issue are substantially higher than the costs involved in retaining earnings" (p. 11). This is precisely the structure imposed in equation (21), where the cost of external finance is positively related to the flow of new issues. Similar concerns with financial decisions are shared by Vickers in his fifth proposition, which states that "investment expenditures are subject not to a savings constraint but to a financing constraint" (p. 36). One way of imbedding such a constraint in an formal framework has been presented in equation (22). As demonstrated in section 4, such concerns in no way undermine "neoclassical"/mainstream models.

The approach taken here is very similar to that of Fried. His essay speaks of implicit prices and frictions (p. 57), concepts represented in the model of section 4 as Φ_t and $i_b[.]$. While Fried's model in chapter 3 differs from that in section 4 in several important respects, both models are based on explicit specification of the environment in which firms operate. Fried conjectures that "incorporating transaction costs and/or rationing would imply that retained earnings will appear to be a signif-

---

[26] One possible definition of a "neoclassical" model is that the benefits and costs facing the decision maker are equated along one or more margins. These margins need not be derived explicitly from an optimization problem, but such a formal analysis is likely to be very useful given the infirmity of intuitions and the vagueness of definitions that are likely to arise otherwise. The "neoclassical" model is sometimes viewed in a rather narrow light, being associated with perfect competition, perfect foresight, and markets that clear instantaneously to their long-run equilibrium. Sections 2 through 4 demonstrate that "neoclassical" models can be derived under more general assumptions.

icant determinant of investment"(p. 58). This conjecture is confirmed by the investment function of Keynes presented in equation (27).

Inappropriate objectives for the firm

The objective functions used in mainstream models are also criticized in the symposium. In his first point, Gordon argues that firms, like individuals, should be thought of as portfolio investors, and hence wealth maximization should be replaced by utility maximization. Clearly, there is nothing in the general optimization framework developed in section 1 that precludes alternative objective functions. Wealth maximization depicted in equation (3) could be replaced by the maximization of an expected utility functional defined with respect to profits or some other variables of interest. The expected utility model is subject to some important qualifications, and it might prove useful to utilize an objective function based on "linearized higher moments" developed by Allais (1952, 1984) and used recently in the study of equity premium puzzles by Golob (1992). Sufficient flexibility exists in the formal framework employed by mainstream economists to accommodate a wide variety of objective functions representing various aspects of economic behavior.

Furthermore, in his second point, Gordon emphasizes that the firm's managers may be the relevant decision makers, and their objective is long-run survival, rather than value maximization. In a similar vein, Crotty argues that "the essence of management's decision-making dilemma is that, at the margin, it confronts a *growth–safety trade-off*" (p. 70). One way to change the model to meet these concerns would be to allow the exogenous output price to follow a random walk,[27] and thus, with probability one, prices will eventually fall so low that the firm will fail. In this model and with the addition of a growth (or profit) constraint, the managers of the firm would choose real and financial policies to maximize the time until failure. The characteristics of these optimal policies remain to be determined. But it is clear that the formal framework is quite adaptable and can accommodate a number of the concerns noted in the Post Keynesian literature.

Ahistoric investment opportunities

An interesting critique, advanced by Gordon as point five, is that mainstream models are deficient in assuming that "the investment

---

[27] See Abel (1983) for the relation between investment and Marginal Q (Λ_t / p^I_t) when output price is a random walk.

opportunities available to a corporation are independent of its history"
(p. 14). Crotty concludes his essay by calling for a Keynesian investment
theory that is *"institutionally specific and historically contingent"* (p.
73). It is straightforward to cast this "path dependence" into a formal
framework by introducing additional state variables (like K_t in equation
(2)) that reflect history and affect the position of the demand schedule.
These state variables can be as complicated as the situation demands,
and can include previous levels of research and development, advertising, sales, or other devices by which the firm might secure market
share.[28] That mainstream investment models have usually omitted the
effects of history on the firm's demand schedule is not a fundamental
deficiency with the analytic apparatus.

Quantifiable risk versus fundamental uncertainty

The modeling of the unknown, and perhaps unknowable, future is the
final concern treated here. This issue is raised by Vickers in his second
point: "The uncertainties that exist in a real-time economy . . . induce
also a recognition of the ignorance in which the human condition and
accordingly economic decision making are bound" (p. 29).[29] As in much
Post Keynesian analysis, the inherent instability of the economy inval-
idates the use of objective or subjective probabilities for describing a
risky situation. Even these extreme circumstances do not undermine the
formal modeling approach. In the models presented here, the $E_t\{.\}$
operator simply refers to the firm's "best guesses" based on available
information, "guesses" that are surely formed notwithstanding the properties or existence of an underlying stochastic structure. A marked
advantage of the models developed in sections 2 through 4 is that all of
the relevant information about future expectations is imbedded in Q.
Instability in expectations will be reflected in instability in Q, not in the
parameters defining the investment function.[30]

[28] It may also be useful to allow the firm to face a downward-sloping demand curve.
Thus, in a given period, prior investment and advertising decisions could determine
the position of the firm's demand schedule, and current pricing decisions could affect
the point at which the firm operates.

[29] Crotty emphasizes (p. 68) that it may be important to focus on higher moments of
the distribution of expected future returns. See Abel (1983) for a model that incorporates both the mean and variance of this distribution, and Chirinko (1993, section
V.C) for references to the literature.

[30] Difficulties may arise in the model with a rising supply price of capital goods because of the presence of the forward-sum in equation (19a). Estimation would pro-

In sum, some of the major criticisms of the "neoclassical"/mainstream model raised in this Post Keynesian symposium can be brought into the formal framework with some additional effort. While not all Post Keynesian concerns have been addressed in this section, the results presented here should, at the least, suggest the possibility for a fruitful exchange between Post Keynesian and mainstream approaches.

6. Summary and epilog

> In order to be able with any safety to interpret economic facts, whether of the past or present time, we must know what kind of effects to expect from each cause and how these effects are likely to combine with one another. This is the knowledge which is got by the study of economic science; while, on the other hand, the growth of the science is itself chiefly dependent on the careful study of facts by the aid of this knowledge. [Marshall, 1885, p. 168]

> Experience has shown that each of these three view-points, that of statistics, economic theory, and mathematics, is a necessary, but not by itself a sufficient, condition for a real understanding of the quantitative relations in modern economic life. It is the *unification* of all three that is powerful. And it is this unification that constitutes econometrics. [Frisch, 1933, p. 2]

This essay has contended that the gap between Post Keynesian and mainstream approaches toward investment behavior is modest. We began by noting that, while dynamics have been taken seriously in Post Keynesian work, they have not been analyzed appropriately. This problem has led to a major discrepancy between the Keynesian investment function—with quantity variables dominating price variables as the primary determinants of investment—and the investment functions of Keynes—based on Keynesian dynamics that impinge on the firm. It has been argued that, in order to understand the fundamental aspects of investment behavior, attention should be focused on the restrictions

---

ceed by quasi-forward differencing equation (19a) so as to eliminate all but the current term in the sum (see Chirinko and Fazzari, 1988). This transformed specification would contain I_{t+1} / K_{t+1} and Q'_t as regressors, which would have to be "forecasted" with a set of instrumental variables. The relation between instrumental variables and these regressors could be affected by the instability due to fundamental uncertainty but, since the forecast horizon is only one period, instability may not prove to be of great moment.

posed by the economic environment and the ways in which firms respond to these restrictions (e.g., expectations, finance constraints, transitional dynamics).[31] As illustrated throughout this study, the implications for investment can be quite subtle, and should be derived formally. While not absolutely required, a formal optimization framework is likely to be very useful given difficulties in analyzing dynamic economic phenomena and drawing relations to fundamental aspects of investment behavior. This approach is not incompatible with some prominent Post Keynesian ideas, and the friendly relations between formal frameworks and several of the concerns expressed in the symposium papers have been highlighted. Based on dynamics arising from internal adjustment costs, a rising supply price of capital goods, and finance constraints, the following four econometric relations have been developed:

Internal adjustment costs

(28a) $$I_t/K_t = (1/\alpha)\, Q_{t-1} + u_t\,;$$

Rising supply price of capital goods

(28b)
$$I_t/K_{t-1} = (1/\beta)\, (Q'_{t-1} - \beta) - E_t\Big\{ \sum_{s=t+1}^{\infty} (R_{t,s}/R_{t,t})\, (p_s^I I_s / p_t^I K_{t-1}) \Big\} + u_t\,;$$

Finance constraints (i_t insensitive to new issues)

(28c) $$0 = Q''_{t-1} + u_t\,;$$

Finance constraints (i_t sensitive to new issues)

(28d) $$I_t/K_{t-1} = (1/\gamma)\, Q''_{t-1} + LIQ_t + u_t\,,$$

where Q_{t-1}, Q'_{t-1}, and Q''_{t-1} have been defined in equations (16), (19b),

---

[31] Some Post Keynesian work is not too distant from this focus on constrained optimization problems. In his preferred Keynesian model, Crotty states that "A realistic theory of investment should incorporate the assumption that the firm is a semiautonomous agent with a preference function of its own" (p. 69). Fried examines the effects of incomplete financial markets in a formal overlapping generations model. Fazzari (1992) concludes that "The debate has focused, correctly in my view, on the environment in which optimization occurs" (p. 128).

and (25b), respectively. As is clear from equation (28), the determinants of investment and the relative roles of quantity and price variables vary greatly depending on the Keynesian dynamics entertained in the optimization problem.

Given the several investment functions associated with Keynesian dynamics, and many more that would follow from non-Keynesian considerations, how are we to discover which elements are essential for understanding investment behavior? The search for an answer must begin with formal theory, which is essential for knowing, as Marshall (1966) wrote, "what kind of effects to expect from each cause and how these effects are likely to combine with one another" (p. 37). While theory is critical for determining the appropriate specification of investment functions, it is silent in discriminating among the various models. To obtain a more precise understanding of investment behavior, we must unify the viewpoints "of statistics, economic theory, and mathematics" by carefully examining the data with econometric equations based on formal optimization.

What are the advantages of such an approach? Working within formal frameworks provides an effective disciplining device that forces a consistent and clear treatment of the issues relevant to firm behavior. At only a theoretical level, however, this discipline is incomplete because a large number of theoretically correct models can be constructed. Econometric models of the firm derived from formal optimization problems and confronted with data provide a means for conducting a *disciplined discourse* that generates productively debatable results and uncovers meaningful answers. The discipline imposed by these models is especially important in the face of severe limitations with the data and the lack of critical experiments. Without some guidance from theory, noisy nonexperimental data are generally insufficient to discriminate among competing hypotheses of economic interest. While formal econometric models may not produce high R^2's relative to distributed lag investment equations and may fail specification tests, they lead to a systematic accumulation of interpretable evidence, and are the preferred vehicle for furthering our knowledge of economic behavior.

The formal approach advocated here may strike some as inappropri-

---

[32] See Summers (1991). Deriving econometric specifications from formal models in no way implies that the equations must be evaluated only by formal statistical tests. While such tests are informative, other considerations—the economic implications of the parameters, the sensitivity of the empirical results to variations in economic and statistical assumptions, and relations among the residuals, the individual instruments, and economic events—can and should be examined.

ate.[32] It may be objected that optimization problems—formulated in this article or elsewhere—will always fail to reflect relevant aspects of economic behavior. Such an objection would be puzzling, since the mathematical and econometric tools are very flexible and can accommodate a wide variety of assumptions. If the economic "reality" under discussion is too complex to be represented formally, then, especially insofar as models are meant to distill the essential aspects of "reality," the ideas themselves may need to be more carefully scrutinized. Keynes was particularly strident about the limitations of mathematical models, claiming that they are "mere concoctions, as imprecise as the initial assumptions they rest on, which allow the author to lose sight of the complexities and interdependencies of the real world in a maze of pretentious and unhelpful symbols" (Keynes, 1936, p. 298). This statement is most certainly wide of the mark. It is precisely the "complexities and interdependencies" uncovered in a formal framework that serve to expose intricate interactions hidden from unaided intuition. The surprising results presented in equations (28a–d) exemplify how formal models can reveal subtle effects and the delicate relations between assumptions and implications.

Are we all Post Keynesians now? While this statement is quite a bit premature, it is hoped that this essay will eliminate the discussion of nonessential differences and stimulate the scrutiny of substantive differences in need of more formal theoretical and empirical investigation.

REFERENCES

Abel, A.B. "Optimal Investment Under Uncertainty." *American Economic Review*, March 1983, *73*, 228–233.

Allais, M. "Fondements d'une Théorie Positive des Choix Comportant un Risque et Critique des Postulats et Axiomes de l'Ecole Américaine." In Econométrie, Colloques Internationaux du Centre National de la Recherche Scientifique, vol. 40, Paris, pp. 257–332. [Trans. as "The Foundations of a Positive Theory of Choice Involving Risk and a Criticism of the American School," in M. Allais and O. Hagen (eds.), *Expected Utility Hypotheses and the Allais Paradox* (Dordrecht: Reidel, 1979), pp. 27–145.]

———. "The Foundations of the Theory of Utility and Risk." In O. Hagen and F. Wenstop (eds.), *Progress in Utility and Risk Theory*. Dordrecht: Reidel, 1984.

Bernanke, B.S., and Blinder, A.S. "Credit, Money, and Aggregate Demand." *American Economic Review*, May 1988, *78*, 435–439.

Bernanke, B.S., and Gertler, M. "Agency Costs, Net Worth, and Business Fluctuations." *American Economic Review*, March 1989, *79*, 14–31.

Bester, H. "Screening vs. Rationing in Credit Markets with Imperfect Information." *American Economic Review*, September 1985, *75*, 850–855.

Blanchard, O.J., and Summers, L.H. "Hysteresis and the European Unemployment Problem." In Stanley Fischer (ed.), *NBER Macroeconomics Annual 1989.* Cambridge, MA: MIT Press, 1986, pp. 1–77.

Brainard, W.C., and Tobin, James. "Pitfalls in Financial Model Building." *American Economic Review,* May 1968, *58,* 99–122.

Chirinko, R.S. "Business Fixed Investment Spending: Modeling Strategies, Empirical Results, and Policy Implications." *Journal of Economic Literature,* 1993, forthcoming. [An extended version of this survey is available as *Center For Economic Studies* (University of Munich) Working Paper No. 27 (November 1992) and Federal Reserve Bank of Kansas City Research Working Paper No. RWP93–01 (February 1993).]

Chirinko, R.S., and Fazzari, S.M. "Tobin's *Q,* Non-Constant Returns to Scale, and Imperfectly Competitive Product Markets." *Recherches Economiques de Louvain,* September 1988, *54,* 259–275.

Coen, R.M. "Tax Policy and Investment Behavior: Comment." *American Economic Review,* June 1969, *59,* 370–379.

Coen, R.M., and Eisner, R. "Investment." In John Eatwell, Murray Milgate, and Peter Newman (eds.), *The New Palgrave: A Dictionary of Economics,* vol. 2. London: MacMillan Press, 1987, pp. 980–986.

Crotty, J.R. "Neoclassical and Keynesian Approaches to the Theory of Investment." *Journal of Post Keynesian Economics,* Summer 1992, *14* (4), 483–496. Chapter 4 of this volume.

Davidson, P. *Money and the Real World,* 2d ed. New York: John Wiley, 1978.

———. "Rational Expectations: A Fallacious Foundation for Studying Crucial Decision-Making Processes." *Journal of Post Keynesian Economics,* Winter 1982–83, *5,* 182–198.

Eichner, A.S., and Kregel, J.A. "An Essay on Post-Keynesian Theory: A New Paradigm in Economics." *Journal of Economic Literature,* December 1975, *13,* 1293–1314.

Eisner, R., and Nadiri, M. Ishaq. "Neoclassical Theory of Investment Behavior: A Comment." *Review of Economics and Statistics,* May 1970, *52,* 216–222.

Eisner, R., and Strotz, R.H. "Determinants of Business Investment." In Commission on Money and Credit, *Impacts of Monetary Policy.* Englewood Cliffs, NJ: Prentice-Hall, 1963, pp. 60–337.

Fazzari, S.M. "Keynesian Theories of Investment and Finance: Neo, Post, and New." In Steven M. Fazzari and Dimitri B. Papadimitriou (eds.), *Financial Conditions and Macroeconomic Performance: Essays in Honor of Hyman Minsky.* Armonk, NY: M.E. Sharpe, 1992, pp. 121–132.

Fazzari, S.M., and Mott, T.L. "The Investment Theories of Kalecki and Keynes: An Empirical Study of Firm Data, 1970–1982." *Journal of Post Keynesian Economics,* Winter 1986–87, *9,* 171–187.

Fazzari, S.M., and Papadimitriou, D.B., eds. *Financial Conditions and Macroeconomic Performance: Essays in Honor of Hyman Minsky.* Armonk, NY: M.E. Sharpe, 1992.

Fried, J., "Financial Theory and the Theory of Investment." *Journal of Post Keynesian Economics,* Summer 1992, *14* (4), 465–481. Chapter 3 of this volume.

Frisch, R. "Founding Editorial." *Econometrica,* January 1933, *1,* 1–4.

Gertler, M. "Financial Structure and Aggregate Economic Activity: An Overview." *Journal of Money, Credit and Banking,* August 1988, *20,* pt 2, pp. 559–588.

Gertler, M., and Hubbard, R.G. "Financial Factors in Business Fluctuations." In *Financial Market Volatility*. Kansas City: Federal Reserve Bank of Kansas City, 1988, pp. 33–72.

Golob, J.E. "Allais Theory Suggests a Solution and an Explanation for the Equity Premium Puzzle." Federal Reserve Bank of Kansas City Research Working Paper 92–04, October 1992.

Gordon, M.J. "The Neoclassical and a Post Keynesian Theory of Investment." *Journal of Post Keynesian Economics*, Summer 1992, *14* (4), 425–443. Chapter 1 of this volume.

Haavelmo, T. *A Study in the Theory of Investment*. Chicago: University of Chicago Press, 1960.

Hall, R.E., and Jorgenson, D.W. "Tax Policy and Investment Behavior." *American Economic Review*, June 1967, *57*, 391–414.

Hayashi, F. "Tobin's Marginal q and Average q: A Neoclassical Interpretation." *Econometrica*, January 1982, *50*, 213–224.

Hubbard, R. G., ed. *Asymmetric Information, Corporate Finance, and Investment*. Chicago: University of Chicago Press (for NBER), 1990.

Jensen, M., and Meckling, W.H. "Theory of the Firm: Managerial Behavior, Agency Costs, and Ownership Structure." *Journal of Financial Economics*, October 1976, *3*, 305–360.

Jorgenson, D.W. "Capital Theory and Investment Behavior." *American Economic Review*, May 1963, *53*, 247–259.

———. "The Theory of Investment Behavior." In R. Ferber (ed.), *Determinants of Investment Behavior*. Universities-National Bureau Conference Series No. 18. New York: Columbia University Press, 1967, pp. 129–155.

Keynes, J.M. *The General Theory of Employment, Interest, and Money*. New York: Harcourt Brace, 1936.

Kleindorfer, G.B.; Kleindorfer, P.R.; and Thompson, G.L. "The Discrete Time Maximum Principle." In Charles Tapiero, *Managerial Planning: An Optimum and Stochastic Control Approach*, vol. 2. New York: Gordon and Breech Science Publishers, 1977, pp. 375–382.

Leijonhufvud, A. *On Keynesian Economics and the Economics of Keynes*. New York: Oxford, 1968.

Leland, H.E., and Pyle, D.H. "Informational Asymmetries, Financial Structure, and Financial Intermediation." *Journal of Finance*, May 1977, *32*, 371–388.

Lucas, R.E., Jr. "Econometric Policy Evaluation: A Critique." In Karl Brunner and Allan H. Meltzer (eds.), *The Phillips Curve and Labor Markets*. Amsterdam: North-Holland, 1976, pp. 19–46. [Reprinted in *Studies in Business Cycle Theory*. Cambridge, MA: MIT, 1981, pp. 104–130.]

Marshall, A. "The Present Position of Economics" [the 1885 inaugural lecture upon election to the professorship in Cambridge]. In A.C. Pigou (ed.), *Memorials of Alfred Marshall*. New York: Augustus M. Kelley, 1966, pp. 152–174.

Milberg, W., ed. *The Megacorp and Macrodynamics: Essays in Memory of Alfred Eichner*. Armonk, NY: M.E. Sharpe, 1992.

Modigliani, F., and Miller, M.H. "The Cost of Capital, Corporation Finance and the Theory of Investment." *American Economic Review*, June 1958, *48*, 261–297.

Mussa, M. "External and Internal Adjustment Costs and the Theory of Aggregate and Firm Investment." *Economica*, May 1977, *44*, 153–178.

Myers, S.C. "Determinants of Corporate Borrowing." *Journal of Financial Economics*, November 1977, *5*, 147–175.

Myers, S.C., and Majluf, N.S. "Corporate Financing and Investment Decisions When Firms Have Information that Investors Do Not Have." *Journal of Financial Economics*, June 1984, *13*, 187–221.

Rothschild, M. "On the Cost of Adjustment." *Quarterly Journal of Economics*, November 1971, *85*, 605–622.

Stiglitz, J.E. "Capital Markets and Economic Fluctuations in Capitalist Economies." *European Economic Review*, April 1992, *36*, 269–306.

Stiglitz, J.E., and Weiss, A. "Credit Rationing in Markets with Imperfect Information." *American Economic Review*, June 1981, *71*, 393–410.

Summers, L.H. "The Scientific Illusion in Empirical Macroeconomics." In Svend Hylleberg and Martin Paldam (eds.), *New Approaches to Empirical Macroeconomics*. Oxford: Blackwell, 1991, pp. 1–20.

Tobin, J. "A General Equilibrium Approach to Monetary Theory." *Journal of Money, Credit, and Banking*, February 1969, *1*, 15–29.

Tobin, J. "Monetary Policies and the Economy: The Transmission Mechanism." *Southern Economic Journal*, January 1978, *44*, 421–431.

Vickers, D. "The Investment Function: Five Propositions in Response to Professor Gordon." *Journal of Post Keynesian Economics*, Summer 1992, *14* (4), 445–464. Chapter 2 of this volume.

Weitzman, M.L., and Schmidt, Alexander G. "The Maximum Principle for Discrete Economic Processes on an Infinite Time Interval." *Kibernetika*, 1971, *5*, 22–35.

Witte, J.G., Jr. "The Microfoundations of the Social Investment Function." *Journal of Political Economy*, October 1963, *71*, 441–456.

8

The user cost of fixed capital in Keynes' theory of investment

JOHAN DEPREZ

"It is by reason," wrote Keynes, "of the existence of durable equipment that the economic future is linked to the present" (1964, p. 146). It was Keynes' opinion that by "the introduction of the concepts of user cost and of the marginal efficiency of capital" one could go beyond the limits of the static nature of classical economics and effectively model the intertemporal aspects of fixed capital and the expectations that surround it "whilst reducing to a minimum the necessary degree of adaption" from the classical theory (1964, p. 146).

User cost is the opportunity cost of currently engaging in production and the using of plant and equipment, as opposed to currently abstaining from production and leaving the fixed capital idle, measured in terms of the expected loss of discounted future profits. Such cost may be expected if current production negatively affects the future productivity of capital, increases the required replacement of capital equipment, negatively affects future expected sales, or increases the cost of future inputs. In the real world where firms face an uncertain future in terms of sales, costs, technological change, and new products, user cost is a pervasive consideration affecting the production and investment decisions of firms.

The emphasis in the literature has generally been on the concept of the marginal efficiency of capital to the neglect of the concept of user cost. This is the way in which Keynes' model is characterized by most textbooks (see Peterson and Estenson, 1992, pp. 303–320). Traditional expositions of Keynes' General Theory,[1] like Hansen's (1953, pp.

The author is an Assistant Professor in the College of Business Administration at Alabama State University.

[1] Following Robinson (1960, p. 134),this does "not mean simply the book called *The General Theory of Employment, Interest, and Money*, but the whole stream of ideas, or rather the analytical system, to which that book made the main contribution,

56–58), have trivialized the role of user cost. Post Keynesian expositions of Keynes' aggregate supply and demand model have tended to ignore the concept completely (see Weintraub, 1957; Davidson and Smolensky, 1964; Wells, 1977)[2] or only mention user cost in passing (see Weintraub, 1958; Casarosa, 1981; Asimakopulos, 1991).

Even those few who point to the importance of Keynes' user cost concept and the need to integrate it explicitly into Keynes' macroeconomic model (see Davidson, 1991b, pp. 139–143) have not carried out this task. The purpose of this article is to make a contribution toward the explicit inclusion of user cost into Keynes' macroeconomic model. Specifically, it seeks to analyze the role that user cost plays in the supply and demand of capital goods. The present study isolates the investment goods sector of Keynes' aggregate supply and demand model and looks at the impact that user cost has on the determination of the overall level of investment. The model of the demand and supply of capital goods that is provided by Davidson (1978, pp. 59–103) provides the basis for the present analysis.

It will be argued that Keynes' notion of user cost plays a crucial role in the determination of the quantity of capital goods purchased and the price at which they are purchased. Given the centrality of investment in Keynes' General Theory, this influence translates into an overall impact on employment, income, and output. Furthermore, the user cost impact on investment has an effect on the rate of capital accumulation and on the future supply possibilities. The inclusion of user cost also opens Keynes' model up to certain considerations linked to technological change. Contrary to what is all too often implied, user cost is not some trivial curiosum. Hence, a full-blown version of Keynes' theory of investment needs to incorporate user cost explicitly. The same must be said of all Post Keynesian extensions of this theory of investment.

The supply and demand of capital goods

Keynes' General Theory is explicitly a *monetary theory of production*, as opposed to a theory set in a real-exchange economy (CWJMK, 13, pp. 408–411).[3] The

---

but which is still in process of developing and perfecting itself, finding new applications and modifying its methods to treat new problems."

[2] Weintraub (1968, pp. 378–381) earlier discussed the concept of user cost in his discussions on the firm, but failed to integrate it systematically into his macroeconomic formulations.

[3] References to Keynes' *Collected Writings* (1971–83) are indicated by CWJMK followed by a volume number.

embracing of this distinction was an important step for Keynes in the process of developing the General Theory, as is illustrated by his lectures in the 1930s (see Rymes, 1989, pp. 93–95). The adoption of the monetary production economy as the appropriate context of analysis is also a fundamental theoretical pillar for Post Keynesian economics (see Dillard, 1954; Davidson, 1991a, pp. 389–407).

The monetary production economy highlights certain special characteristics that are too often left out of economic theory. In this context the prime purpose of the economic activity of the capitalist firm is the search for monetary profit. The production processes that such firms employ are also seen to take real calendar time. This means that short-term expectations need to be formed in order to the determine the optimal amounts to be produced and the quantities of labor and nonlabor inputs that need to be hired in advance of both this production process and the sale of the final output (Keynes, 1964, pp. 46–51). The explicit incorporation of fixed capital brings to the fore another time element in that this capital input to the production process is used for many consecutive production periods and "earns" profits over all these periods.[4] The recognition of fixed capital and its role over many periods leads Keynes to bring in the concept of long-term expectations (1964, pp. 147–164) and to introduce the notion of user cost (1964, pp. 53–59, 66–73).

The monetary production economy is also an economy that directly incorporates the existence of money, financial assets, and monetary and financial institutions. The logical existence of these characteristics is predicated on the existence of true uncertainty—uncertainty that is not reducible to objective probability distributions. In other words, we are dealing with a nonergodic world (see Davidson, 1991b, pp. 159–192). This type of economy is also a money-wage economy and one in which all different types of contracts denominated in terms of money are important. Liquidity considerations are prevalent in this system. Money primarily enters the economy via the production process and "is not created like the manna from heaven of a Patinkinesque world or dropped by helicopter as in Friedman's construction" (Davidson, 1978, p. 147). In order to meet the costs of the working or circulating capital and the direct labor requirements of the firms and to finance the creation of fixed capital, debt contracts and monetary commitments are entered into.

---

[4] For Keynes (CWJMK, 5, p. 116), "working capital is necessary because some goods take time to produce and fixed capital is necessary because some goods take time to use or consume."

Out of these characteristics of the monetary production economy arises the Post Keynesian view of investment as being determined by the supply and demand of capital goods (see Davidson, 1978, 59–103).[5] Crucial here is the separation between the supply and demand of capital goods and the supply and demand for placements—the titles to capital goods. In a monetary production economy, capital goods exist with the main purpose of producing output that is foreseen to be sold for monetary profit. New placements are sold by firms in order to fund expenditures and are held and bought and sold by economic agents as a store of value. In an uncertain world, fixed capital goods, bought new or used, do not serve as an effective store of value because of their illiquid nature and the lack of organized markets. Placements have the liquidity and market characteristics that make them a useful store of value (Davidson, 1978, pp. 61–69).[6]

This approach stands in contradistinction to the classical approach which looks at investment as being determined by the supply and demand of savings. In the classical approach, the supply of savings is equated with the supply of capital and of capital goods. Similarly, investment demand is the demand for capital and for capital goods and is the same as demand for savings. In Keynes' approach saving is not a prerequisite for investment in any form (see CWJMK, 14, pp. 215–223). Nor is there a confusion between capital goods and financial assets. The supply and demand approach to capital goods ignores any significant store of value role for fixed capital. It in essence looks at the investment sector component of the aggregate supply and demand model of Keynes and thus implies a two-sector approach.

Davidson (1978, p. 61) takes the investment decision as "synonymous with the demand for fixed capital."[7] The supply of fixed capital is

---

[5] While the supply and demand of capital goods approach used here is derived from Davidson's work, it should be recognized that the notation has been altered and that there are some substantive alterations from the original in the current presentation and extension. Since the fundamental point of this article revolves around the question of user cost, little or no explanation and justification is given here for these substantive alterations.

[6] When a firm is looking for a profitable way to save its money to be used later—a store of value—it may buy stock in Apple Computers, but it will not buy computers made by Apple. If, on the other hand, this firm is looking for a way to increase its productivity in creating goods and services, then computers by Apple may do the trick, while shares in Apple Computers will be irrelevant.

[7] In other words, Davidson (1978, p. 60) points to the existence of working capital and liquid capital goods.

composed of a stock supply and a flow supply. For a particular universal production period, the stock supply is what exists at the beginning of this production period, time t, and the flow supply is what is produced during this production period and added to the inherited capital stock to end up with the total capital stock available to be used for production at the end of the current production period, time $t+1$, which is also the beginning of the next production period.

The stock supply of fixed capital is simply the quantity of fixed capital in existence at that point in time. This quantity is the cumulative result of investment decisions made at different points in the past. At the beginning of the universal production period in question, the stock supply of capital, $SS_{k,t}$, is the quantity of capital inherited from the past, K_t^s , and can be considered as a given quantity, K_0;

$$(1) \qquad\qquad SS_{k,t} = K_t^s = K_0 .$$

The flow supply of capital is simply the traditional short-period Marshallian supply schedule. Throughout this paper it is assumed that one is dealing with perfectly competitive conditions, so that there is no impact of the degree of monopoly on the supply price. Hence, this "flow supply schedule of capital goods indicates the output quantities which will be offered on the market by the capital-goods industry at alternative expected market prices" (Davidson, 1978, p. 75). Since production takes time, production takes place on the basis of the expected price of capital goods to be sold at the end of the production period, at time $t+1$, $P_{k,t+1}^e$. As usual, the quantity supplied is also a function of the technology employed, TECH, the money wage rate, W, and the spot price of capital at the beginning of the production period, $P_{k,t}$:

$$(2) \qquad FS_{k,t+1} = Q_{k,t+1}^s = f(P_{k,t+1}^e ; TECH ; W ; P_{k,t}) .$$

The partial derivatives with respect to the four variables mentioned carry the usual signs, positive for the expected output price, negative for the input costs, and positive for technological improvements.

The total supply of capital goods available at the end of the current production period (and the beginning of the next period) is the sum of the flow supply of newly produced capital goods plus the stock of capital goods inherited from the beginning of the production period:

$$(3) \qquad S_{k,\,t+1} = SS_{k,t} + FS_{k,t+1}$$

$$= K_t^s + Q_{k,t+1}^s$$

$$= K_0 + f\,(P_{k,t+1}^e\,;\,TECH\,;\,W\,;\,P_{k,t})\,.$$

A question no doubt jumps to mind: what about the depreciation of the capital stock that occurs over the production period? If, as is traditional, one believes that there is a particular fraction of the capital stock that automatically depreciates (by "evaporation"), then equation (3) can be modified to include this consideration.[8] This approach is rejected here in favor of the view that capital goods are replaced when they are deemed economically undesirable for further use in production. Depreciation charges are seen as essentially a financial concept that has no physical equivalent.[9] It is more accurate to see part of the capital stock as being replaced, rather than as disappearing due to use. Hence, depreciation considerations are left out on the supply side and replacement considerations are included on the demand side.

As was done with the supply part of the capital goods market, the demand for capital goods can also be separated into stock and flow demand schedules for capital goods. For each production period there is an optimal stock of capital that is desired by the firm, given its price expectations and its technology and labor cost. The stock demand for the production period in question depends on what firms feel their profits will be by using capital goods in production. This demand for capital goods could be broken down according to whether it comes from the capital goods sector, $K_{k,t}^d$, or the consumer goods sector, $K_{c,t}^d$. These stock

---

[8] With this type of inclusion the total supply of capital goods would be:

$$(3')$$

$$S_{k,\,t+1} = SS_{k,t} - DEP_{k,t} + FS_{k,t+1}$$

$$= K_t^s - \delta K_t^s + Q_{k,t+1}^s$$

$$= K_0 - \delta K_0 + f\,(P_{k,t+1}^e\,;\,TECH\,;\,W\,;\,P_{k,t})\,.$$

[9] The value of a car may depreciate 10 percent over a year in the eyes of its owner or "the market" because of expected increases in repair costs, reduced performance, the car being less fashionable, or other similar reasons. In no way, however, has this car lost 10 percent of its engine, steering wheel, gas tank, or any other physical components.

demand functions are just the factor demand functions derived from the profit maximization decisions of the firms in each sector. Hence, each sectoral function depends upon each sector's expectation of its sale price, on its technology, and on its factor costs:

$$(4) \quad SD_{k,t} = K_t^d = K_{k,t}^d + K_{c,t}^d$$

$$= h_k \, (P_{k,t+1}^e \quad ; TECH_k \, ; W_t \, ; P_{k,t})$$

$$+ \, h_c \, (P_{c,t+1}^e \quad ; TECH_c \, ; W_t \, ; P_{k,t})$$

$$= h \, (P_{k,t+1}^e \quad ; P_{c,t+1}^e \quad ; TECH_k \, ; TECH_c \, ; W_t \, ; P_{k,t}).$$

The partial derivatives with respect to the six variables in this equation carry the usual signs, positive for the expected output price of each sector, negative for the price of current capital goods, and ambiguous for the wage rate and for technological improvements.

In conjunction with the stock supply of capital, equation (1), this equation determines the equilibrium spot price of capital, $P_{k,t}^*$. In a simple model where the transferability of fixed capital between the consumption goods and the capital goods is allowed for—a "putty–putty" model—this spot price of capital then determines the distribution of the existing capital stock between the two sectors. In a "putty–clay" model, this spot price is purely notional in that the amount of capital in each sector is fixed by previous purchases. It should also be recognized that this spot price may be different from the contract price at which capital goods were bought at different points in the past, reflecting the potential disappointment of the expectations that were used to make these previous decisions.

What about the demand for currently produced capital goods? This demand is, in part, derived form the stock demand for the capital stock to be used in the next production period. Hence, it is subject to the same influences as the stock demand for capital in the current period, except it is looking one period further into the future and it includes the rate at which future profits are discounted, i (Davidson, 1978, p. 72). It is the current view of what the capital needs will be in the next period. If, as Davidson (pp. 76–77) argues, the capital goods market is one organized on a "custom building" or "to contract" basis, then expectations as to the future use of fixed capital need to exist so that firms are able to place the orders for the new capital goods that take time to produce. Hence, the stock demand for capital at the end of the period is:

(5) $\quad SD_{k,t+1} = K^d_{t+1} = K^d_{k,t+1} + K^d_{c,t+1}$

$$= h_k \, (P^e_{k,t+2} \,;\, TECH_k \,;\, W^e_{t+1} \,;\, P^e_{k,t+1} \,;\, i \,)$$

$$+ h_c \, (P^e_{c,t+2} \,;\, TECH_c \,;\, W^e_{t+1} \,;\, P^e_{k,t+1} \,;\, i \,)$$

$$= h \, (P^e_{k,t+2} \,;\, P^e_{c,t+2} \,;\, TECH_k \,;\, TECH_c \,;\, W^e_{t+1} \,;\, P^e_{k,t+1} \,;\, i \,) .$$

The partial derivatives all keep the same sign as they have for the function relating to the previous period and the one with respect to the rate of discount is negative.

On top of this stock demand for fixed capital goods one must add the replacement demand for fixed capital. This capital demand is to replace the capital stock that has "depreciated" or that has been deemed obsolete. As mentioned before, the underlying view is that the capital stock does not depreciate as such. Machines can always be repaired, but the question is whether or not it is worthwhile to do so.[10] Hence, this replacement investment is another expectational element, just as is the overall desire for a particular capital stock.[11] Davidson (1978, p. 74) refers to this replacement demand as the flow demand for capital. The role of replacement investment is a component of total investment that tends to be ignored, though some have drawn attention to it (see Perelman, 1989). In the most simple version of this, a particular percentage of the existing capital stock is replaced, δ, with this percentage being the same in each sector, $\delta = \delta_k = \delta_c$:

(6) $\qquad FD_{k,t+1} = KREP_{t+1} = KREP_{k,t+1} + KREP_{c,t+1}$

$$= \delta_k K_{k,t} + \delta_c K_{c,t} = \delta K_t = \delta K_0 .$$

The total demand for capital is the sum of the stock demand and the

[10] The office photocopying machine can always be repaired (and often is), but the costs of repair and the advancing technology embodied in new machines make it, under particular circumstances, more economical to replace the photocopying machine rather than repair it.

[11] Another way to understand this supply and demand presentation is to realize that the end-of-period capital stock is the capital stock inherited from the beginning of the period, less the quantity thereof that has "depreciated," plus the new capital goods that have been added (equation 3′). Instead of presenting two stock supply schedules, one can just add this depreciation quantity to the end of period capital demand function. This may be a simpler, but less conceptually accurate, way of looking at the problem.

replacement or flow demand:

(7) $D_{k,t+1} = SD_{k,t+1} + FD_{k,t+1} = K^d_{t+1} + KREP_{t+1}$

$= h(P^e_{k,t+2}; P^e_{c,t+2}; TECH_k; TECH_c; W^e_{t+1}; ; P^e_{k,t+1}; i) + \delta K_0.$

Total investment demand is, consequently, the sum of the desired additions to the capital stock and the desired replacement of the existing capital stock:

(8)

$ID_{g,k,t+1} = D_{k,t+1} - SD_{k,t} = SD_{k,t+1} - SD_{k,t} + FD_{k,t+1}$

$Q^d_{k,t+1} = K^d_{t+1} - K^d_t + KREP_{t+1}$

$= h(P^e_{k,t+2}; P^e_{c,t+2}; TECH_k; TECH_c; W^e_{t+1}; P^e_{k,t+1}; i) - (1 - \delta) K_0.$

Under conditions of a perfect and competitive market, the short-period equilibrium of the demand and supply of capital goods to be produced for use in the next production period is derived by the equality of the total supply, equation (3), and total demand, equation (7). This can also be determined by the equality of the flow supply of capital goods, equation (2), with the total (gross) investment demand, equation (8). This equality determines the forward price of capital goods (Davidson, 1978, pp. 77–78)—the price at which contracts are signed for the delivery of capital goods at the end of the current production period. Also determined is the amount of gross investment that occurs and how this is split between replacement investment and net additions to the capital stock. The key variables involved in this determination are the cost and technology of production in the capital goods sector, expected future sales and profits in both sectors, the discount rate, and the rate of fixed capital replacement.

Keynes' notion of user cost

The *user cost* of fixed capital is the loss of expected future profit incurred by currently using fixed capital as opposed to leaving it idle. User cost is the opportunity cost of employment and production "today"—using fixed capital in the current period—as opposed to leaving the fixed capital idle "today" and having it fully available in a series of "tomorrows." Current production may impact on the future conditions of production by altering the "amount" of capital available by depreciating it in some fashion or by altering the productivity of capital and labor in the future. These effects could occur by increased wear and tear, increased congestion,[12] and the need to meet increased health, pollution, and replacement standards. Current production may also influence the future by changing the expected market conditions for the firm's output or the expected costs of the labor and capital inputs of the firm (Davidson, 1991b, p. 139).[13]

Keynes put it this way:

> User cost constitutes one of the links between the present and the future. For in deciding his scale of production an entrepreneur has to exercise a choice between using up his equipment now and preserving it to be used later on. It is the expected sacrifice of future benefit involved in present use which determines the amount of the user cost, and it is the marginal amount of this sacrifice which, together with the marginal factor cost and the expectation of the marginal proceeds, determine his scale of production. [Keynes, 1964, pp. 69–70]

Keynes derived the notion of user cost from discussions on natural resources like copper (CWJMK, 6, pp. 116–131). For these inputs it is obvious that user cost must be allowed for in that what is used up today cannot be used tomorrow (Keynes, 1964, p. 73). Keynes (1964, p. 73) argued that user cost considerations should be extended to fixed capital, which also experiences disinvestment, though only of a partial nature and stretched over a number of production periods.

If current production has no impact upon the production and the sales conditions in future periods, then the user cost of fixed capital is zero. This is what is implicitly and explicitly assumed in many microeconomic and macroeconomic models, and one of the things for which Keynes (1964, p. 72) criticizes Pigou. The intertemporal aspects of production and fixed capital utilization are what Keynes aims to capture by "the introduction of the concepts of user cost and of the marginal efficiency of capital" (Keynes, 1964, p. 146). Conse-

---

[12] An example along these lines might be increasing the number of flights at an airport, thereby reducing the ability to effectively service these flights and get them off the ground on time.

[13] An increase in the current production of a particular type of automobile, say a Miata, leading to the expectation of lower sales in the future is one example of this type of user cost. The current increased use of a particular type of skilled labor, say chemical engineers, resulting in the expectation of higher cost for the same type of labor in the future is another example of user cost in this category.

quently, firms need to form expectations about both the short-term and the long-term future. The marginal efficiency of capital, on its own, captures only the future profitability of capital independent of the current production decisions. User cost adds the influence of current production decisions on future profitability, how this needs to be considered in the present production decision, and how current production decisions influence the investment decision.

Keynes (1964, p. 53) defines *prime cost* as the sum of factor cost and user cost. Since both factor cost and user cost vary with the level of output, marginal prime cost is equal to the sum of marginal factor cost and marginal user cost (Keynes, 1964, p. 67). Consequently, under competitive conditions, the unit supply price of the firm's output is equal to marginal prime cost and not equal to marginal factor cost as is usually assumed. The exception is, of course, the special case where marginal user cost is equal to zero. Since Keynes (1964, p. 67) generally sees marginal user cost as being positive, unit supply prices are for him greater than marginal factor cost. Monopoly is usually seen as the key reason why supply prices (or short-period equilibrium prices) are greater than marginal factor cost (see Davidson and Smolensky, 1964, pp. 128–131). Positive marginal user cost provides a reason why this would be so under perfectly competitive conditions.

User cost and the supply conditions of fixed capital goods

The profit-maximizing production decisions made by firms are generally conceived of as independent of considerations outside the production period in question. The usual exception is the role played by the capital stock that is inherited from the past. With the recognition that there may be user cost involved in current production, the profit-maximizing production decisions made by firms are decisions that interrelate considerations associated with different time periods. It is not only conditions and expectations related to the current production period that matter, but also the expectations related to revenues, costs, and technology in future periods (Davidson, 1991b, p. 140).

As pointed out above, this time interdependence in production means that marginal prime cost is the sum of marginal factor cost and marginal user cost. If marginal user cost is positive for all levels of output in the capital goods sector, then marginal prime cost will be higher than marginal factor cost. This means that the flow supply price for capital goods will be higher at any level of output when user costs are included, as opposed to when they are not included. Consequently, the flow supply curve with user cost lies above the curve without user cost. This is seen as the usual case.[14]

The stock supply of capital is not affected by the inclusion of user cost in the production decisions of the capital goods sector.[15] The flow supply function is what is modified by the existence of non-zero marginal user cost in the capital goods sector, $MUC_{k,t}$. The modified flow supply function of fixed capital goods can be specified as follows:

$$(9) \quad FS_{k,t+1} = Q^s_{k,t+1} = f(P^e_{k,t+1} ; TECH ; W ; P_{k,t} ; MUC_{k,t}) .$$

Within a monetary production economy, the existence of true uncertainty creates two important considerations. First, marginal user cost is, potentially, the most volatile aspect of marginal prime cost (Keynes, 1964, p. 302). Changes in expectations may cause marginal user cost to vary significantly, even when marginal factor cost is constant. These variations in marginal user cost vary marginal prime cost and may then be the key element varying the supply price of output. The factors that could change are the perceptions of the firm of the impact of current employment and production on the future technological productivity of capital and the expectations of input costs and output prices.[16] Even when the perceptions of the degree to which current output and employment will impact on the expected profit of the future are constant, there may be changes in what may be considered parameter values. These parameter values include the depreciation (or desired replacement) of the current capital stock, the future technology in use, and the expected output and input prices (see Keynes, 1964, pp. 70–71).[17]

The second consideration relates to the heterogeneity of the expectations that firms hold (Davidson, 1991b, p. 141). In an uncertain world, it is likely that different firms foresee different futures. These heteroge-

[14] Keynes (1964, p. 54) argued that the possibility of negative marginal user cost is limited to very special conditions.

[15] In a sophisticated conceptualization of the role of user cost, one can conceive that user cost has an impact on the stock of capital that is allowed to be used, that is, the reservation demand conditions.

[16] The expectations of the introduction of new products and technologies in the consumer electronics industry are quite volatile and impact on the pricing and production decisions of firms and their introduction of new products.

[17] The desire for shorter payback periods for new fixed capital is an example of an influence that usually results in higher prices for output.

neous expectations mean that, even when all firms face the same factor costs and production technology, the individual firm supply functions will differ because of different perceptions of the user cost involved in production.[18] This discussion essentially ignores this important complication. This heterogeneity also means that "there can be no such thing as a unique path of optimal resource allocation over future time" (Davidson, 1991b, p. 141).

Marginal user cost can then be written as a function of a number of variables itself:

$$(10) \quad MUC_{k,t} = g_k \left(P^e_{k,t+2} ; TECH_k ; W^e_{t+1} ; P^e_{k,t+1} ; i \right) ;$$

$$MUC_{c,t} = g_c \left(P^e_{c,t+2} ; TECH_c ; W^e_{t+1} ; P^e_{k,t+1} ; i \right) .$$

The marginal user cost function can shift for a number of reasons. First is a direct change in the degree to which current output changes impact on future technological or market conditions. The inclusion of user cost brings to the fore a number of other factors. Changes of the firm's expectations of what parameter values will be in the future and how future profits need to be discounted will also shift the marginal user cost function. The depreciation (or desired replacement) of the current capital stock, the future technology in use, and the expected output and input prices (see Keynes, 1964, pp. 70–71) are additional variables that can shift the entire marginal user cost function.

Within the context of a fixed-capital-using monetary economy working under conditions of uncertainty, this means that the expectations on the economic lifespan of fixed capital and on the technological obsolescence thereof have an impact on the current period production decisions. Changes in these expectations will shift the marginal user cost function and, consequently, affect current output and employment decisions. Keynes (1964, pp. 71–72, 302) acknowledged this type of influence in *The General Theory.*

At the macroeconomic level, Keynes' model is fully capable of analyzing the output, employment, and income effects arising from user cost and changes in user cost. It is also able to look at the general price or inflation effects brought about by user cost (Deprez, 1993b). As has been argued elsewhere (Deprez, 1993a), Keynes' model, with the inclu-

---

[18] An example along these lines would be the effect that the wide diversity of opinion about future oil prices had on the output and exploration decisions in the oil and related industries in the 1970s (see Davidson, 1991b, pp. 407–421).

sion of user cost considerations, can explain the causes of the stagflation of the 1970s as being rooted in technological change and the expectations thereof. This emphasis on the importance of a changing general structure or *regime of accumulation* of fixed capital depreciation, obsolescence, and replacement in explaining stagflation has been the focus of the French Regulation School (see Aglietta, 1979; Lipietz, 1985; Boyer, 1990).

User cost and the demand conditions for fixed capital goods

The impact of user cost is not limited to the supply side of Keynes' aggregate supply and demand model. The demand for capital goods is derived from the optimal intertemporal production decisions of firms in both the consumption goods and the capital goods sectors. Consequently, the existence of user cost impacts on both the demand for capital goods to be used in the current period and the demand for capital goods to be used in the future period. The stock demand functions for fixed capital goods need to be modified to include the user cost considerations involved in production in both sectors.

For the current stock demand this includes the current user cost and for the end of period stock demand this includes the next period's expected user cost. For the current period, the stock demand for fixed capital goods is:

(11)

$$SD_{k,t} = K^d_t = K^d_{k,t} + K^d_{c,t}$$

$$= h_k(P^e_{k,t+1}; TECH_k; W_t; P_{k,t}; MUC^e_{k,t})$$

$$+ h_c(P^e_{c,t+1}; TECH_c; W_t; P_{k,t}; MUC^e_{c,t})$$

$$= h(P^e_{k,t+1}; P^e_{c,t+1}; TECH_k; TECH_c; W_t; P_{k,t}; MUC^e_{k,t}; MUC^e_{c,t}).$$

The additional influence comes from the current expected user cost in both the consumer goods sector and the capital goods sector. Since user cost, *ceteris paribus*, reduces the optimal amount of output and employment offered by each sector, it also reduces the demand for capital in each sector. Consequently, the spot price for capital goods will be lower than it is in the case without user cost. If this price allocates the stock supply of capital goods between the two sectors, then the relative user cost between the two sectors will play a role in this allocation. The lower the relative user cost of a particular sector, the greater will be the percentage of the inherited capital stock allocated to that sector. Because user cost is an expectational element, variations in these expectations, under the same marginal factor cost conditions, will have an effect on the spot price of fixed capital and may affect the allocation of this fixed capital between the sectors of the economy.[19]

The stock demand for fixed capital goods to be used in the next production period now becomes:

(12)

$$SD_{k,t+1} = K^d_{t+1} = K^d_{k,t+1} + K^d_{c,t+1}$$

$$= h_k (P^e_{k,t+2} ; TECH_k ; W^e_{t+1} ; P^e_{k,t+1} ; i ; MUC^e_{k,t+1})$$

$$+ h_c (P^e_{c,t+2} ; TECH_c ; W^e_{t+1} ; P^e_{k,t+1} ; i ; MUC^e_{c,t+1})$$

$$= h (P^e_{k,t+2} ; P^e_{c,t+2} ; TECH_k ; TECH_c ; W^e_{t+1} ; P^e_{k,t+1} ; i ; MUC^e_{k,t+1} ; MUC^e_{c,t+1}).$$

As with the current period stock demand for fixed capital goods, the demand for capital goods to be used in the next production period will depend negatively on the value of the expected marginal user cost in that period. The inclusion of user cost means that the quantity of capital demanded by each sector for future use, *ceteris paribus*, will be lower compared with what would be demanded where no user cost is considered. Variations in the expectation of user cost will vary this stock demand. Reductions in user cost will increase the demand for capital goods, while increases in this expected cost will dampen the demand for capital goods. The composition of total stock demand between the demand from the capital goods sector and the demand from the consumer goods sector may also vary with changes in these expectations. This, of course, affects the relative growth of the productive capacity in the different sectors.

The expectations of prices, costs, and technology that are usually seen to enter the marginal efficiency of capital schedule do not include user cost. What equation (12) points out is that user cost does have an influence on this schedule and contributes to its possible volatility

---

[19] User cost may influence which product line, say, in women's fashions, a firm decides to emphasize in production.

(Keynes, 1964, pp. 135–164). Consequently, the exclusion of user cost leaves even the marginal efficiency of investment element of Keynes' investment theory incomplete.

User cost also affects the replacement demand for capital in both sectors. Hence, the flow demand function needs to be modified and becomes:

$$(13)\ FD_{k,t+1} = KREP_{t+1} = KREP_{k,t+1} + KREP_{c,t+1}$$

$$= \delta_k K_{k,t} + l_k\,(MUC^e_{k,t}\,;\,MUC^e_{k,t+1})$$

$$+\ \delta_c K_{c,t} + l_c\,(MUC^e_{c,t}\,;\,MUC^e_{c,t+1})$$

$$= \delta K_t + l\,(MUC^e_{k,t}\,;\,MUC^e_{k,t+1}\,;\,MUC^e_{c,t}\,;\,MUC^e_{c,t+1})\,.$$

The replacement demand for capital goods by each sector depends upon the expected user cost of both the current period and the future period. If the current use of fixed capital goods inhibits their physical ability to produce in the future, then there is an increased need to replace these machines with new ones or to bring these machines back to the production capability they would have had if they had not been used in production. This type of user cost requires investment in order to maintain the capital stock.

User cost may also occur because current production affects future market conditions. If user cost occurs because current production is "spoiling the market", then the desire for capital to be used in production in the next period will be less. This aspect is captured by a negative impact of marginal user cost on the stock demand for the next period. There is, however, no reason why this would necessarily have a negative impact on the replacement demand for fixed capital goods.

If, on the other hand, the "spoiling of the market" is of the output produced by specific technology of specific output, then one would expect an increase in replacement demand. This replacement demand would be in order to replace old machines with new machines that embody a new technology or with machines that are capable of producing new types of output. In this case, replacement is not occurring by substituting identical machines, but by substituting technologically different machines. This type of substitution means that user cost has a positive impact on the replacement demand for capital goods. Increases in the expected marginal user cost in either sector will increase the replacement demand for capital goods.[20]

When the different influences that user cost can have on the replacement demand for fixed capital goods are grouped together, then the general effect can be seen as increasing this flow demand. Increases in marginal user cost will, generally, increase the replacement demand for capital goods. Consequently, the influence of the variations in the expectations of user cost on the replacement demand for fixed capital is one step in arguing that the characterization of depreciation or replacement as some given percentage of the capital stock is inaccurate. The replacement of fixed capital is always based on expectations of the future. The inclusion of user cost highlights this aspect and points out the variability of replacement demand on the basis of current economic circumstances and the expectations of future profitability. The employment- and income-generating effects of this replacement investment are also important and variable. They cannot be deemed something of secondary importance or ignored completely, as is done in too many macroeconomic models.

The total demand for capital is the sum of the stock demand function for capital to be used in the next period plus the replacement demand of capital goods. Having discussed the component parts above, it is obvious that marginal user cost needs to be included here as well:

$$(14) \quad D_{k,t+1} = SD_{k,t+1} + FD_{k,t+1} = K^d_{t+1} + KREP_{t+1}$$

$$= h \, (P^e_{k,t+2} ; P^e_{c,t+2} ; TECH_k ; TECH_c ; W^e_{t+1} ;$$

$$P^e_{k,t+1} ; i ; MUC^e_{k,t+1} ; MUC^e_{c,t+1})$$

$$+ \delta K_0 + l \, (MUC^e_{k,t} ; MUC^e_{k,t+1} ; MUC^e_{c,t} ; MUC^e_{c,t+1}) \, .$$

The impact of user cost on the total demand for capital goods is ambiguous. It is, in general, negative when it comes to the stock demand and positive when one is considering replacement demand. The same

---

[20] The previous example of consumer electronics, such as CD players and VCRs, illustrates this. Higher current production and sales may logically lead to expectations that there are fewer potential costumers—ones without a compaprable CD player or VCR—to whom sales could be made in the future. This "spoiling of the market" increases the need to come up with a new generation of sound and video equipment or find ways to improve significantly the current generation of products. New machines are needed to replace the old ones in order to produce these new and improved products. This also highlights how important it is to firms to predict these product innovation cycles correctly.

can be said for the modified gross investment demand function:

$$(15) \quad ID_{g,k,t+1} = D_{k,t+1} - SD_{k,t} = SD_{k,t+1} - SD_{k,t} + FD_{k,t+1}$$

$$Q^d_{k,t+1} = K^d_{t+1} - K^d_t + KREP_{t+1}$$

$$= h \left(P^e_{k,t+2} ; P^e_{c,t+2} ; TECH_k ; TECH_c ; W^e_{t+1} ; \right.$$

$$\left. P^e_{k,t+1} ; i ; MUC^e_{k,t+1} ; MUC^e_{c,t+1} \right)$$

$$- (1 - \delta) K_0 + l \left(MUC^e_{k,t} ; MUC^e_{k,t+1} ; MUC^e_{c,t} ; MUC^e_{c,t+1} \right).$$

From what has been presented above, the quantity of capital goods supplied will be less, *ceteris paribus*, when user cost is included compared with the theoretical case where it is excluded. The investment demand for newly produced capital goods when user cost is included may either be larger or smaller when compared with when user cost is excluded. This means that what the equilibrium amount of capital goods that are produced and sold will be and what their price will be is an open question. Clearly, if the same quantity is produced as where user cost is ignored, then the supply price will be higher. It is possible that the influences of user cost on the demand for capital goods are such as to lead to exactly the same equilibrium quantity produced and sold as without the inclusion of user cost. It is possible to argue that the pushing of user cost into the background of the General Theory by Keynes (1964, p. 55) is based on this reasoning.[21] For user cost to be neutral with respect to output and employment, the user cost influences in both the investment and consumption goods sectors need to be just right. This is only the special case, with all the other possible influences of user cost not being neutral with respect to equilibrium output and employment in both the investment goods sector and the consumer goods sector. Examining the specifics of this question is, however, for another paper.

Conclusions

Keynes' aggregate supply and demand model is meant to be a strong and general alternative to the classical model, without moving too far away from the classical frame of reference. With the resurrection of formal, micro-based macroeconomic models and these becoming the center of textbook macroeconomics (see Abel and Bernanke, 1992;

[21] This is the belief expressed to me by Paul Davidson.

Mankiw, 1992), Keynes' own model provides a direct and effective counterpoint to these models because it can comprehensively incorporate a wide range of demand and supply considerations. This is something that the traditional "Keynesian" models cannot do. Going back to Keynes' model and the extensions and articulations of the aggregate supply and demand model provides an important basis for discussing current macroeconomic theory and policies. A look at the microeconomics of Keynes' model is one element of this reexamination. The role of user cost highlights the difference between the classical and Keynesian models and the temporal nature of Keynes' model versus the static nature of the classical model.

As has been illustrated here, user cost is an important element that comes to the fore in a fully developed version of Keynes' intertemporal model. User cost is crucial to the understanding of the determination of investment and, consequently, to the general determination of output, income, and employment. User cost has an impact on the supply conditions of capital goods. It also has an impact on the stock demand for capital goods. Finally, user cost has an important influence on the replacement demand for fixed capital goods. In combination, these considerations have an impact on the quantity of capital goods produced and sold and the price at which they are sold.

By looking only at the supply and demand of capital goods, certain important considerations arising from the inclusion of user cost into Keynes' model have not been discussed. The expected user cost in the consumption goods sector will also affect production, employment, and pricing in that sector. The distribution of income is also affected by the inclusion of user cost. Equilibrium prices are not equal to marginal factor cost, as is usually assumed. User cost adds another element to the margin above average factor cost. This shifts the distribution of income in favor of capital and reduces the real wage. Hence, as Keynes (1964, p. 66) pointed out, "user cost . . . has an importance for the classical theory of value which has been overlooked." This impact on the distribution of income may translate into an impact on the propensity to consume, expectations of future profitability, liquidity preference, and the propensity to buy placements. All these variables would have an impact on the economy's generation of output, income, and employment.

The role of user cost is not limited to Keynes' own model. The Post Keynesian models that include significant alterations of the original also need to take user cost into consideration when aiming at a complete model. For example, when one moves forward to different production and firm structures, certain elements of Keynes' own model are modified. Yet, no matter what the modifications are, the essential characteristics and the role of user cost need to be included. The impact of current production on future profitability is always a relevant consideration for production using fixed capital in a monetary production economy where uncertainty is pervasive. These extensions are where future research must be concentrated.

REFERENCES

Abel, A.B., and Bernanke, Ben S. *Macroeconomics.* Reading, MA: Addison-Wesley, 1992.

Aglietta, M. *A Theory of Capitalist Regulation: The US Experience.* London: NLB, 1979.

Asimakopulos, A. *Keynes's General Theory and Accumulation.* Cambridge: Cambridge University Press, 1991.

Boyer, R. *The Regulation School: A Critical Introduction.* New York: Columbia University Press, 1990.

Casarosa, C. "The Microfoundations of Keynes's Aggregate Supply and Expected Demand Analysis." *Economic Journal,* March 1981, *91* (361), 188–194.

Crotty, J.R. "Neoclassical and Keynesian Approaches to the Theory of Investment." *Journal of Post Keynesian Economics,* Summer 1992, *14* (4), 483–496. Chapter 4 of this volume.

Davidson, P. *Money and the Real World,* 2d ed. London: Macmillan, 1978.

———. *Money and Employment. The Collected Writings of Paul Davidson,* vol. 1, ed. L. Davidson. New York: New York University Press, 1991a.

———. *Inflation, Open Economies and Resources. The Collected Writings of Paul Davidson,* vol. 2, ed. L. Davidson. New York: New York University Press, 1991b.

Davidson, P., and Smolensky, E. *Aggregate Supply and Demand Analysis.* New York: Harper and Row, 1964.

Deprez, J. "Modes of Regulation and Stagflation: A Post Keynesian Analysis of a Marxian Problem." Paper presented at "Comparisons of Post Keynesian, Classical, and Marxian Economic Theories," conference at the University of Utah, January 8–9, 1993a.

———. "Fixed Capital and Inflation: An Analysis Applying Keynes' Notion of User Cost." *Review of Radical Political Economics.* September 1993b, *25* (3), forthcoming.

Dillard, D. "The Theory of a Monetary Economy." In Kenneth K. Kurihara (ed.), *Post Keynesian Economics.* New Brunswick, NJ: Rutgers University Press, 1954.

Fried, J. "Financial Theory and the Theory of Investment." *Journal of Post Keynesian Economics,* Summer 1992, *14* (4), 465–481. Chapter 3 of this volume.

Gordon, M.J. "The Neoclassical and a Post Keynesian Theory of Investment." *Journal of Post Keynesian Economics,* Summer 1992, *14* (4), 425–443. Chapter 1 of this volume.

Hansen, A.H. *A Guide to Keynes.* New York: McGraw-Hill, 1953.

Keynes, J.M. *The General Theory of Employment, Interest, and Money.* New York: Harcourt Brace Jovanovich, 1964 (originally published 1936).

————. *The Collected Writings of John Maynard Keynes.* London: Macmillan, and Cambridge: Cambridge University Press, 1971–83.

Lipietz, A. *The Enchanted World: Inflation, Credit and the World Crisis.* London: Verso, 1985.

Mankiw, N.G. *Macroeconomics.* New York: Worth, 1992.

Perelman, M. *Keynes, Investment Theory and the Economic Slowdown: The Role of Replacement Investment and q-Ratios.* New York: St. Martin's Press, 1989.

Peterson, W.C., and Estenson, P.S. *Income, Employment, and Economic Growth,* 7th ed. New York: W.W. Norton, 1992.

Robinson, J.V. "Marx and Keynes." *Collected Economic Papers,* vol. 1. Oxford: Basil Blackwell, 1960.

Rymes, T.K. *Keynes's Lectures, 1932–35: Notes of a Representative Student.* Ann Arbor: University of Michigan Press, 1989.

Vickers, D. "The Investment Function: Five Propositions in Response to Professor Gordon." *Journal of Post Keynesian Economics,* Summer 1992, *14* (4), 445–464. Chapter 2 of this volume.

Weintraub, S. *Price Theory.* New York: Greenwood Press, 1968 (originally published 1949).

————."The Micro-Foundations of Aggregate Demand and Supply." *Economic Journal,* September 1957, 67 (267), 455–470.

————. *An Approach to the Theory of Income Distribution.* Philadelphia: Chilton Books, 1958.

Wells, P. "Keynes' Disequilibrium Theory of Employment." In Sidney Weintraub (ed.), *Modern Economic Thought.* Philadelphia: University of Pennsylvania Press, 1977.

Index

Achievement motive, 118
Adjustment costs, 66–67*n.7*, 139*n.11*, 144–46, 158
Agency, 116 costs, 51, 51*n.9*, 89 and financial markets, 92–93 layers, 87, 89–91 *see also* Principal agent problem
APMs. *See* Asset pricing models
APT. *See* Asset pricing theory
Arbitrage pricing model, 102 Asset pricing models (APMs), 99–100
Asset pricing theory (APT), 100
Asymmetric information, 12

Bankruptcy, 18, 47, 66, 99, 149
Banks and banking, 38
Barsky, R.B., 51*n.8*
Baumol, W.J., 119–20
Belief, 106
Berle, A.A., 86
Bernanke, Benjamin S., 131
Black, F., 11
Blanchard, Olivier J., 132
Blinder, Alan S., 131
Bonding costs, 89
Boom-bust cycles, 72
Borrowing constraint, 48, 51
Brigham, E.F., 9
Brothwell, J.F., 32
Budgeting, 116

Capital
  accumulation, 67, 69–70
  budgeting, 113
  cost of, 13–14, 26–27, 34–35, 43, 57–58
  demand, 138, 166–73
    for fixed, 178–82
    flow, 172
    price for, 57
    total, 181–82

Capital *(continued)*
  depreciation of, 170, 170*n.9*, 172
  entrepreneurial theory of, 116–25
  fixed, 167, 168–70
  as liquid asset, 66–67, 68–69
  marginal efficiency of, 165, 175, 179–81
  marginal product of, 145
  rising supply price of goods, 146–48, 158
  spot price of, 171, 178–79
  supply of, 166–73, 170*n.8*
  user cost of, 173
  see also Investment; Marginal efficiency of capital; Perfectly competitive capital markets
Capital asset pricing model (CAPM), 54, 57, 100, 102
Capital structure, 17–18
Capital structure theorem, 8–10
Capital theoretic critique, 34–35
CAPM. *See* Capital asset pricing model (CAPM)
Carvalho, F., 32
Causality in Economics (Hicks), 30
Choice, Complexity and Ignorance (Loasby), 29
Choice. *See* Rational choice
Coen, Robert M., 143*n.16*
Coherence, 26
Confidence, 65
Consumption goods, 183
Contracts, 105–6, 112
Conventions, 64–66, 65*n.5*, 108
Corporations, 4–5, 84–85
  agency and financial markets, 92–93
  agency layers in, 87, 89–91

About the Editor

Professor Paul Davidson has held the Holly Chair of Excellence in Political Economy at The University of Tennessee since 1986. His previous experience includes Professor of Economics and Associate Director of the Bureau of Economics and Research at Rutgers University (1966–86), Associate Professor of Economics at the University of Pennsylvania (1961–66), and Assistant Director of the Economics Division of Continental Oil Company (1960–61). He has also been Visiting Professor at the University of Strasbourg, Institute for Advanced Studies in Vienna, University of Nice (France), and Senior Visitor at Cambridge University, Cambridge, England. He is author and co-author of 12 books including *Controversies in Post Keynesian Economics*, *Money and the Real World*, *Economics for a Civilized Society*, and *Aggregate Demand and Supply Analysis*. He is also the author of more than 105 professional journal articles. He has been the editor of the *Journal of Post Keynesian Economics* since 1978. He received his Ph.D. at the University of Pennsylvania in 1959, an MBA at the City University of New York in 1955, and BS at Brooklyn College in 1950.

For Product Safety Concerns and Information please contact our EU
representative GPSR@taylorandfrancis.com
Taylor & Francis Verlag GmbH, Kaufingerstraße 24, 80331 München, Germany

www.ingramcontent.com/pod-product-compliance
Lightning Source LLC
Chambersburg PA
CBHW050441280326
41932CB00013BA/2202

9 781563 243073